aRM

LifeSongs

Leader Book

D1308252

Table of contents

Hymns and Songs

Indexes

LIFESONGS Leader Book

Also available:
LifeSongs Songbook (11-10940) ISBN 0-8066-4271-8
LifeSongs compact discs
Volume 1 ages 3 and up (11-10941) ISBN 0-8066-4272-6
Volume 2 ages 7 and up (11-10942) ISBN 0-8066-4273-4

The paper used in this publication meets the minimum requirements of American National Standard for Information Sciences—Permanence of Paper for Printed Materials, ANSI Z329.48-1984.

Manufactured in the U.S.A. ISBN 0-8066-4270-X 11-10939

05 04 03 02 01 00 99 2 3 4 5 6 7 8 9 10

Preface

To sing of faith is to sing of the life that is God's gift. *LifeSongs* opens new avenues of exploration through which children of various ages may discover the ways that their lives are a song to God. This resource links music, education, and worship so that children may grow in and celebrate their life together with God, with one another, and with the church.

LifeSongs gathers 200 musical items, carefully selected to meet the needs of children from early through later childhood years, for use in learning, worship, recreational, and home environments. A range of age appropriate music has been chosen to meet children at their own level of understanding. Included here are traditional and new children's songs, call and response songs, rounds and action songs, scripture songs, contemporary worship songs, songs from various cultures, as well as representative hymns, carols, and refrains of the church and its liturgy. The leader book contains an appendix of early childhood piggyback songs, short song texts set to nursery and folk tunes.

The *LifeSongs* **songbook**, containing words and melody lines only, can be placed directly into the hands of children. The *LifeSongs* **leader book** contains a variety of helpful features for teachers and other leaders, whether or not they have musical training. Many of the songs include teaching notes. These notes may offer insight into the words and music of the songs by noting scriptural connections or historical background. Creative movement and sign language suggestions engage children's bodies as well as their voices. Possible uses of the songs in worship and daily life are noted. Additional musical features include practical methods of teaching the songs, the nurturing of the singing voice while promoting good listening skills, basic techniques for learning to read music, and optional instrumental accompaniments for simple percussion and Orff instruments. The leader book includes a full accompaniment (keyboard and guitar chord symbols) for all but a few songs. Musicians will note that in the case of some hymns with a more complex harmonic structure, the chord symbols offer a simplified accompaniment that may not match the keyboard part. In addition to these two print resources, *LifeSongs* **recordings** include a representative selection of songs both for younger children (age 3 and up) and older children (age 7 and up).

LifeSongs is a musical companion to the materials in the Life Together family of resources available from Augsburg Fortress. The three-year lectionary and the seasons of the church year are important organizing principles for these resources, as can be seen in the *LifeSongs* index of hymn and song suggestions. The *LifeSongs* package, however, is also recommended for use independently, wherever churches are seeking to encourage children to sing. As they listen, move, play, sing, and pray together, children who encounter these songs can begin to build their own understanding of the Christian story, enjoy the life they share with all God's children, and develop a lifelong love for lifting their voices in worship and song.

Stay awake, be ready

1

See LifeSongs *recording Volume 2*

We hear the call to be alert and expectant, to change our lives, and to prepare for the advent of Christ as we would ready ourselves to greet a new day.

• Introduce the meaning of Advent by playing a game of telephone. Begin by whispering the words *stay awake* to one child and inviting the child to whisper it to the next person. The last person announces what was heard. If the words have changed, then discuss how Advent is our "wake-up call" to create a space for the one who is coming.

• Now whisper the words *be ready* and pass them on. How was this message carried? Were the children more alert?

• Using the echo method, teach the melody with claps.

• The four stanzas reflect the gospel readings for Advent in year A.

Stanza 1: Matthew 24:35-44
Stanza 2: Matthew 3:1-12
Stanza 3: Matthew 11:2-11
Stanza 4: Matthew 1:18-25

Sing a stanza each week during Advent as the gospel acclamation.

F C
1 Stay a - wake, (clap, clap) be read - y. You
2 Change your lives, he's com-ing. The
3 Go . . . . back, tell John
4 By the pow'r of the Spir - it
F Gm C
do not know the hour when the Lord is com - ing. Stay a -
one who is the light of the world is com - ing. Change your
all that you have heard and have seen me do - ing. Go . . . .
Mar - y will give birth to a son called Je - sus. By the
F C Gm C7 F
wake, be read - y. The Lord is com-ing soon!
lives, he's com - ing. The reign of God is near!
back, tell John the won-ders that you see.
pow'r of the Spir - it Em - man - u - el is near.
C F B♭ C F
Al-le - lu - ia, al-le - lu - ia!
The Lord is com-ing soon.
The reign of God is near.
The won-ders that you see.
Em - man - u - el is near.

Text: Christopher Walker
Music: Christopher Walker

2 Soon and very soon

F Bb F
1 Soon and ver - y soon
2 No more cry - in' there,
3 No more dy - in' there,
4 Soon and ver - y soon
we are goin' to see the King,
C7 F
soon and ver - y soon
no more cry - in' there,
no more dy - in' there,
soon and ver - y soon
we are goin' to see the King,
Bb F
soon and ver - y soon
no more cry - in' there,
no more dy - in' there,
soon and ver - y soon
we are goin' to see the King.
F7 Bb Bbm F C7
1, 2
F
Hal-le - lu - jah, hal-le - lu - jah, we're goin' to see the King!

3, 4
F G7 C7 F G7 C7
Hal - le - lu - jah, hal - le - lu -
F G7 C7 F G7 C7 F
jah, hal - le - lu - jah, hal - le - lu - jah.

Text: Andraé Crouch
Music: Andraé Crouch

Advent is often portrayed in scripture and poetry as a longing for light. Engage the children in an exercise around light and darkness. Find a way to darken the room, then light a candle. Discuss how the light overcomes the darkness and is not swallowed up by it. The Word made flesh breaks into our darkened world in the same way. What does this mean for our own lives?

- To begin teaching the melody sing the first five notes on *bah* with the children echoing. Play the notes on an Orff instrument. Give each child an opportunity to play the pattern as the others sing.

- Sing the song for the children, asking them to raise their hand every time they hear the five-note pattern (three times). If the leader sings on *bah*, the children will recognize the pattern more easily.

- Sing the song with the words. Teach by phrases, inviting the children to echo.

- Add a combination of signing and movement. Sign the words *Christ* and *come* (see p. 212).

Candle: hold up the number of fingers being lit in each verse.

World: bring arms in a side-swooping movement to form a circle above head.

Use during the lighting of the Advent candles on each of the four Sundays in Advent.

3 Light one candle: Christ is coming

Advent candle song

1*
G (throughout)
2
1 Light one can - dle: Christ is com - ing, Christ, the hope of the world.
2 Light two can - dles: Christ is com - ing, Christ, the way of the world.
3 Light three can - dles: Christ is com - ing, Christ, the joy of the world.
4 Light four can - dles: Christ is com - ing, Christ, the peace of the world.
Light one can - dle: Christ is com - ing, Christ is com - ing soon!
Light two can - dles: Christ is com - ing, Christ is com - ing soon!
Light three can - dles: Christ is com - ing, Christ is com - ing soon!
Light four can - dles: Christ is com - ing, Christ is com - ing soon!

may be sung as a round

Bells used: 2 oct. (6 bells)
Alto xylophone
Last time
Handbells/chimes
LV
Last time
SK
Alto metallophone
Last time

Text: Sally Ahner
Music: Sally Ahner

He came down

4

See LifeSongs *recording Volume 1*

From the Cameroon tradition comes this delightful song that answers the question, "Why did Jesus come?" The answer is easy: that we might have a more abundant life, one secure in God's love, light, peace, and joy.

Share with the children information about Cameroon. Locate the country on a map or globe. Cameroon is a republic in western Africa. The country is shaped like an elongated triangle and forms a bridge between western and central Africa. The average temperature is 77 degrees and the rainfall is plentiful, 160 inches in a year.

- The rhythm is constant for each measure. Don't rush the triplet, which is spread over two beats.

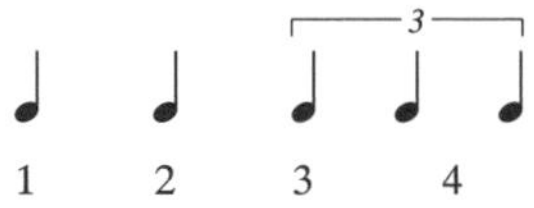
3
1 2 3 4

- Experience the triplet by inviting one child to play the four beats of each measure on claves. Speak the words rhythmically over this pattern.
- Musically, each phrase is slightly different. Teach the melody one phrase at a time. A leader or a group of voices may sing the question. Keep the rhythm flowing between stanzas.
- Play this pattern lightly on a drum:

- Add different rhythm instruments to play on the words *love, light, peace,* and *joy.*

Sing in Advent, adding a new stanza each week.

G D7
1 He came down that we may have love; he came down
2 He came down that we may have light; he came down
3 He came down that we may have peace; he came down
4 He came down that we may have joy; he came down
G
that we may have love; he came down that we may
that we may have light; he came down that we may
that we may have peace; he came down that we may
that we may have joy; he came down that we may
C G D G
Leader
Why did he come?
have love;
have light;
have peace;
have joy;
hal - le - lu - jah for - ev - er - more.

Text: Cameroon traditional
Music: Cameroon traditional; arr. John L. Bell

5 The King shall come

Written by the prolific Scottish hymn writer, John Brownlie, this hymn was first published in 1907. Although the text has an emphasis on light that is characteristic of early Greek hymnody, no Greek source has ever been found. It is believed to be an original poem by Brownlie, reflecting his vast knowledge of Greek hymnody.

- Read through the stanzas, encouraging children to pull from the text images of light and life.
- This hymn is set in a minor key. Teach it with a bright, uplifting tone.
- Create a word picture for each stanza with suggestions from the children. Draw symbols on poster board.
- During the four weeks in Advent build on each of the stanzas by adding an instrument.

Week 1: stanzas 1, 2—alto glockenspiel.

Week 2: stanzas 1, 2, 3—add alto metallophone.

Week 3: stanzas 1, 2, 3, 4—add soprano and/or alto xylophone.

Week 4: stanzas 1, 2, 3, 4, 5—add bass xylophone (a flute may double the vocal line).

1 The King shall come when morn - ing dawns and
2 Not as of old a lit - tle child, to
3 Oh, bright - er than the ris - ing morn when
4 Oh, bright - er than that glo - rious morn shall
5 The King shall come when morn - ing dawns and
light tri - um - phant breaks, when beau - ty gilds the
bear and fight and die, but crowned with glo - ry
Christ, vic - to - rious, rose and left the lone - some
dawn up - on our race the day when Christ in
light and beau - ty brings. Hail, Christ the Lord! Your
east - ern hills and life to joy a - wakes.
like the sun that lights the morn - ing sky.
place of death, de - spite the rage of foes.
splen - dor comes, and we shall see his face.
peo - ple pray: come quick - ly, King of kings.

Alto glockenspiel
Last time
Soprano/alto xylophone
Last time
Alto metallophone
Last time
Bass xylophone
Last time

Text: John Brownlie
Music: A. Davisson, *Kentucky Harmony*; arr. Betty Ann Ramseth

On Jordan's banks the Baptist's cry

Bm D A D
1 On Jor - dan's banks the Bap - tist's cry an - nounc - es
2 Then cleansed be ev - 'ry life from sin; make straight the
3 Stretch forth your hand, our health re - store, and make us
4 All praise to you, e - ter - nal Son, whose ad - vent
A D G D Bm A
that the Lord is nigh; a - wake and hear - ken,
way for God with - in, and let us all our
rise to fall no more; oh, let your face up -
has our free - dom won, whom with the Fa - ther
G D A G A D
for he brings glad tid - ings of the King of kings!
hearts pre - pare for Christ to come and en - ter there.
on us shine and fill the world with love di - vine.
we a - dore, and Ho - ly Spir - it, ev - er - more.

Text: Charles Coffin
Music: European tune, adapt. Michael Praetorius

7 Prepare the royal highway

This Swedish folk tune has a lilting, dance-like quality that conveys the joy of preparing to greet the coming Savior. Younger singers may learn to sing the refrain only.

Em G D G C D G
1 Pre - pare the roy - al high - way; the King of kings is near!
2 God's peo - ple, see him com - ing: your own e - ter - nal king!
3 Then fling the gates wide o - pen to greet your prom - ised king!
4 His is no earth - ly king - dom; it comes from heav'n a - bove.
Em G D G C D G
Let ev - 'ry hill and val - ley a lev - el road ap - pear!
Palm branch - es strew be - fore him! Spread gar - ments! Shout and sing!
Your king, yet ev - 'ry na - tion its trib - ute too may bring.
His rule is peace and free - dom and jus - tice, truth, and love.
Em D A7 D A D Em D
Then greet the King of glo - ry, fore - told in sa - cred sto - ry:
God's prom - ise will not fail you! No more shall doubt as - sail you!
All lands will bow be - fore him; their voic - es join your sing - ing:
So let your praise be sound - ing for kind - ness so a - bound - ing:
Refrain Bm Em D Em C D G
Ho - san - na to the Lord, for he ful - fills God's Word!

Text: Frans Mikael Franzén; tr. *Lutheran Book of Worship*
Music: Swedish traditional

The King of glory

Refrain
Em Bm7 Em
The King of glo - ry comes, the na - tion re - joic - es.
Em Bm7 Em
O - pen the gates be - fore him, lift up your voic - es.
G C Bm D7 G
1 Who is the King of glo - ry; how shall we call him?
2 In all of Gal - i - lee, in cit - y or vil - lage,
3 Sing then of Da - vid's Son, our Sav - ior and broth - er;
4 He gave his life for us, the pledge of sal - va - tion;
5 He con - quered sin and death; he tru - ly has ris - en,
Em C G C D7 G
Refrain
He is Em - man - u - el, the prom - ised of ag - es.
he goes a - mong his peo - ple, cur - ing their ill - ness.
in all of Gal - i - lee was nev - er an - oth - er.
he took up - on him - self the sins of the na - tion.
and he will share with us his heav - en - ly vi - sion.

Text: Willard F. Jabusch
Music: Israeli traditional; arr. *Worship & Praise*

9 We light the Advent candles

Capo 1 D A D Em A D
E♭ B♭ E♭ Fm B♭ E♭
1 We light the Ad-vent can-dles a-gainst the win-ter night
2 The first one will re-mind us that Christ will soon re-turn.
3 We light the sec-ond can-dle, and hear God's ho-ly word.
4 Three can-dles now are gleam-ing and show us the true way.
5 Four can-dles burn-ing bright-ly an-nounce that Christ has come.
G D Em A D
A♭ E♭ Fm B♭ E♭
to wel-come our Lord Je-sus, who is the world's true light;
We light it in the dark-ness and watch it gleam and burn.
It tells us, cling to Je-sus, pre-pare to meet your Lord.
Re-joice, the Bap-tist cries out: your Lord has come to-day!
Pre-pare, my heart, be-lieve it, and give the Christ child room!
G D Em A D
A♭ E♭ Fm B♭ E♭
to wel-come our Lord Je-sus, who is the world's true light.
We light it in the dark-ness and watch it gleam and burn.
It tells us, cling to Je-sus, pre-pare to meet your Lord.
Re-joice, the Bap-tist cries out: your Lord has come to-day!
Pre-pare, my heart, be-lieve it, and give the Christ child room!

Text: Gracia Grindal
Music: German traditional

Oh, come, oh, come, Emmanuel

Em Bm Am Em Bm C
1 Oh, come, oh, come, Em - man - u - el, and ran - som cap - tive
2 Oh, come, blest Day-spring, come and cheer our spir - its by your
3 Oh, come, O Key of Da - vid, come, and o - pen wide our
Am Bm Em Am G D
Is - ra - el, that mourns in lone - ly ex - ile here
ad - vent here; dis - perse the gloom - y clouds of night,
heav'n - ly home; make safe the way that leads on high,
Am G C D G Refrain D Bm
un - til the Son of God ap - pear.
and death's dark shad - ows put to flight. Re - joice! Re - joice!
and close the path to mis - er - y.
Am Em Bm C Am Em
Em - man - u - el shall come to you, O Is - ra - el.

Text: *Psalteriolum Cantionum Catholicarum*, Köln; tr. John M. Neale
Music: French processional

11 People, look east

See LifeSongs *recording Volume 2*

This text by Eleanor Farjeon invites us to prepare as we are able. The text, set to a lilting French carol, reminds us of the one who brings new life to earth.

• Invite the children to be silent, to watch, and to listen. Set the rhythmic tone of this carol by clapping the following pattern three times.

• Practice clapping with the children and encourage them to sway from side to side, feeling two pulses for each of the measures.

• Prepare two flash cards:

1 

2 

• Sing the carol showing the card that introduces each of the three phrases: card 1, phrase 1; card 2, phrases 2 and 3.

• Practice singing each card.

• Add the words from stanza 1 to introduce each of the three phrases.

• Finish teaching the carol using the echo method.

• Learn one stanza for each week in Advent. The carol in its entirety could be sung on one of those Sundays.

D A Bm A D Bm
1 Peo - ple, look east. The time is near of the
2 Fur - rows, be glad. Though earth is bare, one more
3 Stars, keep the watch. When night is dim, one more
4 An - gels an - nounce with shouts of mirth him who
A D E A A7 D A
crown - ing of the year. Make your house fair as you are
seed is plant - ed there. Give up your strength the seed to
light the bowl shall brim, shin - ing be - yond the frost - y
brings new life to earth. Set ev - 'ry peak and val - ley
D Bm Em D A7
a - ble, trim the hearth and set the ta - ble. Peo - ple look
nour - ish, that in course the flower may flour - ish. Peo - ple, look
weath - er, bright as sun and moon to - geth - er. Peo - ple, look
hum - ming with the word, the Lord is com - ing. Peo - ple, look
D A D A Em G A D
east, and sing to - day— Love, the Guest, is on the way.
east, and sing to - day— Love, the Rose, is on the way.
east, and sing to - day— Love, the Star, is on the way.
east, and sing to - day— Love, the Lord, is on the way.

Text: Eleanor Farjeon
Music: French carol; arr. *LifeSongs*

Get ready!

See LifeSongs *recording Volume 1*

Young children experience Advent as a time of thanksgiving and joy. Help them to understand that Advent is a season of thanksgiving for what God has done for us and joyful anticipation of that great day we prepare to celebrate.

• Introduce first as chant or rhythmic speech (see chant A below).

• Clap or add a drum or tambourine on accented beats.

• Before teaching the melody give attention to the first three notes, *sol-mi-do*. Sing to the children on *bah*. Ask them to listen carefully and repeat. Then sing with the words *Get ready!*

• Teach the melody by phrases.

• After each stanza finish with chant B (below).

Sing one stanza each of the four weeks in Advent. When singing the entire piece, use the chanting between stanzas and at the song's conclusion.

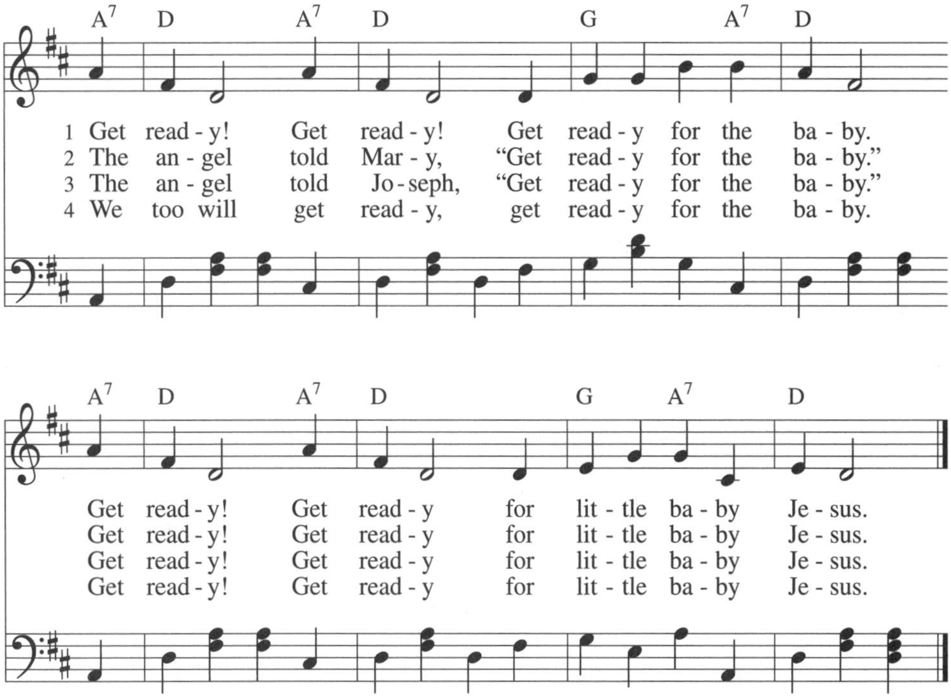
A7 D A7 D G A7 D
1 Get read - y! Get read - y! Get read - y for the ba - by.
2 The an - gel told Mar - y, "Get read - y for the ba - by."
3 The an - gel told Jo - seph, "Get read - y for the ba - by."
4 We too will get read - y, get read - y for the ba - by.
A7 D A7 D G A7 D
Get read - y! Get read - y for lit - tle ba - by Je - sus.
Get read - y! Get read - y for lit - tle ba - by Je - sus.
Get read - y! Get read - y for lit - tle ba - by Je - sus.
Get read - y! Get read - y for lit - tle ba - by Je - sus.

Text: Linda Carpenter
Music: Lois Holck; arr. Edward Damerau, Jr.

A

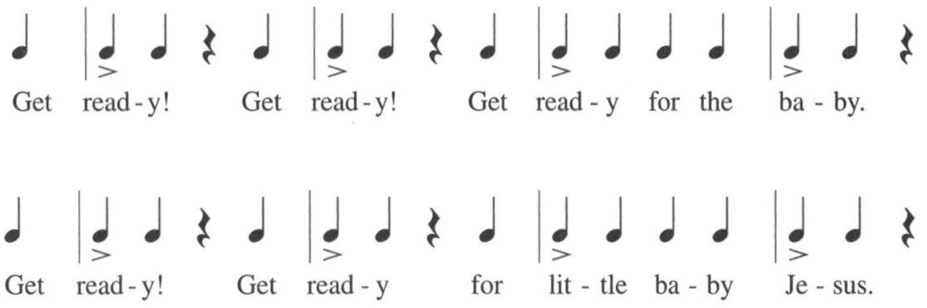
Get read - y! Get read - y! Get read - y for the ba - by.
Get read - y! Get read - y for lit - tle ba - by Je - sus.

B

Get read - y! Get read - y! Get read - y! Get read - y!

13 Come now, O Prince of Peace

This traditional Korean melody, with words originally written to express the hope for peace in that divided country, also makes a fine Advent song. As with many songs from various parts of the Asian continent, it is best sung without accompaniment. A finger cymbal or triangle may sound on the first beat of each measure.

1 Come now, O Prince of peace, make us one bod - y.
2 Come now, O God of love, make us one bod - y.
3 Come now and set us free, O God, our Sav - ior.
4 Come, Hope of u - ni - ty, make us one bod - y.
O - so - sŏ o - so - sŏ, pyong - hwa - ŭi - im - gŭm
Come, O Lord Je - sus, re - con - cile your peo - ple.
Come, O Lord Je - sus, re - con - cile your peo - ple.
Come, O Lord Je - sus, re - con - cile all na - tions.
Come, O Lord Je - sus, re - con - cile all na - tions.
u - ri - ga han - mom i - ru - ge ha - so - sŏ.

Text: Geonyong Lee; tr. Marion Pope
Music: Korean traditional

That boy-child of Mary

14

See LifeSongs *recording Volume 2*

While a missionary in Malawi, Africa, Tom Colvin wrote this Christmas carol after learning that a child's name is often chosen by parents based on their hopes for the child's future. Using a Malawian dance tune, Colvin wrote words about the birth of Jesus. This song celebrates the naming of the babe of Bethlehem.

- Feel the rhythm of three beats in each measure (***1***-2-3-***4***-5-6-***7***-8-9) by clapping and rocking from side to side on beats 1, 4, and 7.
- Add the following pattern to the clapping before teaching the melody.

- Teach the refrain.
- Add rhythm instruments: beat 1, tambourine; beat 4, guiro; beat 7, triangle.

Use during the Christmas season with children singing the refrain and stanza 1. Include the congregation on stanzas 2–6.

Refrain
F C
That boy-child of Mary was born in a stable,
F C7 F
a manger his cradle in Bethlehem.
F Gm C Am Dm
1 What shall we call him, child of the manger?
2 His name is Jesus, God ever with us,
3 How can he save us, how can he help us,
4 Gift of the Father, to human mother,
Gm C7 F Refrain
What name is given in Bethlehem?
God given for us in Bethlehem.
born here among us in Bethlehem?
makes him our brother in Bethlehem.

5 One with the Father,
he is our Savior,
heaven-sent helper
in Bethlehem. *Refrain*

6 Gladly we praise him,
love and adore him,
give ourselves to him
in Bethlehem. *Refrain*

Text: Tom Colvin
Music: Malawian traditional, adapt. Tom Colvin

15 'Twas in the moon of wintertime

See LifeSongs *recording Volume 2*

This hymn is the earliest known Canadian carol. It is attributed to Jean de Brebeuf, a Jesuit priest and missionary to the Iroquois and Huron tribes. Father de Brebeuf brought them the good news that God had sent Jesus to bring light and love to the world. The moon was a special symbol of light to the Hurons. The author used language and concepts (hunters, forest, the winter moon) that would be familiar to the people of that region.

- Introduce this hymn without singing the melody, as if telling a story. Discuss the images of stanzas 1–2: the moon of wintertime, birds, angel choirs, wandering hunters, ring of glory, shepherds.
- Invite the children to close their eyes and visualize the story as it is being told.
- Distribute paper, pencils, and crayons and ask the children to draw the images they saw.
- Teach the first two stanzas, encouraging the children to look at their drawings.
- Using the half-note pattern of the alto metallaphone, alternate patting thighs while singing.
- If the notated rhythms of the xylophone and hand drum parts are too difficult, substitute a steady quarter note pattern.

Sing during the Christmas season. Stanza 3 may be sung as a solo with children joining on the refrain.

Am
Em
Am
1 'Twas in the moon of win - ter - time when all the birds had fled,
2 The ear - liest moon of win - ter - time is not so round and fair
3 O chil - dren of the for - est free, the an - gels' song is true.
Em
Am
that God, the Lord of all the earth, sent an - gel choirs in - stead.
as was the ring of glo - ry a - round the in - fant there.
The ho - ly child of earth and heav'n is born to - day for you.
Be - fore their light the stars grew dim, and wan - d'ring hunt - ers
And when the shep - herds then drew near the an - gel voic - es
Come, kneel be - fore the ra - diant boy, who brings you beau - ty,
Refrain
Em
Am
heard the hymn:
rang out clear:
peace and joy.
Je - sus your king is born!
Em
Am
Em
Am
Je - sus is born! Glo - ry be to God on high!

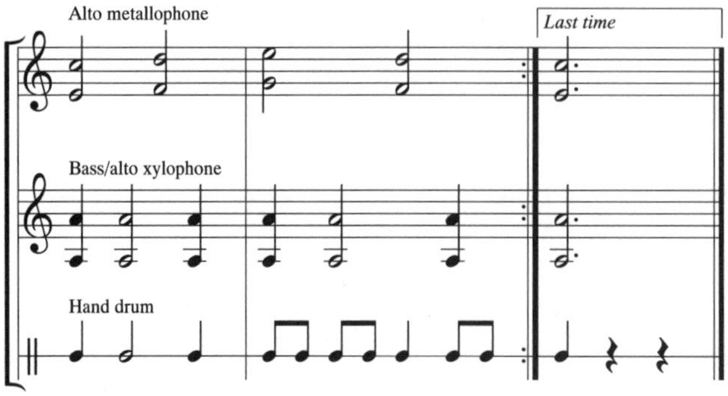
Alto metallophone
Last time
Bass/alto xylophone
Hand drum

Text: Jean de Brebeuf; tr. Jesse E. Middleton, alt.
Music: French traditional; arr. Melinda Ramseth and Betty Ann Ramseth

Young children will enjoy singing the refrain only. Teach the simple Latin pronunciation: *gloh-ree-ah een ehk-shel-sees deh-oh* (glory to God in the highest).

Angels we have heard on high 16

F Am C F C F C F
1 An - gels we have heard on high, sweet - ly sing - ing o'er the plains,
2 Shep-herds, why this ju - bi - lee? Why your joy - ous strains pro - long?
3 Come to Beth - le - hem and see him whose birth the an - gels sing;
Am C F C F C F
and the moun-tains in re - ply, ech - o - ing their joy - ous strains.
What the glad - some tid - ings be which in - spire your heav'n - ly song?
come, a - dore on bend - ed knee Christ the Lord, the new - born king.
Refrain
F Dm Gm C F B♭ C
Glo - - - ri - a
F C F Dm Gm C
in ex - cel - sis De - o; glo - -
F B♭ C F C F
- - ri - a in ex - cel - sis De - o.

Text: French carol; tr. "Crown of Jesus"
Music: French carol

17 Away in a manger

See LifeSongs *recording Volume 1*

This beloved Christmas carol is often sung to the two tunes presented here. Older singers may enjoy the challenge of singing both tunes simultaneously.

F Bb F
1 A - way in a man - ger, no crib for his bed,
2 The cat - tle are low - ing; the poor ba - by wakes,
3 Be near me, Lord Je - sus; I ask you to stay
C F
the lit - tle Lord Je - sus laid down his sweet head;
but lit - tle Lord Je - sus no cry - ing he makes.
close by me for - ev - er and love me, I pray.
Bb F
the stars in the sky looked down where he lay;
I love you, Lord Je - sus; look down from the sky
Bless all the dear chil - dren in your ten - der care
C F Bb C F
the lit - tle Lord Je - sus a - sleep on the hay.
and stay by my cra - dle till morn - ing is nigh.
and fit us for heav - en, to live with you there.

Text: North American, anonymous
Music: North American, anonymous; arr. Richard W. Hillert

Away in a manger

18

F Gm
1 A - way in a man - ger, no crib for his bed,
2 The cat - tle are low - ing; the poor ba - by wakes,
3 Be near me, Lord Je - sus; I ask you to stay
C F G7 C
the lit - tle Lord Je - sus laid down his sweet head;
but lit - tle Lord Je - sus no cry - ing he makes.
close by me for - ev - er and love me, I pray.
F Am D Gm
the stars in the bright sky looked down where he lay;
I love you, Lord Je - sus; look down from the sky
Bless all the dear chil - dren in your ten - der care
C F C7 F
the lit - tle Lord Je - sus a - sleep on the hay.
and stay by my cra - dle till morn - ing is nigh.
and fit us for heav - en, to live with you there.

Text: North American, anonymous
Music: William J. Kirkpatrick

19 Sing we now of Jesus

This French carol tune, Noël Nouvelet, has received a new text by Michael Burkhardt. In three short sentences it sets forth the who, when, where, and why of Christmas and Easter.

• Identify the three sentences and the repetitive melody as the A section. Show the contrast in the B section, pointing out the song's AABA form.

• Consider this plan for singing with handbell accompaniment:

1. Soloist sings song a cappella.
2. All sing song in unison with handbell accompaniment.
3. All sing canon in two parts, a cappella, repeating as desired.
4. As the canon concludes, ring the first eight measures of accompaniment twice as a coda.

The canon may be sung as a processional on Christmas Eve, Christmas Day, and on the Sundays after Christmas; as a processional on Easter and throughout the Easter season; or as a response to the gospel reading on Christmas or Easter (using the appropriate text).

1*
2
Em A Em
Christmas: Sing we now of Je - sus, born on Christ-mas day.
Easter: Sing we now of Je - sus, ris'n on Eas - ter day.
A Em
Sing we now of Je - sus, born on bed of hay.
Sing we now of Je - sus, ris'n from death's dark grave.
B7 Em B7
Lift up your voice, with all the world re - joice;
Lift up your voice, with all the world re - joice;
Em A Em
sing we now of Je - sus, born to light our way.
sing we now of Je - sus, ris'n the world to save.

*may be sung as a round

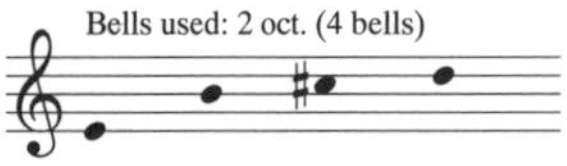
Bells used: 2 oct. (4 bells)

Handbells (metallophone)
*

*triangle

Text: Michael Burkhardt
Music: French carol

Glory to God

This refrain, from the *Bread of Life* liturgical setting by Jeremy Young, may be sung independently, or children may sing the refrain while a leader sings the rest of the "Glory to God" text from *With One Voice*, page 29.

D A G D C
Glo - ry to God, glo - ry to God, glo - ry to
G A D A
God in the high - est; glo - ry to God,
G D C G A D
glo - ry to God, and peace to God's peo-ple on earth.

Text: "Gloria," tr. English Language Liturgical Consultation
Music: Jeremy Young

21 Gloria

1*
2
Glo - ri - a, glo - ri - a, in ex - cel - sis De - o!
Glo-ry to God, glo-ry to God, glo - ry in the high - est!
3
4
Glo - ri - a, glo - ri - a, al - le - lu - ia, al - le - lu - ia!
Glo-ry to God, glo-ry to God, al - le - lu - ia, al - le - lu - ia!
Capo 3 Bm Em A D Bm Em A D
Dm Gm C F Dm Gm C F
Bm Em A D Bm Em A D
Dm Gm C F Dm Gm C F

*may be sung as a round

Text: traditional
Music: Jacques Berthier

I am so glad each Christmas Eve

22

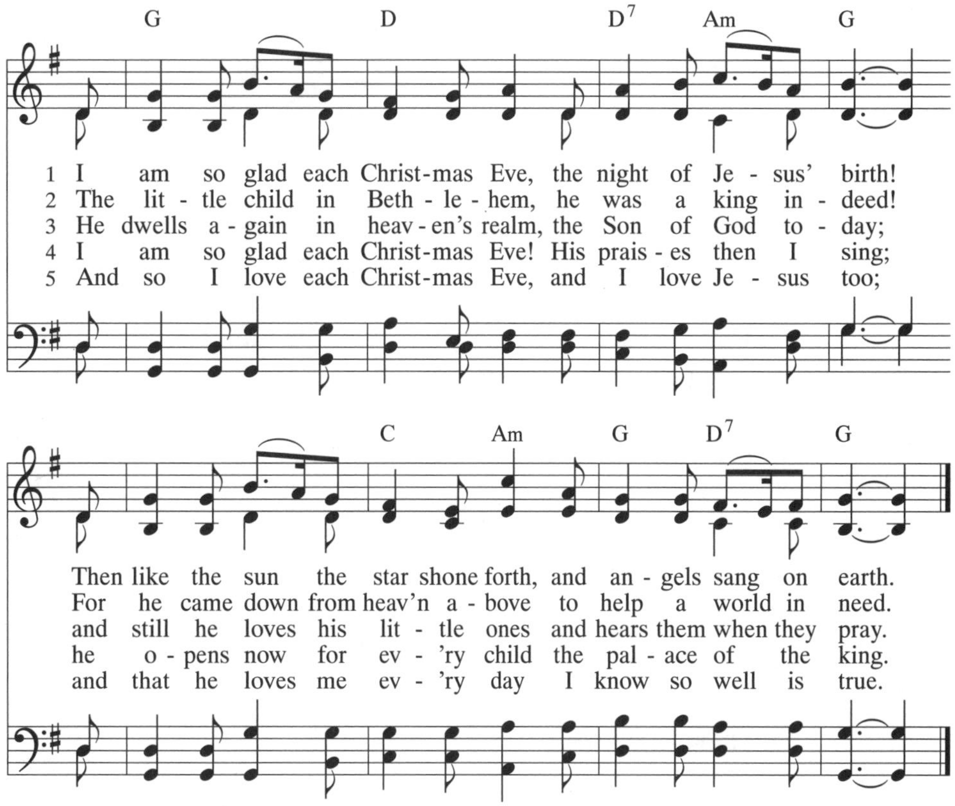
G D D7 Am G
1 I am so glad each Christ-mas Eve, the night of Je - sus' birth!
2 The lit - tle child in Beth - le - hem, he was a king in - deed!
3 He dwells a - gain in heav - en's realm, the Son of God to - day;
4 I am so glad each Christ-mas Eve! His prais - es then I sing;
5 And so I love each Christ-mas Eve, and I love Je - sus too;
C Am G D7 G
Then like the sun the star shone forth, and an - gels sang on earth.
For he came down from heav'n a - bove to help a world in need.
and still he loves his lit - tle ones and hears them when they pray.
he o - pens now for ev - 'ry child the pal - ace of the king.
and that he loves me ev - 'ry day I know so well is true.

Text: Marie Wexelsen; tr. Peter A. Sveeggen, alt.
Music: Peder Knudsen

23 Go tell it on the mountain

See LifeSongs *recording Volume 1*

This rousing spiritual celebrates the birth of Jesus Christ as told in Luke 2:8-20. Its origins are uncertain; like most spirituals, it evolved through group singing. Echoing Isaiah 40:9-10, the text urges the faithful to climb to the highest mountaintop to proclaim the news of Jesus' birth.

• Begin by teaching actions to illustrate the refrain.

Go: Cup hands around mouth.

Mountain: Touch fingertips with palms facing.

Over: Make a wavy movement with one hand.

Everywhere: Thrust both arms outward.

Jesus Christ is born: Cradle arms.

• Teach the refrain. Stanzas can be sung as solos.

Refrain
Go tell it on the moun - tain, o-ver the hills and ev - 'ry - where;
go tell it on the moun - tain that Je - sus Christ is born!
1 While shep-herds kept their watch-ing o'er si - lent flocks by night,
2 The shep-herds feared and trem - bled when, lo, a - bove the earth
3 Down in a lone - ly man - ger the hum-ble Christ was born;
be - hold, through-out the heav-ens there shone a ho - ly light.
rang out the an - gel cho - rus that hailed our Sav - ior's birth.
and God sent us sal - va - tion that bless-ed Christ-mas morn.
Refrain

Text: African American spiritual, refrain; John W. Work, Jr., stanzas
Music: African American spiritual

Joy to the world

24

D A D G
1 Joy to the world, the Lord is come! Let earth re -
2 Joy to the earth, the Sav - ior reigns! Let all their
3 He rules the world with truth and grace and makes the
A D
ceive its King; let ev - 'ry heart pre - pare him
songs em - ploy, while fields and floods, rocks, hills, and
na - tions prove the glo - ries of his righ - teous -
A
room and heav'n and na - ture sing, and heav'n and na - ture
plains re - peat the sound-ing joy, re - peat the sound-ing
ness and won-ders of his love, and won-ders of his
D A D
sing, and heav'n and heav'n and na - ture sing.
joy, re - peat, re - peat the sound - ing joy.
love, and won - ders, won - ders of his love.

Text: Isaac Watts
Music: George F. Handel, adapt.

25 Hark! The herald angels sing

F C F B♭ F C F
1 Hark! The her - ald an - gels sing, "Glo - ry to the new-born king;
2 Hail the heav'n - born Prince of Peace! Hail the sun of righ-teous-ness!
F Dm G7 Am C F G7 C
peace on earth, and mer - cy mild, God and sin - ners rec - on - ciled."
Light and life to all he brings, ris'n with heal - ing in his wings.
F C7 F C F C7 F C
Joy - ful, all you na-tions, rise; join the tri-umph of the skies;
Mild he lays his glo - ry by, born that we no more may die,
B♭ D Gm C7 F C F
with an - gel - ic hosts pro-claim, "Christ is born in Beth - le - hem!"
born to raise each child of earth, born to give us sec-ond birth.
Refrain
B♭ F Gm D Gm C F C7 F
Hark! The her - ald an-gels sing, "Glo - ry to the new-born king!"

Text: Charles Wesley, alt.
Music: Felix Mendelssohn

Silent night, holy night! 26

Capo 1
A
B♭
E7
F7
1 Si - lent night, ho - ly night! All is calm,
2 Si - lent night, ho - ly night! Shep - herds quake
3 Si - lent night, ho - ly night! Son of God,
A
B♭
D
E♭
A
B♭
all is bright round yon vir - gin moth - er and child.
at the sight; glo - ries stream from heav - en a - far,
love's pure light ra - diant beams from your ho - ly face,
D
E♭
A
B♭
E
F
E7
F7
Ho - ly In - fant, so ten - der and mild, sleep in heav - en - ly
heav'n - ly hosts . . . sing, al - le - lu - ia! Christ, the Sav - ior, is
with the dawn of re - deem - ing grace, Je - sus, Lord, at your
A
B♭
A/D
B♭/D
A
B♭
E
F
E7
F7
A
B♭
peace, sleep in heav - en - ly peace.
born! Christ, the Sav - ior, is born!
birth, Je - sus, Lord, at your birth.

Text: Joseph Mohr; tr. John F. Young
Music: Franz Gruber

27 Oh, come, all ye faithful

G D G C G D
1 Oh, come, all ye faith - ful, joy - ful and tri - um - phant! Oh,
2 Sing, choirs of an - gels, sing in ex - ul - ta - tion,
3 Yea, Lord, we greet thee, born this hap - py morn - ing;
Em D A D G D A D
come ye, oh, come ye to Beth - le - hem;
sing, all ye cit - i - zens of heav - en a - bove!
Je - sus, to thee be . . . glo - ry giv'n!
G D7 G D G Em D
come and be - hold him, born the king of an - gels:
Glo - ry to God . . . . . in . . . the . . . high - est:
Word of the Fa - ther, now in flesh ap - pear - ing:
Refrain G C G D
Oh, come, let us a - dore him, oh, come, let us a - dore him,
G D A7 D7 G C G D G
oh, come, let us a - dore him, Christ the Lord!

Text: attr. John F. Wade, tr. Frederick Oakeley
Music: attr. John F. Wade

Oh, sleep now, holy baby 28

D A7 D Bm G Bm F♯
1 Oh, sleep now, ho - ly ba - by, with your head a - gainst my breast;
1 Duér-me-te, ni - ño lin-do, en los bra-zos del a - mor
Bm DM7 GM7 F♯ D A D
mean-while the pangs of my sor - row are soothed and put to rest.
mien - tras que duer-me y des - can - sa la pe - na de mi do - lor.
Refrain/Estribillo
D7 G A7 D B7 Em A D
A la ru, a la mé, a la ru, a la mé,
D7 G A7 B7 E7 D A7 D
a la ru, a la mé, a la ru, a la ru, a la mé.

2 You need not fear King Herod,
he will bring no harm to you;
so rest in the arms of your mother
who sings you a la ru. *Refrain*

2 No temas al rey Herodes
que nada te ha de hacer;
en los brazos de tu madre
y ahi nadie te ha de ofender. Estribillo

Text: Hispanic folk song; tr. John Donald Robb
Music: Hispanic folk tune; arr. John Donald Robb

29 The virgin Mary had a baby boy

F C7
1 The vir - gin Mar - y had a ba - by boy, the
2 The an - gels sang . . . . when the ba - by was born, the
3 The shep - herds came. . . . where the ba - by was born, the
4 The wise men saw . . . . where the ba - by was born, the
B♭ C7 F F7
vir - gin Mar - y had a ba-by boy, the vir - gin Mar - y had a
an - gels sang . . when the ba-by was born, the an - gels sang . . when the
shep-herds came. . where the ba-by was born, the shep-herds came. . where the
wise men saw . . where the ba-by was born, the wise men saw . . where the
B♭ F C7 F
3
ba-by boy, and they say that his name is Je - sus.
ba-by was born, and they sang that his name is Je - sus.
ba-by was born, and they say that his name is Je - sus.
ba-by was born, and they say that his name is Je - sus.

Refrain
He come from the glo - ry, he come from the glo-rious king-dom.
Oh, yes, be-liev-er! Oh, yes, be-liev-er! He come from the
glo - ry, he come from the glo-rious king-dom.

Text: West Indian carol
Music: West Indian carol; arr. John Barnard

30 We three kings of Orient are

1 We three kings of O - ri - ent are; bear - ing gifts we tra - verse a - far,
2 Born a king on Beth - le - hem's plain, gold I bring to crown him a - gain;
3 Frank - in - cense to of - fer have I; in - cense owns a de - i - ty nigh;
4 Myrrh is mine; its bit - ter per - fume breathes a life of gath - er - ing gloom;
5 Glo - rious now be - hold him a - rise, King and God and Sac - ri - fice;
field and foun - tain, moor and moun - tain, fol - low - ing yon - der star.
king for - ev - er, ceas - ing nev - er, o - ver us all to reign.
prayer and prais - ing, glad - ly rais - ing, wor - ship - ing God Most High.
sor - rowing, sigh - ing, bleed - ing, dy - ing, sealed in the stone - cold tomb.
heav'n sings al - le - lu - ia: al - le - lu - ia the earth re - plies.
Refrain
Oh, star of won - der, star of night, star with roy - al beau - ty bright;
west - ward lead - ing, still pro - ceed - ing, guide us to thy per - fect light!

Text: John Henry Hopkins, Jr.
Music: John Henry Hopkins, Jr.

Open our eyes, Lord

D G2 G Em7 A7 G
O - pen our eyes, Lord; we want to see Je -
D A Bm D Em A7
sus, to reach out and touch him, and
G D D A/G
say that we love him. O - pen our ears,
G Em7 A7 G D Bm7 D
Lord, and help us to lis - ten. O - pen our
GM7 Em7 A7 Em/D D
eyes, Lord, we want to see Je - sus.

Text: Bob Cull
Music: Bob Cull

32 This little light of mine

Whether sung by adults or children, this familiar song reminds us that we are sent to enlighten others who sit in darkness. Our mission is to spread the good news and share the light.

• Sing the song, tapping the two beats per measure on your knees.

• Practice the following movements with the children:

1. Hold up the index finger to make the light.
2. Hide the light under your other hand.
3. Blow out the light.
4. Share your light by touching index fingers with another child.

• Sing the song, adding the following stanzas:

Hide it under a basket? No!
Don't let anyone (pretend to blow) *it out.*
Share my light with others! Yes!

• Play a singing game. Ask everyone to stand in a circle, holding hands. Choose children to stand in the center, holding up index fingers to make lights. Sing the first stanza with those in the circle walking around the "candles."

For *Hide it under a basket? No!* have everyone in the circle walk in while those in the center "hide" the "candles." Those in the circle walk back out on the word *No!* Repeat movement.

For *Don't let anyone* (blow) *it out*, have everyone in the circle run in and pretend to blow the candles out. Walk back out and repeat the movement.

For *Share my light with others! Yes!* the children in the center share their light with those in the circle.

Give all the children a chance to be candles.

C Dm7 G7 C C7
1 This lit-tle light of mine, I'm goin'-a let it shine;
F Refrain G7 C
this lit-tle light of mine, I'm goin'-a let it shine,
A7 Dm7 G7 C Fine
let it shine, let it shine, let it shine.
C Dm7 G7
2 Hide it un-der a bas-ket? No! I'm goin'-a let it
3 Don't let a-ny-one (blow) it out. I'm goin'-a let it
4 Share my light with . . . oth-ers! Yes! I'm goin'-a let it
C C7 F Refrain
shine. Hide it un-der a bas-ket? No!
shine. Don't let a-ny-one (blow) it out.
shine. Share my light with . . . oth-ers! Yes!

Text: traditional
Music: traditional

This little light of mine

See LifeSongs *recording Volume 2*

Here is another version of "This little light of mine," developed among African Americans during the time of slavery. Handclaps may be added on the second and fourth beats.

G D G
1 This lit - tle light of mine, I'm goin'-a let it shine;
2 Ev - 'ry - where I go, I'm goin'-a let it shine;
3 Je - sus gave it to me, I'm goin'-a let it shine;
C G
this lit - tle light of mine, I'm goin'-a let it shine;
ev - 'ry - where I go, I'm goin'-a let it shine;
Je - sus gave it to me, I'm goin'-a let it shine;
G B Em
this lit - tle light of mine, I'm goin'-a let it shine,
ev - 'ry - where I go, I'm goin'-a let it shine,
Je - sus gave it to me, I'm goin'-a let it shine,
G A D7 G C G
let it shine, let it shine, let it shine.
let it shine, let it shine, let it shine.
let it shine, let it shine, let it shine.

Text: African American spiritual
Music: African American spiritual; arr. Horace Clarence Boyer

34 I am the light of the world

See LifeSongs *recording Volume 1*

Children are often fearful of the dark. This verse from John 8:12 teaches us who really is the light of the world and the light of life.

- Bring a world globe and a candle. Light the candle and turn out the lights. Rotate the globe slowly, showing how the light continues to shine on it.
- Go one step further and ask the children if there are ever dark times in their lives when they feel sad. It is important to remember that the light of Christ comes to dispel the darkness of our hearts and minds. Encourage the children to think of this verse from John during those times.
- Sing the song with a simple movement. Standing straight, slowly move downward to a squatting position through the first phrase. On the second phrase slowly move upward to a standing position and jump on the word *life*. Invite the children to enter into the movement.
- Teach the song, adding a triangle each time the word *light* is sung.

F
B♭
I am the light of the world, I am the light of the world. Who-
F
C7
F
ev - er fol-lows me will nev-er walk in the dark, will nev-er
B♭
F
C7
F
walk in the dark, but have the light of life.

Text: John 8:12
Music: June Fischer Armstrong

Bring forth the kingdom

In the Sermon on the Mount one of Jesus' teachings was about salt and light (Matthew 5:13-16). To a child these are simple words. Invite children to share what salt and light mean to them. In Jesus' day salt was used for flavoring and preserving. Clay lamps burning olive oil drawn up by a wick were used for light. Both salt and light were an important part of living.

Discuss how we are called to be salt for the earth, a light on a hill, and seed of the word. Point out that we are scattered in the world as salt is shaken. We are sent into the world as lights that point to the greater light of God's grace. We plant seeds of God's word by living in a manner that leads others to praise God.

- Divide each stanza into a call and response. Teach the second and fourth phrases to the children; have a soloist sing phrases one and three. Everyone learns the refrain.

- Add rhythm instruments to each stanza:

Salt: rainstick or tree chimes
Light: finger cymbals
Seed: maracas

Leader
All
1 You are salt for the earth, O people: salt for the kingdom of God!
2 You are a light on the hill, O people: light for the city of God!
3 You are a seed of the word, O people: bring forth the kingdom of God!
4 We are a blest and a pilgrim people: bound for the kingdom of God!
Share the flavor of life, O people: life in the kingdom of God!
Shine so holy and bright, O people: shine for the kingdom of God!
Seeds of mercy and seeds of justice, grow in the kingdom of God!
Love our journey and love our homeland: love is the kingdom of God!
Refrain
Bring forth the kingdom of mercy, bring forth the kingdom of peace; bring forth the kingdom of justice,
bring forth the city of God!

Text: Marty Haugen
Music: Marty Haugen

36 I want to walk as a child of the light

Epiphany begins with a star pointing the way toward the light of the world. As that light shines forth, this hymn invites us to seek and to find, to walk and to follow Jesus.

• Invite older children to read the text of stanza 1 together. Make a list of words and phrases pertaining to light *(child of the light, stars, light to the world, star of my life, no darkness, light, shine)*. Discuss what meaning these light images have in our lives.

• Refer to Isaiah 42:6, "I have called you . . . I have given you as a covenant to the people, a light to the nations." This love of Christ shines in us, who share Christ's baptismal life and calling.

• Experience the triple meter by rocking from side to side. Speak the beats in each measure giving accent to the first beat as in the pattern below.

3
4
du - du - du du - du - du
du - du - du du

• Repeat several times. Add a rhythm instrument to the first beat of each measure (drum, cowbell, tambourine, or triangle).

• Teach by four-measure phrases, encouraging children to echo.

Sing during the season of Epiphany or in any service where we are called to follow Jesus.

D A G A
1 I want to walk as a child of the light.
2 I want to see . . . the bright - ness of God.
3 I'm look - ing for . . . the com - ing of Christ.
D G A7 G
I want to fol - low Je - sus.
I want to look at Je - sus.
I want to be with Je - sus.
D G A
God set the stars to give light to the world.
Clear Sun of righ - teous - ness, shine on my path,
When we have run . . . . with pa - tience the race,
D A G E A
The star of my life is Je - sus.
and show me the way to the Fa - ther.
we shall know the joy of Je - sus.

Refrain
D G D
In him there is no dark - ness at all.
Bm D Bm A
The night and the day are both a - like.
Em D G E A
The Lamb is the light of the cit - y of God.
D A G A7 D
Shine in my heart, Lord Je - sus.

Text: Kathleen Thomerson
Music: Kathleen Thomerson

37 We are called

What does the Lord ask of us? To do justice, to love kindness, and to walk humbly with God. These simple words from Micah 6:8 remain a challenge today for anyone who recognizes the injustice and suffering in the world. But there is hope. Through baptism we are called to enlighten those who sit in darkness, to live in the light, to open our hearts, and to sing a new song.

- What does it mean to *act with justice* (to be fair and impartial), to *love tenderly* (to be sensitive to others' feelings), to *serve* (to prepare and offer), to *walk humbly* (to be modest, not proud)? Print the italicized phrases on poster board and encourage responses from children.
- Teach the refrain. Ask children on which beat the word *we* begins (beat 2). How many times do they sing *we are called*?
- Children do their best singing when they learn how to shape sounds. Show them how to drop the jaw forming "tall sounds" on such words as *come, light, shine, called,* and *God*. Practice speaking with this more open sound.
- Pay close attention to pronunciation and encourage good breath support for tied notes.
- Clap lightly on the first beat of each measure to establish the pulse.

Sing in a service when Micah 6:8 is one of the readings or when the emphasis is on our call to serve others.

G C D
1 Come! Live in the light!
2 Come! O - pen your heart!
3 Sing! Sing a new song!
G C D
Shine with the joy and the love of the Lord! We are
Show your . . . mer - cy to all those in fear! We are
Sing of that great day when all will be one! God will
Em Em7 C G
called to be light for the king - dom, to
called to be hope for the hope - less so all
reign, and we'll walk with each oth - er as
Am7 G C D
live in the free - dom of the cit - y of God.
ha - tred and blind - ness . . . will be . . . no more.
sis - ters and broth - ers . . . . u - nit - ed in love.

Refrain
Am G C D C G
We are called to act with jus-tice, we are
C D Em Em7 G C
called to love ten-der - ly; we are called to
D C G Am7 G C
serve one an - oth-er, to walk
D C D G
hum - bly with God.
C
1, 2
D
3
D G

Text: David Haas
Music: David Haas

38 Shine, Jesus, shine

See LifeSongs *recording Volume 2*

Epiphany is a feast of light. We see that this radiance is not of our own doing, but the love of God shining on us and all around us. When we live as people upon whom the light has shined, we see differently. We become aware that the whole earth is full of God's glory. The light shines and draws our attention outside of ourselves so we can see those who are weak, in need, poor, and hungry. We live as reflections of that light, radiating love.

• Bring a flashlight (large, if possible) to class. Shine it around the room and on the children. Discuss how we take on God's light and love in the same way.

• Each phrase of the refrain begins with the same note pattern. Teach these action words to younger children: *shine, Jesus, shine; blaze, Spirit, blaze; flow, river, flow; send forth your Word*. Older children will enjoy learning all of the refrain. Stanzas can be sung by a soloist.

Useful for the Epiphany season, Pentecost, and at other times. Stanza 2 is especially fitting on Transfiguration Day.

Refrain
A E D A Bm B7 E
Shine, Je-sus, shine, fill this land with the Fa-ther's glo-ry;
A E D A Bm Bm G E
blaze, Spir-it, blaze, set our hearts on fire.
A E D A Bm B7 E
Flow, riv-er, flow, flood the na-tions with grace and mer-cy;
A E D A Bm E7 A D
To stanzas
E D
Last time
A
send forth your Word, Lord, and let there be light!

A D A E A D
1 Lord, the light of your love is shin - ing, in the midst of the
2 As we gaze on your king - ly bright-ness, so our fac - es dis-
A E D E7 C♯m F♯m
dark - ness, shin - ing; Je - sus, light of the world, shine up - on us,
play your like - ness, ev - er chang-ing from glo - ry to glo - ry,
D E7 C♯m F♯m
set us free by the truth you now bring us.
mir - rored here, may our lives tell your sto - ry.
G E G E Refrain
Shine on me, shine on me:
Shine on me, shine on me:

Text: Graham Kendrick
Music: Graham Kendrick

39 Jesus brings a message

The call of the disciples, told in the stories of the Epiphany season, is celebrated in this song. We are called as disciples, too. Personalize this song by substituting the names of children in the fourth line.

C G7 Am C7
Je - sus brings to the world a spe - cial mes - sage. Ev - 'ry -
Je - sús tra - e u - na no - ti - cia. To - do el
F G7 C E7
bo - dy lis-ten up, it's meant for you. There will come a time of peace and of
mun-do se de-be en - te - rar. Vie-ne un tiem - po de paz y jus-
Am C7 F Dm G7
jus - tice. Who will help him spread the news?
ti - cia. ¿Quién le a - yu - da a pro - cla - mar?
C F G C
Si-mon, let's go! An-drew, you too! Come James and John, to -
Va-mos, Si - món, va - mos, An - drés, va - mos, San - tia - go y
G D G7 C F
geth-er we'll march on. Leave ev - 'ry-thing and fol-low me.
Juan . . . tam - bién, de - jen to - do y sí - gan - me,
C G C F C
Come one, come all, come fol - low me.
va - mos, ... sí - gue - me tú tam - bién.

Text: Alejandro Zorzin; tr. William Dexheimer Pharris
Music: Alejandro Zorzin

Come to the mountain

In the Bible, mountains often serve as places of revelation. We are invited to come to the mountain and be tranformed by the light, love, and power of God. We are transformed when our inner nature is forever changed and we walk in the reflected light of God's eternal presence. How are we affected by this transformation?

- Clap each rhythm, inviting children to echo. Show them a different way to clap by extending one hand, palm up, with the other hand clapping into the extended hand.

A
B

- Teach the melody. Add a rhythm instrument such as claves or tambourine and play the rhythm of the words.
- Sign the word *come* (see p. 212), adding motions for other words.

Mountain: With palms facing, touch fingertips together.

Transformed: With hands in front of chest, rotate in a circular motion on *be trans-*, ending with palms up on *formed.*

- Finish teaching the song.
- Add signing to the words *light, love*, and *power* (see p. 213).

Sing on the last Sunday after the Epiphany, the Transfiguration of Our Lord.

D Em A7 D
Come to the moun-tain. Come to the moun-tain. Come to the moun-tain and
Em A7 D Em A7
be trans-formed. Come to the moun-tain. Come to the moun-tain.
D G A7 D
Come to the moun-tain and be trans - formed:
A7 D
changed by the light of God, changed by the love of God,
A7 D
changed by the pow'r of God on the moun-tain - top.

Text: Pamela L. Hughes
Music: Pamela L. Hughes

41 I want Jesus to walk with me

See LifeSongs *recording Volume 1*

In this African American spiritual we are reminded that our lives can be described as a journey or a walk where we encounter trials of all kinds. We are helpless to face our troubles alone. The walk of faith invites the presence of Christ in all life's relationships and decisions.

• Can the children identify what is meant by trials and troubles? Encourage them to share.

• Know the melody well enough to be able to sing this spiritual unaccompanied. Invite the children to pat their thighs with the palms of their hands, alternating between left and right. Then sing the hymn again for the children as they pat the rhythm.

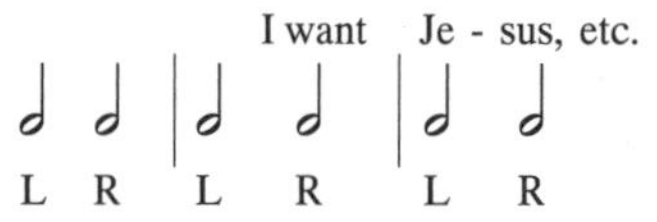
I want Je - sus, etc.
L R L R L R

• Teach by phrases. Children can continue feeling the pulse of the rhythm by patting thighs lightly.

• Transfer the rhythm to temple blocks or drums. Use two different pitches for left (low) and right (high).

• Add other rhythm instruments: finger cymbals on the first syllable of *Jesus*; claves playing three quarter notes (♩ ♩ ♩) when singing *walk with me*.

Sing in worship when the theme focuses on seeking the presence and comfort of Christ.

Capo 3
1 I want Je - sus to walk with me;
2 In my tri - als, Lord, walk with me;
3 When I'm in trou - ble, Lord, walk with me;
I want Je - sus to walk with me;
in my tri - als, Lord, walk with me;
when I'm in trou - ble, Lord, walk with me;
all a - long my pil - grim jour - ney,
when my heart is al - most break - ing,
when my head is bowed in sor - row,
Lord, I want Je - sus to walk with me.
Lord, I want Je - sus to walk with me.
Lord, I want Je - sus to walk with me.

Text: African American spiritual
Music: African American spiritual; arr. J. Jefferson Cleveland and Verolga Nix

Is there anybody here who loves my Jesus? 42

There is nothing complicated about this African American spiritual. Based on the pentatonic scale *(do-re-mi-sol-la),* it is straightforward and very simple in witnessing to the love of Christ.

- Teach the melody to the children. Sing by dividing into two sections. Assign the first and third phrases to one section, the second and fourth phrases to the other.
- Consider using the hymn "There's new life in Jesus" (#59) in alternation with the refrain, *Is there anybody here who loves my Jesus?*
- A leader or group of voices may sing the stanzas, with all joining on the refrain.
- Sign the words *love, Jesus, Lord,* and *know* (see pp. 212–213), adding movement to these two additional words:

Here: Palm down, move right arm waist high away from body in a half circle.

I: Point to self.

Sing in worship when the day's theme reminds us that life in Christ strengthens us to witness and serve.

Refrain
F
Is there an - y - bod - y here who loves my Je - sus,
C7 F
an - y - bod - y here who loves my Lord? I want to know if you
B♭ F B♭ F
love my Je - sus; I want to know if you love my Lord.
1 This world's a wil - der - ness of woe,
2 When I was blind and could not see,
so let us all to glo - ry go.
King Je - sus brought the light to me.
Refrain

Text: African American spiritual
Music: African American spiritual

43 Walk in God's ways

Moving to music comes naturally to young children. Providing opportunities for their spontaneity and creativity in a "doing" environment is of primary importance. To have success with this kind of experience, it is necessary that children learn to listen.

- Begin by playing a game. Using a hand drum, strike the drum with palm of the hand or a mallet. Tell the children to walk anywhere in the room while the drum is playing walking beats. Let them know when they are to stop by giving this directive: *Ready . . . and . . . stop.*

- Invite them to think of other activities that can be reflected by the drum. Example: *running, running, running, running, ready . . . and . . . stop.* The directive to stop is very important.

- Without any movement, teach the melody.

- Add other activity suggestions from the children.

- Now experience the singing with the movement. For the final phrase, *singing God's praise*, all activity stops. The children place both hands on their lips on the word *singing*, and slowly move them forward, palms up, as a singing gesture. This becomes their signal to finish their activity.

- Using this song in a classroom setting is one way to assist children in growing in their faith by teaching them to give thanks and sing praises even when they are walking, jumping, and hopping.

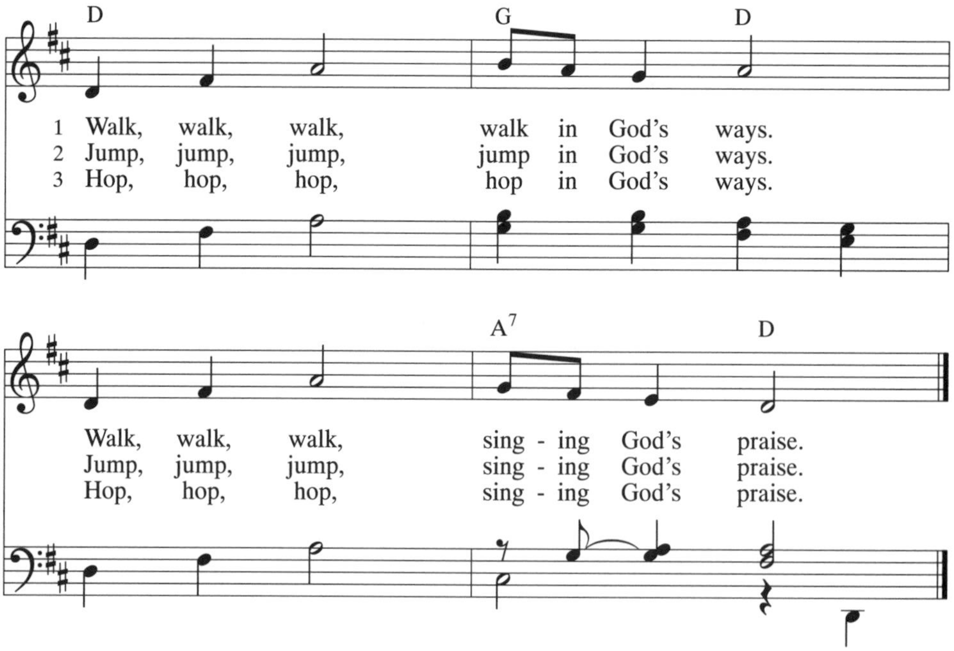
D
G
D
1 Walk, walk, walk, walk in God's ways.
2 Jump, jump, jump, jump in God's ways.
3 Hop, hop, hop, hop in God's ways.
A7
D
Walk, walk, walk, sing - ing God's praise.
Jump, jump, jump, sing - ing God's praise.
Hop, hop, hop, sing - ing God's praise.

Text: Pamela L. Hughes
Music: Pamela L. Hughes

Jesus, remember me

44

This short response takes us to the time when Jesus was crucified. Hanging on a nearby cross was a criminal who said these words, "Jesus, remember me when you come into your kingdom" (Luke 23:42-43). To the criminal and to us, through the gift of his body and blood, Christ gives a share in his own life, saying, "today you will be with me in Paradise."

This creative musical ostinato from the Taizé monastic community is intended to be repeated many times until we no longer focus on the words or the melody. Instead, we meditate on the promise of Jesus to remember us.

- The melody can be easily taught. Encourage the use of a light voice. Take special note to observe the rests.

- Teach the children to sign *Jesus, remember, me, come,* and *kingdom* (see pp. 212–213).

Sing on Christ the King Sunday (year C) or anytime during Holy Week.

Capo 1
D Em A D
E♭ Fm B♭ E♭
Je - sus, re - mem-ber me when you come in-to your king - dom.
Bm Em A D
Cm Fm B♭ E♭
Je - sus, re - mem-ber me when you come in-to your king - dom.

Text: Luke 23:42
Music: Jacques Berthier

45 For God so loved the world

Refrain
For God so loved the world that God gave the on - ly Son,
that who - ev - er be - lieves in him shall have e - ter - nal life.
1 As Mo - ses lift - ed the ser - pent in the wil - der - ness,
2 For God sent Je - sus from heav - en to this world of ours
3 For sure - ly Je - sus has taught us that we must be born
so the Son of God must be lift - ed that we may have life.
not to curse the world but to save us, that we may have life.
of the wa - ter and of the Spir - it, that we may have life.
Refrain

Text: Rusty Edwards
Music: Rusty Edwards

Lamb of God

See LifeSongs *recording Volume 2*

Jesus is spoken of as the Lamb of God in several places in the scriptures. As recorded in John 1:29, John the Baptist saw Jesus coming toward him and declared, "Here is the Lamb of God who takes away the sin of the world!" This song has long been sung in worship as the bread is broken for communion. It is a prayer addressed to Christ, who is present in the bread and wine for the forgiveness of sin. Sing the music softly with a spirit of devotion.

• Teach by phrases. Ask children to identify the phrases that are the same (the first two phrases are identical).

• Sign the words *Lamb* and *peace* (see pp. 212–213). Enhance other words with movement:

Sin: Arms crossed and placed on forehead, head bowed slightly.

World: Sweep arms in a circle bringing fingertips to meet above head.

Mercy: Arms straight in front, at waist.

On us: Spread arms out in a gentle gesture intended to include all people.

In addition to its usefulness during Lent and as a part of the liturgy, this hymn may be sung when John 1:29-42 is the appointed gospel reading.

F Gm Am Dm Em C F
Lamb of God, you take a-way the sin of the world; have
Dm F C F Gm Am Dm Em
mer-cy on us. Lamb of God, you take a-way the sin of the
C F Dm F C F B♭
world; have mer-cy on us. Lamb of God, you take a-way the
E♭ Fm B♭ Dm G C
sin of the world; grant us peace.

Text: traditional; tr. International Consultation on English Texts
Music: Richard W. Hillert

47 Hosanna! the little children sing

Holy Week begins on the Sunday before Easter, called Palm Sunday or Sunday of the Passion. On the first Palm Sunday, the people celebrated Jesus the king. As he rode into Jerusalem on a donkey, they remembered the promise of the Messiah coming just that way, in Zechariah 9:9. But when he did not show his power in the way they thought he should, their hosannas ended.

• Sing the song for the children asking them to tap the beat on their knees, two pulses in each measure.

• Teach the song by inviting the children to repeat each phrase after it is sung.

• If possible, have in hand a palm branch saved from the previous Palm Sunday. Make a palm branch from construction paper for each child.

• Practice waving the palm branch in the air to the rhythm. Invite the children to play follow the leader while singing. March around the room as if in a procession.

Sing on the Sunday of the Passion. Following the singing of the hymn "All glory, laud, and honor" the children could sing "Hosanna! the little children sing"

Capo 1 A B♭
D E♭ E7 F7 A B♭
"Ho - san - na! Ho - san - na!" the lit - tle chil - dren sing;
"Ho - san - na! Ho - san - na! For Christ our Lord is King."
"Pre - pare the way," the chil - dren sing, "Ho - san - na to our
Lord and King!" "Ho - san - na! Ho - san - na!" the lit - tle chil - dren
sing; "Ho - san - na! Ho - san - na! For Christ our Lord is King."

Text: Helen Kemp
Music: Helen Kemp

All glory, laud, and honor

Refrain
Capo 3
G C Em C D G
B♭ E♭ Gm E♭ F B♭
All glo - ry, laud, and hon - or to you, re - deem - er, king,
C Em C D G
E♭ Gm E♭ F B♭
to whom the lips of chil - dren made sweet ho - san - nas ring.
G D Bm Em A D
B♭ F Dm Gm C F
1 You are the king of Is - rael and Da - vid's roy - al Son,
2 The com - pa - ny of an - gels is prais - ing you on high;
3 The mul - ti - tude of pil - grims with palms be - fore you went.
4 To you, be - fore your Pas - sion, they sang their hymns of praise.
5 Their prais - es you ac - cept - ed; ac - cept the prayers we bring,
G C D Em Am D G
B♭ E♭ F Gm Cm F B♭ Refrain
now in the Lord's name com - ing, our King and Bless - ed One.
cre - a - tion and all mor - tals in cho - rus make re - ply.
Our praise and prayer and an - thems be - fore you we pre - sent.
To you, now high ex - alt - ed, our mel - o - dy we raise.
great au - thor of all good - ness, O good and gra - cious King.

Text: Theodulph of Orleans; tr. John M. Neale
Music: Melchior Teschner

49 Filled with excitement

See LifeSongs *recording Volume 2*

This Spanish hymn depicts Jesus' triumphal entry into Jerusalem. Explain to the children that in Jesus' time, to spread cloaks and branches (in Spanish, *mantos y palmas*), was an act of homage to a king. The excitement builds as the crowd breaks into hosannas. We are called today to praise Christ with our hosannas and to follow him in love and faith.

- Clap the rhythm of each phrase for stanza 1.
- To establish the rhythm, teach the stanzas before moving on to the refrain.
- Rhythm instruments will enhance the text. Add maracas playing an eighth-note pattern throughout. For the *hosanna* section a soprano glockenspiel can play the melody. Sound a pair of large cymbals (or one cymbal struck with a mallet) on the *ho* of *hosanna* each time.

Sing on the Sunday of the Passion.

C F
1 Filled with ex - cite - ment, all the hap - py throng
2 As in that en - trance to Je - ru - sa - lem,
1 Man - tos y pal - mas es - par - cien - do va
2 Co - mo en la en - tra - da de Je - ru - sa - lén,
Fm C
spread cloaks and branch - es on the cit - y streets.
ho - san - nas we will sing to Je - sus Christ,
el pue - blo a - le - gre de Je - ru - sa - lén,
to - dos can - ta - mos a Je - sús, el rey,
F
There in the dis - tance they be - gin to see,
to our re - deem - er who still calls to - day,
a - llá a lo le - jos se em - pie - za a mi - rar
al Cris - to vi - vo que nos lla - ma hoy
Fm C
there on a don - key comes the Son of God.
asks us to fol - low with our love and faith.
en un po - lli - no al Hi - jo de Dios.
pa - ra se - guir - le con a - mor y fe.
Refrain
F Em
From ev - 'ry cor - ner a thou - sand voic - es sing
Mien - tras, mil vo - ces re - sue - nan por do - quier: Ho -

F G7 C
praise to the one who comes in the name of God.
san - na al que vie - ne en el nom - bre del Se - ñor.
F Em D7
With one great shout of ac - cla - ma - tion loud, tri - um - phant song breaks
Con un a - lien - to de gran ex - cla - ma - ción pro - rrum - pen con voz triun -
G C F
forth: Ho - san - na!
fal: ¡Ho - san - na!
G C
Ho - san - na to the king! Ho -
¡Ho - san - na al rey! ¡Ho -
F G C
san - na! Ho - san - na to the king!
san - na! ¡Ho - san - na al rey!

Text: Rubén Ruiz Avila; tr. Gertrude C. Suppe
Music: Rubén Ruiz Avila; arr. Alvin Schutmaat

50 Hosanna! This is a special day

To shouts of "Hosanna!" Jesus made his triumphal entry into Jerusalem. Palm branches are blessed and waved in procession to begin the liturgy that announces the first day of Holy Week. Palm branches symbolize victory, but the mood shifts quickly as one of the passion accounts is read. Children can participate in the processional gospel with this joyful song.

- Begin by singing *sol-mi-sol*, asking children to echo. Finish the phrase with the words and melody. Sing the second phrase with syllables, children echoing. Finish the phrase with the words and melody.
- Practice speaking *ho-***zah***-na* in rhythm. The third syllable should be pronounced softly. Add the melody line.
- Finish teaching the song. Discuss the form: AABA.
- Add an Orff instrument such as a bass xylophone. Or, sound the first and third beats on wood blocks or claves to create the sound of a donkey walking.
- Include the song on Palm Sunday in the reading of the processional gospel when one of the following is appointed:

Matthew 21:1-11: sing stanza 1 after verse 5, stanza 2 after verse 9.
Mark 11:1-11: sing stanza 1 after verse 7, stanza 2 after verse 10.
Luke 19:28-40: sing stanza 1 after verse 36, stanza 2 after verse 38.
John 12:12-15: reverse the stanzas to complement the text. Sing stanza 2 after verse 13, stanza 1 after verse 15.

I II (echo) All
C G
1 Ho - san-na! Ho - san-na! This is a spe-cial
2 Ho - san-na! Ho - san-na! Oh, how the voic-es
I II (echo) All
C G C
day. He's com-ing! He's com-ing! The king is on his way.
ring. We see him! We see him! He is our King of kings.
I II (echo) All
F C D G
Did you hear? Can it be? Rid-ing on a colt is he.
Wave the palms, sing a song! We have wait-ed for so long.
I II (echo) All
C G C
Ho - san-na! Ho - san-na! Bless-ed be our Lord.
Ho - san-na! Ho - san-na! Bless-ed be our Lord.

Text: Kathleen Donlan Tunseth
Music: Kathleen Donlan Tunseth

Bass xylophone

Were you there

51

Capo 1
D Em A D G D
E♭ Fm B♭ E♭ A♭ E♭
1 Were you there when they cru - ci - fied my Lord?
2 Were you there when they nailed him to the tree?
3 Were you there when they pierced him in the side?
G D A G A
A♭ E♭ B♭ A♭ B♭
Were you there when they cru - ci - fied my Lord?
Were you there when they nailed him to the tree?
Were you there when they pierced him in the side?
Refrain
D G D G D F♯ Bm
E♭ A♭ E♭ A♭ E♭ G Cm
Oh! some - times it caus - es me to
G D G A G
A♭ E♭ A♭ B♭ A♭
trem - ble, trem - ble, trem - ble. Were you
D Em A D G D
E♭ Fm B♭ E♭ A♭ E♭
there when they cru - ci - fied my Lord?
there when they nailed him to the tree?
there when they pierced him in the side?

4 Were you there when the sun refused to shine?
5 Were you there when they laid him in the tomb?

Text: African American spiritual
Music: African American spiritual; arr. *LifeSongs*

52 Glory be to Jesus

This familiar hymn has been given newer words that are more accessible to children. Learn stanza 1 during Lent; add stanza 2 during Easter.

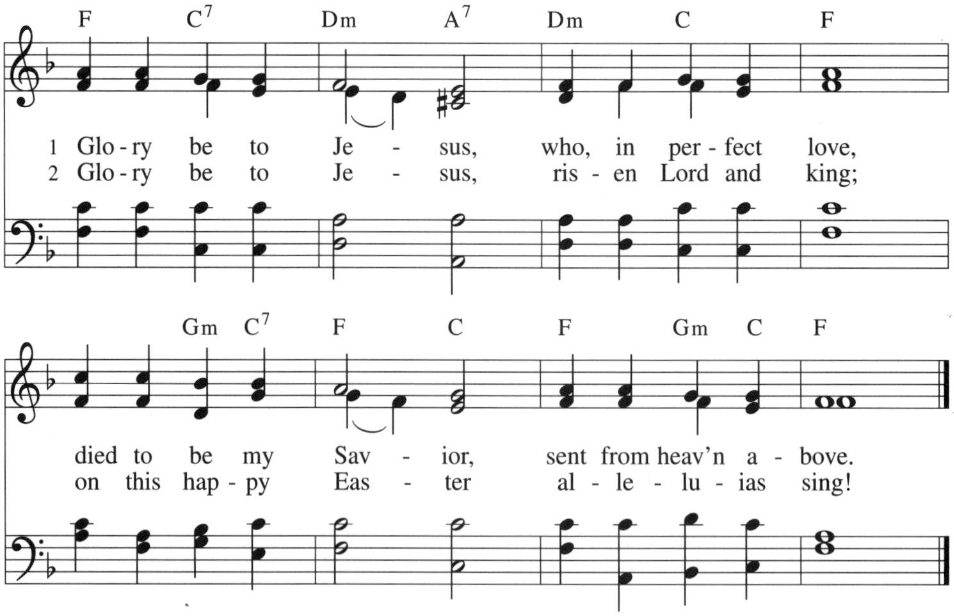
F C7 Dm A7 Dm C F
1 Glo-ry be to Je - sus, who, in per-fect love,
2 Glo-ry be to Je - sus, ris - en Lord and king;
Gm C7 F C F Gm C F
died to be my Sav - ior, sent from heav'n a - bove.
on this hap-py Eas - ter al - le - lu - ias sing!

Text: Dorothy N. Schultz
Music: Friedrich Filitz

53 Do you know who died for me?

See LifeSongs *recording Volume 1*

Children like to ask questions. To be a part of the Christian community leads children to inquisitiveness about God and Jesus. Who are they? Where are they? Why can't I see them? This simple song is a beginning for the young child in taking steps toward growing in faith.

• Begin by teaching the children to speak, with expression, the words *Jesus did. Jesus did*, and *Yes, he really did*. The leader then speaks the questions with the children speaking the answer.

• Teach the children the melody for their answer. Now the leader sings the questions, children sing the answers.

• Continue this pattern changing the word *did* to *does*.

Surprise the children by singing the questions without any announcement and see how spontaneous their answers will be.

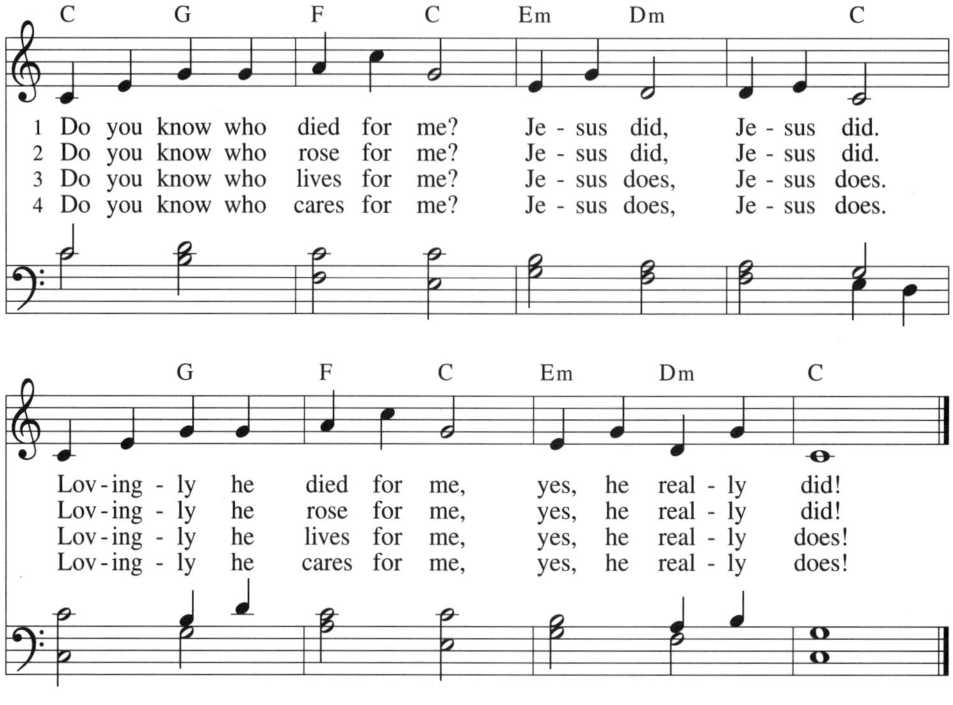
C G F C Em Dm C
1 Do you know who died for me? Je - sus did, Je - sus did.
2 Do you know who rose for me? Je - sus did, Je - sus did.
3 Do you know who lives for me? Je - sus does, Je - sus does.
4 Do you know who cares for me? Je - sus does, Je - sus does.
G F C Em Dm C
Lov-ing - ly he died for me, yes, he real - ly did!
Lov-ing - ly he rose for me, yes, he real - ly did!
Lov-ing - ly he lives for me, yes, he real - ly does!
Lov-ing - ly he cares for me, yes, he real - ly does!

Text: O. William Luecke
Music: O. William Luecke, arr. Richard W. Gieseke

This is the feast 54

See LifeSongs *recording Volume 1*

Even the youngest children can be taught to sing parts of the liturgy. Short responses are most easily learned. This refrain is especially meaningful since it is repeated several times within the hymn of praise, "Worthy is Christ." The theme of this canticle comes from Revelation 5:12, "Worthy is the Lamb that was slaughtered to receive power and wealth and wisdom and might and honor and glory and blessing!"

- Sing this refrain to younger children, inviting them to tap the beat on their knees. Transfer to rhythm sticks, if available.
- Teach by short phrases.
- Add movement. Walk the beat while singing *This is the feast*. Stand still and clap the beat on the alleluias. It is important to stop moving on the word *God*. Teach the children to listen.
- This canticle is often sung in worship during the season of Easter and on other festivals. When the children participate, instruct the congregation that the children will sing the opening refrain. The congregation continues with the words *Worthy is Christ*.

D G F♯m G A Bm
This is the feast of vic-to-ry for our God.
Em A D F Em A
Al-le-lu-ia, al-le-lu-ia, al-le-lu-ia.

Text: John W. Arthur
Music: Richard W. Hillert

55 Now the green blade rises

Set to the French carol NOËL NOUVELET, this song compares the resurrection of Christ to wheat sprouting from the earth. Wheat that once lay in the depths of the earth now lives. Love lives again! Stanza 4 reminds us there are times when we are weighed down with troubles. The presence of Christ calls us back to life once again.

• Younger children can understand the burying of a seed in the dark earth and how it bursts forth into a living plant. During the third or fourth week in Lent, arrange for each child to plant seeds (of wheat, if possible) in a small container. By Easter the green shoots will be bursting forth through the dark soil.

• For older children add the following movements as suggested by Shirley W. McRae: In a circle formation, the children are linked together by holding colored scarves. The group does a grapevine step (or walks) to the right for phrase one, to the left for phrase two, to the center and back for phrases three and four. For the interludes, step the rhythm of the accompaniment in a clockwise direction.

Introduction: measures 1–8 of AX/AM, BX/BM.

Stanza 1: sung with instruments and dance.

Interlude: measures 1–8 of AX/AM, BX/BM, with movement.

Continue singing stanzas 2–4 with interludes, concluding with stanza 4.

• Soprano recorder (or flute) may double the melody.

Dm G Dm
1 Now the green blade ris - es from the bur - ied grain,
2 In the grave they laid him, love by ha - tred slain,
3 Forth he came at Eas - ter, like the ris - en grain,
4 When our hearts are win - try, griev - ing, or in pain,
SG
AG SM
Trgl.
AX AM
Tamb.
BX BM
G Dm
wheat that in dark earth man - y days has lain;
think - ing that he would nev - er wake a - gain,
he that for three days in the grave had lain;
your touch can call us back to life a - gain,

A7 Dm A7
love lives a - gain, that with the dead has been;
laid in the earth like grain that sleeps un - seen;
raised from the dead my ris - en Lord is seen;
fields of our hearts that dead and bare have been;
Dm G Dm
love is come a - gain like wheat a - ris - ing green.
love is come a - gain like wheat a - ris - ing green.
love is come a - gain like wheat a - ris - ing green.
love is come a - gain like wheat a - ris - ing green.

Text: John M. C. Crum
Music: French carol; arr. Shirley W. McRae

56 In the bulb there is a flower

Hymn of promise

See LifeSongs *recording Volume 2*

Trying to understand why a loved one dies can be extremely traumatic for a young person. Nature supplies many images that suggest the truth of death and resurrection. Phyllis Wezeman suggests a creative way to introduce this Easter hymn:

• Prepare these symbols as pieces of a puzzle: a flower bulb and a flower; a small seed and an apple tree; a picture of a cocoon and a butterfly; a cold, wintery scene (maybe from a picture) and an orchard of beautiful, flowery trees; a cross and an empty tomb.

• Say: I have a game for us to play. Perhaps you can help me complete this puzzle. The idea is to match the two symbols that go together. We might be able to tell just by looking at the symbol, but each puzzle piece will only fit with the one that is the correct answer. Let's look at each piece and see if we can figure it out. (Hold up each piece and name the symbol. Then choose enough participants to help match the correct pieces.)

Can you find the one that matches the flower? How do you know the bulb matches the flower? (Flowers come from bulbs.) What about the apple? Why does the seed match? (Apple trees grow from seeds.) We know what goes with the butterfly, but why would these two be partners? (Butterflies come from cocoons.)

continued on next page

F Gm7
1 In the bulb there is a flow - er; in the seed, an ap-ple tree;
2 There's a song in ev-'ry si - lence, seek-ing word and mel-o - dy;
3 In our end is our be - gin - ning; in our time, in - fin - i - ty;
C7 F
in co-coons, a hid-den prom - ise: but - ter-flies will soon be free!
there's a dawn in ev-'ry dark-ness, bring-ing hope to you and me.
in our doubt there is be - liev - ing; in our life, e - ter - ni - ty;
B♭ F Gm A7 Dm
In the cold and snow of win - ter there's a spring that waits to be,
From the past will come the fu - ture; what it holds, a mys-ter - y,
in our death, a res - ur - rec - tion; at the last, a vic - to - ry,
B♭ F Dm Gm7 C7 F
un-re - vealed un-til its sea - son, some-thing God a-lone can see.

Text: Natalie Sleeth
Music: Natalie Sleeth

continued from previous page

• All of these symbols teach us the same lesson. Can you guess what it is? (Listen to speculations.) Actually, I was thinking that these symbols from nature teach us that the end is just the beginning. When a plant dies in the fall, all that is left is the dead-looking bulb. Yet in the spring, that dead-looking bulb becomes a flower! When an apple falls to the ground, the outer layer rots away leaving only the seeds. In time, those seeds can produce new apple trees that blossom and produce more fruit! And we all know that the caterpillar seems to die inside a cocoon, but soon the caterpillar becomes a new creature transformed into a beautiful butterfly! Each time, what seems to be the end becomes a new beginning!

• Isn't that the message of Easter? (Hold up the additional puzzle pieces containing the Easter symbols, the cross and the empty tomb.) Can you explain why these two symbols are related? (Wait while children explain the story of the resurrection. Let one begin and another add to the story, filling in details as needed.) What looked like the end of Jesus' life as he died on the cross was actually a new beginning for everyone. Jesus rose from the dead and promised that those who believe will have eternal life, too.

• Sometimes we don't know how God will solve the puzzle of life's mysteries. But whenever we feel that we have reached an end, we might look at flowers, apples, and butterflies, and remember that in each end is a beginning. Easter teaches us to remember that even death is simply the beginning of a new kind of life with God. That is the promise God makes to each one of us. That is the promise of Easter.

Sing anytime during the Easter season. Or include in a service for the burial of the dead, especially when young children are part of the family.

Jesus Christ is risen today — 57

Young children can begin to sing well-known Easter hymns by learning a phrase such as this and using it as a classroom response.

Je - sus Christ is ris'n to - day, al - le - lu - ia!

Text: Latin carol; tr. *Lyra Davidica*
Music: *Lyra Davidica*

58 Alleluia, alleluia, give thanks

Alleluia No. 1

Refrain
F Dm Gm C
Al - le - lu - ia, al - le - lu - ia, give thanks to the ris - en Lord;
F Dm Gm C F
al - le - lu - ia, al - le - lu - ia, give praise to his name.
F Dm B♭ C
1 Je - sus is Lord of all the earth;
2 Spread the good news o'er all the earth:
3 We have been cru - ci - fied with Christ;
4 Come, let us praise the liv - ing God,
F Dm B♭ C
Refrain
he is the king of cre - a - tion.
Je - sus has died and has ris - en.
now we shall live . . . for - ev - er.
joy - ful - ly sing to our Sav - ior.

Text: Donald Fishel
Music: Donald Fishel; arr. Betty Pulkingham

There's new life in Jesus

Easter is the season of new life. "See, I am making all things new," says the voice from the throne (Revelation 21:5). All things are new and in this we rejoice. We raise our voices in singing about this new life.

• Clap each of the phrases, inviting children to echo. Discuss which phrases are the same and which ones are different (the first, second, and fourth phrases are the same; the third phrase is different). The form of this song is AABA.

• Write the melody of the first and third phrases on poster board (11" x 17") or on a chalkboard (see below). Sight read the phrases using syllables *(do, re, mi)*. The key is F.

• Add a simple Orff accompaniment. A tambourine can play on beats two and four.

• Relate scripture to each of the stanzas. Rotate the reading of scripture among the children each time the song is sung in class. A suggested pattern is that the scripture for stanza 1 be read, followed by the singing of stanza 1, and so on.

Stanza 1: John 8:12
Stanza 2: 1 Peter 2:24

F C F
1 There's new life in Je - sus, lift up your heart!
2 There is heal - ing in his love, lift up your heart!
C F
There's new life in Je - sus, lift up your heart!
There is heal - ing in his love, lift up your heart!
Lift up your heart! Lift up your heart!
Lift up your heart! Lift up your heart!
C7 F
There's new life in Je - sus, lift up your heart!
There is heal - ing in his love, lift up your heart!

Text: anonymous
Music: anonymous; arr. *LifeSongs*

do do do re mi do mi mi re do
sol sol la sol mi mi fa mi

60 This is the day

Easter means new life for us. This joyful Easter song pairs a refrain based on Psalm 118:24 with two stanzas celebrating Christ's resurrection. Children will enjoy learning the words and the melody. Its bright uplifting mood and short phrases will assist in the teaching.

- Teach the refrain. Clap on the word *rejoice*. Sign the word *hallelujah* (see *Alleluia*, p. 212).

- Write the notes of the first measure of stanza 1 on a chalkboard or poster board.

If the children have music in hand ask them how many times this phrase appears (four times, once at the beginning of each of the phrases). If teaching by rote, sing the phrase for them. Invite them to listen and raise their hands each time it is heard.

- Add a simple dance movement to the refrain.

This is the day: Beginning with either foot, step forward on the first beat, then back on the third beat. Repeat the movement with the other foot.

Rejoice, rejoice: Clap hands in rhythm.

And be exceeding glad: Turn around once in place; repeat, then conclude by signing *hallelujah*.

Remain in place while singing the stanzas.

Sing the refrain as a response to the reading or chanting of Psalm 118, or sing the entire song in place of the psalm on Easter Sunday.

Refrain
This is the day that the Lord has made! Re - joice! Re - joice, and be ex-ceed-ing glad! This is the day that the Lord has made! Re - joice! Re-joice! Hal-le - lu - jah!
1 Christ has con-quered death at last, left the tomb that held him fast!
2 Je - sus lives who once was dead, crown of glo - ry on his head.
Gone the sor-row, gone the night. Dawns the morn-ing clear and bright!
Ris - en now our Lord and King: songs of glad-ness let us sing.
Refrain

Text: Natalie Sleeth
Music: Natalie Sleeth

Come and see

See LifeSongs *recording Volume 2*

Doubting Thomas is the name often given to the person referred to in this song. Thomas did not believe the reports that Christ was alive. Based on John 20:19-29, Thomas had a second chance to see Jesus when he appeared again. The risen Lord appeared again to the disciples to help Thomas believe.

Like Thomas, doubt has a way of hindering our belief. When that occurs we need to remember the gift of Christ's presence with us. He continues to seek those who may have missed the offer of peace and life through his resurrection.

• Speak the stanzas with expression to the children, asking them to respond in speech with the words *Come and see! Come and see*.

• Teach the melody to the response *Come and see*. Keep the syncopation accented and accurate.

• As the children become more familiar with the song divide them into two groups, with one taking the part of leader. All join on the refrain.

Leader
All
1 The night was dark and filled with gloom. They
2 Then sud-den-ly the Lord ap-peared (Come and see! Come and see.) to
3 Well, Thom-as said, "My God, my Lord!" Now
hid with-in a se-cret room. Now
see his friends and calm their fears. (Come and see! Come and see.) To
I be-lieve the liv-ing Word. Go
Thom-as had not seen the Lord. He
Thom-as he said, "See my hand." (Come and see! Come and see.) It
tell the peo-ple far and wide, 'twas
doubt-ed ev-'ry sin-gle word.
hap-pened just as God had planned. (Come and see! Come and see.)
for their sins that Je-sus died.
Refrain
I be-lieve this is Je-sus! Come and see! Come and see. Oh,
I be-lieve this is Je-sus! Come and see! Come and see.

Text: John Ylvisaker, based on John 20:24-28
Music: African American spiritual

62 Alleluia! Jesus is risen!

How does a child come to know the risen Christ? Where do we find Christ today? In conversation with the children, recognize the actions that reveal Christ's presence with us. Christ welcomes people and turns no one away, speaks words of hope rather than words that hurt others, washes and refreshes people, clothes and gives light, feeds the hungry, heals the sick, sings with his friends, and cares for the poor. In all these actions, present in the church's liturgy, Christ is revealed. Engage the children in discussing how one of these actions is carried out in their own church setting.

- Teach the refrain and add signing to the words *Jesus, risen, God, glory*, and *Alleluia* (see pp. 212–213).
- Before teaching each stanza invite older children to discuss the actions that reveal the risen Christ.
- Share the various "I am" sayings of Jesus. Refer to John 6:48, "I am the bread of life"; John 6:51, "I am the living bread that came down from heaven"; John 8:12, "I am the light of the world"; John 10:11, "I am the good shepherd"; John 11:25, "I am the resurrection and the life"; John 14:6, "I am the way, and the truth, and the life"; John 15:5, "I am the vine, you are the branches."

G C G D Em Bm
1 Al - le - lu - ia! Je - sus is ris - en!
2 Walk - ing the way, Christ in the cen - ter
3 Je - sus the vine, we are the branch - es;
4 Weep - ing, be gone; sor - row, be si - lent:
5 Cit - y of God, Eas - ter for - ev - er,
C Am7 G C D G
Trum - pets re - sound - ing in glo - ri - ous light!
tell - ing the sto - ry to o - pen our eyes;
life in the Spir - it the fruit of the tree;
death put a - sun - der, and Eas - ter is bright.
gold - en Je - ru - sa - lem, Je - sus the Lamb,
Am G D G D A D
Splen - dor, the Lamb, heav - en for - ev - er!
break - ing our bread, giv - ing us glo - ry:
heav - en to earth, Christ to the peo - ple,
Cher - u - bim sing: "O grave, be o - pen!"
riv - er of life, saints and arch - an - gels,
C Am7 G C D G
Oh, what a mir - a - cle God has in sight!
Je - sus our bless - ing, our con - stant sur - prise.
gift of the fu - ture now flow - ing to me.
Clothe us in won - der, a - dorn us in light.
sing with cre - a - tion to God the I AM!

Refrain
Je - sus is ris - en and we shall a - rise:
Give God the glo - ry! Al - le - lu - ia!

Text: Herbert F. Brokering
Music: David N. Johnson

He is Lord 63

He is Lord, he is Lord, he is ris - en from the dead and he is Lord;
ev - 'ry knee shall bow, ev - 'ry tongue con - fess that Je - sus Christ is Lord.

Text: Philippians 2:10-11, adapt.
Music: traditional

64 Christ the Lord is risen today!

This joyful Easter hymn rings clear with the message of the resurrection and our joy at this crowning event. The words were written by Charles Wesley in the first year following his conversion, 1739. For more information on Charles Wesley see "Oh, for a thousand tongues to sing" (#185).

The tune is a French melody from the 13th century. Matched with the words by Wesley, the tune today is sung in triumphal praise of the resurrection.

• Introduce by lightly clapping a steady beat, chanting:

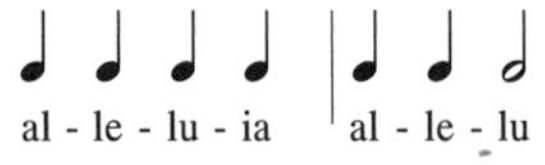
al - le - lu - ia
al - le - lu

Invite children to join in.

• Chant two measures of *Alleluia, allelu*, then speak the first phrase of the text in rhythm (leader first, children echo). Chant two more measures of *Alleluia, allelu*, then speak the second phrase in rhythm. Continue this pattern for phrases three and four, concluding with two measures of *Alleluia, allelu*.

• Teach the melody substituting the words *Alleluia, allelu* for each phrase. Once the melody is learned, add the text.

• Play finger cymbals on the first word of each phrase.

• Children can sing an introduction to this hymn in worship using the words *Alleluia, allelu*. The congregation follows with the singing of stanza 1.

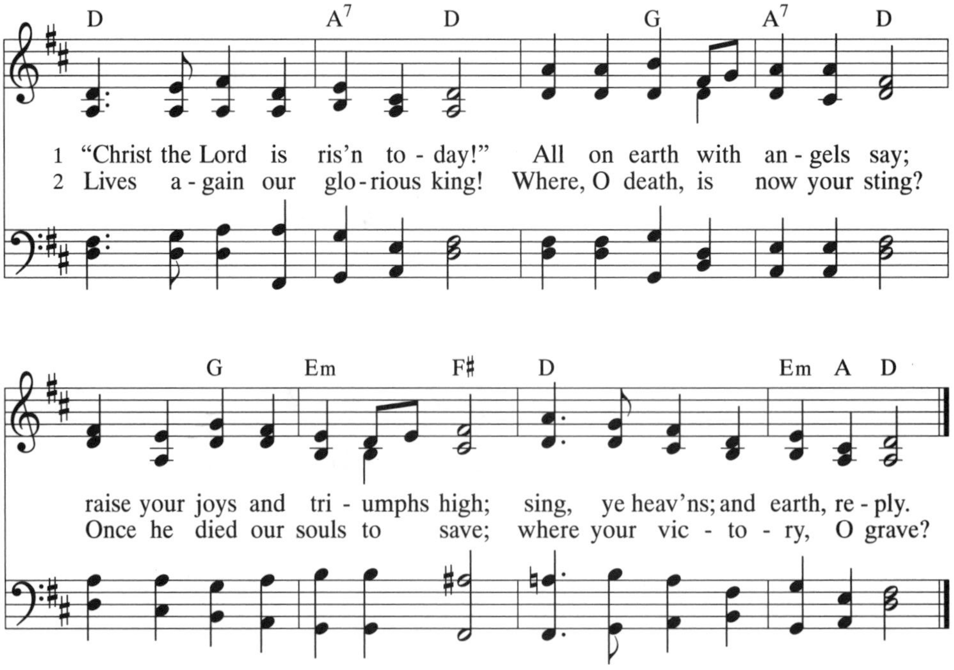
D A7 D G A7 D
1 "Christ the Lord is ris'n to - day!" All on earth with an - gels say;
2 Lives a - gain our glo - rious king! Where, O death, is now your sting?
G Em F♯ D Em A D
raise your joys and tri - umphs high; sing, ye heav'ns; and earth, re - ply.
Once he died our souls to save; where your vic - to - ry, O grave?

Text: Charles Wesley
Music: French traditional

The Lord is my shepherd

See LifeSongs *recording Volume 1*

Children may have no experience of sheep or shepherds. Show pictures and talk with them about the shepherds who care for the flock. Point out that by overseeing the well-being of the flock, the shepherd helps the sheep do what they do best—eat and grow. The shepherd seeks safe places for the sheep, stands watch in the night, and constantly searches for green pastures. All this is done for the sake of the flock. Jesus promises to be our shepherd. He knows what is safe for us, stands watch in our most troublesome times, and constantly turns us toward ways that will help us grow into all we have been baptized to be.

- Teach by two-measure phrases.
- Feel the rhythm by clapping on the first beat and then moving the hands up in the air making a circle to prepare to clap on the first beat of the next measure. Keep the hands moving while singing the first eight measures (A section).
- Fold hands for next eight measures (B section).
- Repeat clapping movement (A section) to *Fine*.
- Sing the first eight measures (A section) as an antiphon to Psalm 23 before verses 1 and 4, and after verse 6. Accompany with Orff instruments, keyboard, or guitar. Include the children as active participants when Psalm 23 is included in worship.

1*
F C F
The Lord is my shep-herd; I'll walk with him al - ways.
C F Fine
He leads me by still wa - ters; I'll walk with him al - ways.
2
C F
Al - ways, al - ways, I'll walk with him al - ways.
D.C. al fine
C F
Al - ways, al - ways, I'll walk with him al - ways.

**may be sung as a round*

Second piano part, for playing as a duet or bass metallophone

Text: Psalm 23:1-2
Music: traditional, arr. Charlotte Larsen

66 Gracious Spirit, heed our pleading

See LifeSongs *recording Volume 1*

Howard Olson has given us a gift of song from his days as a missionary in Tanzania (see "Listen, God is calling," #79). In the text we call on the Spirit for vitality and inspiration to guide us, to teach us, and to nourish our unity in worship and witness. *Come, Holy Spirit, come!*

- Write the rhythm of the first and third measures on a chalkboard or poster board. Clap each rhythm. Can children find these rhythms in the song? (Measures one and two are the same, measures three and four are the same.)
- Sign the words *come* and *Holy Spirit* (see pp. 212–213). Teach the Swahili. Pronounced: *Njoh-ho, njoh-ho, njoh-ho, row-ho mway-mah*.
- Add a hand drum or a conga. Find two sounds on the instrument, one near the rim with fingertips, another with the palm of the hand played in the middle.

Stanzas:

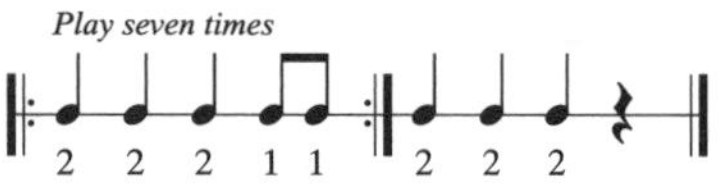
Play seven times
2 2 2 1 1 2 2 2

Refrain:

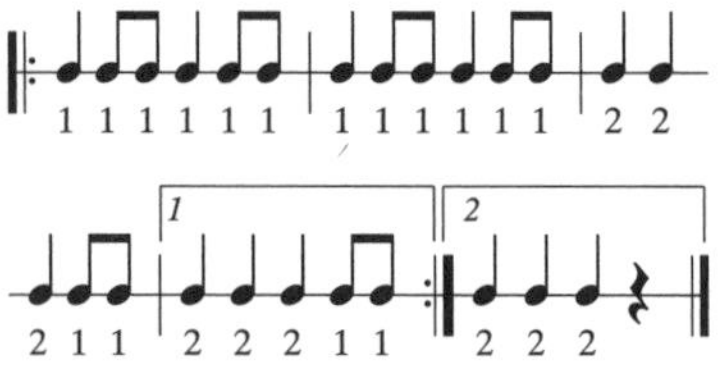
1 1 1 1 1 1 1 1 1 1 1 1 2 2
1
2
2 1 1 2 2 2 1 1 2 2 2

Have children sing stanza 1 and refrain on the Day of Pentecost. Children can also lead the congregation in singing one phrase of the refrain as a response to petitions offered in the prayers of the church.

G D7 G D G
1 Gra - cious Spir - it, heed our plead - ing, fash - ion us all a - new.
2 Come to teach us, come to nour - ish those who be - lieve in Christ.
3 Guide our think - ing and our speak - ing done in your ho - ly name.
4 Not mere knowl - edge, but dis - cern - ment, nor root - less lib - er - ty;
5 Keep us fer - vent in our wit - ness; un - swayed by earth's al - lure.
D7 G D G
It's your lead - ing that we're need - ing, help us to fol - low you.
Bless the faith - ful, may they flour - ish, strength - ened by grace un - priced.
Mo - ti - vate all in their seek - ing, free - ing from guilt and shame.
turn dis - qui - et to con - tent - ment, doubt in - to cer - tain - ty.
Ev - er grant us zeal - ous fit - ness, which you a - lone as - sure.
Refrain/Kipokeo
G Am D G Am7 D G
Come, come, come, Ho - ly Spir - it, come.
Njo - o, njo - o, njo - o, Ro - ho mwe - ma.
Am D G Am7 D G
Come, come, come, Ho - ly Spir - it, come.
Njo - o, njo - o, njo - o, Ro - ho mwe - ma.

Text: Wilson Niwagila; tr. Howard S. Olson
Music: Wilson Niwagila; arr. Egil Hovland

Come, O Holy Spirit, come

67

This joyful Nigerian song may be repeated a number of times and makes a rousing Pentecost processional. A hand drum and shakers may be added. Teach the pronunciation of the original text: *wah wah wah eh-mee-mee-moh, eh-mee-oh-loh-yeh; wah wah wah ah-lahg-bah-rah, ah-lahg-bah-rah-meh-tah, wah-oh . . .*

All
Come, O Ho-ly Spir-it, come,
Wa wa wa E-mi-mi-mo,
Come, al-might-y Spir-it,
Wa wa wa A-lag-ba-
Leader
Ho-ly Spir-it, come.
E-mi-o-lo-ye.
come,
ra,
Come, come, come.
Wa-o wa-o wa-o.
al-might-y Spir-it, come.
A-lag-ba-ra-me-ta.
O Spir-it, come.
E-mi-mi-mo.

Text and music: The Church of the Lord (Aladura); transc. and para. I-to Loh

68 Spirit, Spirit of gentleness

Refrain
Spir - it, Spir-it of gen-tle-ness, blow through the wil-der-ness
call-ing and free; Spir - it, Spir-it of rest-less-ness,
stir me from plac-id-ness, wind, wind on the sea.
1 You moved on the wa - ters, you called to the
2 You swept through the des - ert, you stung with the
3 You sang in a sta - ble, you cried from a
4 You call from to - mor - row, you break an - cient

D A D Bm
deep, then you coaxed up the moun - tains from the
sand and you goad - ed your peo - ple with a
hill, then you whis - pered in si - lence when the
schemes. From the bond - age of sor - row all the
E A D G
val - leys of sleep; and o - ver the e -
law and a land; and when they were blind -
whole world was still; and down in the cit -
cap - tives dream dreams; our wom - en see vi -
A G D Bm
ons you called to each thing: "A - wake from your
ed with i - dols and lies, then you spoke through your
y you called once a - gain, when you blew through your
sions, our men clear their eyes. With bold new de -
GM7 Em7 A7 D
Refrain
slum - bers and rise on your wings."
proph - ets to o - pen their eyes.
peo - ple on the rush of the wind.
ci - sions your peo - ple a - rise.

Text: James K. Manley
Music: James K. Manley

69 Spirit Friend

Help the children to understand that God sent the Holy Spirit to help us live Christ-like lives. It all began with baptism, when the Spirit claimed us, transformed us, and made us one in Christ. The Spirit inspires our faith over and over again, pointing us always to God. In times of doubt the Spirit helps us to say, "I believe that Jesus Christ died for me."

• Talk with the children about key words in stanza 1 and their meaning: *befriend* (to act as a friend), *enliven* (to make active and lively), *sanctifies* (to make holy), *enlighten* (to inform).

• Chant stanza 1 in rhythm by phrases for children to echo. Encourage good diction.

• The first three eighth notes of each measure establish the piece's rhythm. Invite children to clap the three notes with an accompanying drum.

Clap:

Drum:

• Teach the melody with the words, in short one-measure phrases.

• Sing accompanied only by claps (a rhythm instrument such as claves could be substituted) and drum.

Am Em F C
1 God sends us the Spir - it to be - friend and help us,
2 Dark - ened roads are clear - er, heav - y bur - dens light - er,
3 Now we are God's peo - ple, bond - ed by God's pres - ence,
Em G C
re - cre - ate and guide us, Spir - it Friend.
when we're walk - ing with our Spir - it Friend.
a - gents of God's pur - pose, Spir - it Friend.
Am Em F C
Spir - it who en - liv - ens, sanc - ti - fies, en - light - ens,
Now we need not fear the pow - ers of the dark - ness.
Lead us for - ward ev - er, slip - ping back - ward nev - er,
Em G C
sets us free, is now our Spir - it Friend.
None can o - ver - come our Spir - it Friend.
to your re - made world, our Spir - it Friend.

Em G C Em G
*
Spir-it of our mak - er, Spir-it Friend. Spir-it of our Je - su,
C Em G C
Spir-it Friend. Spir-it of God's peo - ple, Spir-it Friend.

*hand claps

Text: Tom Colvin
Music: Gonja traditional, adapt. Tom Colvin; arr. Marty Haugen

70 Holy, Holy Spirit

Refrain
C G Am F Dm7
Ho - ly, Ho - ly Spir - it, ho - ly, ho - ly
G C G Am
dove, ho - ly, ho - ly help - er,
F G Am Em F G C
ho - ly fire of love, ho - ly fire of love.

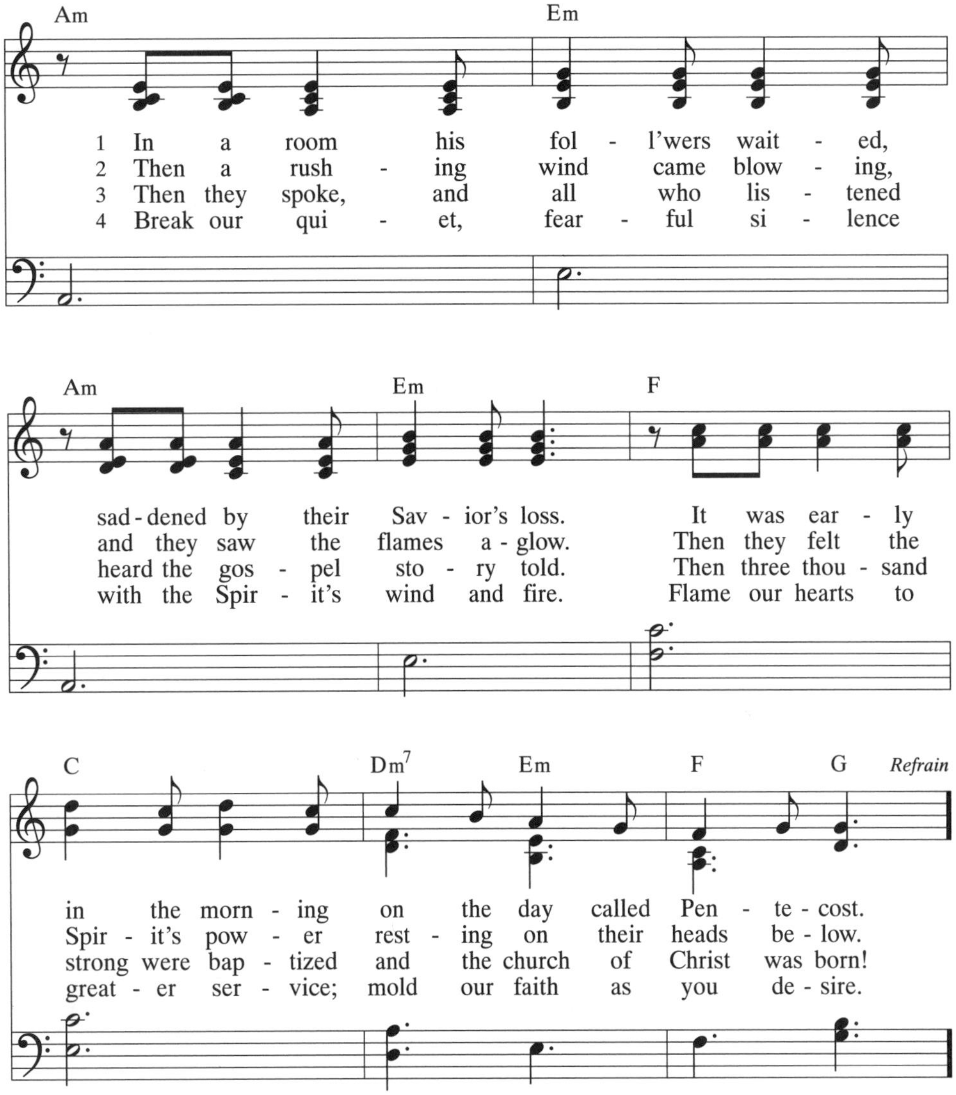
Am
Em
1 In a room his fol - l'wers wait - ed,
2 Then a rush - ing wind came blow - ing,
3 Then they spoke, and all who lis - tened
4 Break our qui - et, fear - ful si - lence
Am
Em
F
sad - dened by their Sav - ior's loss. It was ear - ly
and they saw the flames a - glow. Then they felt the
heard the gos - pel sto - ry told. Then three thou - sand
with the Spir - it's wind and fire. Flame our hearts to
C
Dm7
Em
F
G
Refrain
in the morn - ing on the day called Pen - te - cost.
Spir - it's pow - er rest - ing on their heads be - low.
strong were bap - tized and the church of Christ was born!
great - er ser - vice; mold our faith as you de - sire.

Text: Scott Tunseth
Music: Kathleen Donlan Tunseth

71 O day full of grace

C Am G F C F
1 O day full of grace that now we see ap - pear - ing on
2 God came to us then at Pen - te - cost, his Spir - it new
3 When we on that fi - nal jour - ney go that Christ is for
G7 C G Em D G
earth's ho - ri - zon, bring light from our God that we may
life re - veal - ing, that we might no more from him be
us pre - par - ing, we'll gath - er in song, our hearts a -
D G Am D G C
be re - plete in his joy this sea - son. God, shine for us
lost, all dark - ness for us dis - pel - ling. His flame will the
glow, all joy of the heav - ens shar - ing, and walk in the
F C Am G G7 C
now in this dark place; your name on our hearts em - bla - zon.
mark of sin ef - face and bring to us all his heal - ing.
light of God's own place, with an - gels his name a - dor - ing.

Text: Danish folk hymn; tr. Gerald Thorson
Music: Christoph E. F. Weyse

Spirit of the living God

F Gm F C7 F
1 Spir - it of the liv - ing God, fall fresh on me,
2 Spir - it of the liv - ing God, move in us all;
F Gm F C7 F
Spir - it of the liv - ing God, fall fresh on me.
make us one in heart and mind, one in your love;
B♭ F G7 C C7
Melt me, mold me, fill me, use me.
hum - ble, car - ing, self - less, shar - ing.
F Gm F C7 F
Spir - it of the liv - ing God, fall fresh on me.
Spir - it of the liv - ing God, fill us with love.

Text: Daniel Iverson, st.1; Michael Baughen, st. 2
Music: Daniel Iverson

73 Come! Come! Everybody worship

See LifeSongs *recording Volume 1*

For Christians, every Sunday is Easter Sunday. What is most important is "joyful worship that restores us to communion with the risen Christ" and each other (*Practicing Our Faith*, Dorothy C. Bass, ed., Jossey-Bass Publishers, pp. 86–87). It is a festival time in which God is shaping a new creation. It is a foretaste of the feast to come.

"Come! Come! Everybody worship" is accessible to children from preschool to upper elementary. It invites us to come and worship and calls us to remember and keep the day of rest.

- Draw children into a discussion about sabbath. Where do we first hear about sabbath? Read the third commandment (Exodus 20:8-10) to the children. What does it mean to keep sabbath when we live in a world of so many pressures? How do we unwrap the gift of sabbath? Prepare for this discussion by reading chapter 6, "Keeping Sabbath," from *Practicing Our Faith*.
- Show how stanzas 2–5 continue to refer to worship and how we are to live our lives apart from worship.
- Teach by phrases.
- Add signs for the words *come, worship, prayer, song,* and *God* to the refrain (see pp. 212–213).

Sing as an invitation to worship. If used immediately before the entrance hymn, check that the keys are the same or compatible.

Refrain
F Dm F Gm7 C7
Come! Come! Ev-'ry-bod-y wor-ship with a prayer or song of praise!
¡Ven - gan to-dos a-do-re-mos con can-tos y o - ra-ción!
F Dm F Gm7 C F
Come! Come! Ev-'ry-bod-y wor-ship! Wor-ship God al - ways!
¡Ven - gan to-dos a-do-re-mos a nues-tro Se - ñor!
C F C F
1 Wor-ship and re - mem-ber to keep the Sab-bath day.
2 Wor-ship and re - mem-ber the Lord's un - end - ing care,
3 Wor-ship and re - mem-ber your bless-ings great and small.
4 Wor-ship and re - mem-ber how Je - sus long a - go
5 Wor-ship and re - mem-ber that God is like a light:
C F Dm7 G C7 Refrain
Take a rest and think of God; put your work a - way.
reach-ing out to love and help peo - ple ev - 'ry - where.
Give to God an of - fer - ing; show your thanks for all.
taught us how to talk to God; some-thing we should know.
show-ing you the way to go, ev - er burn-ing bright!

Text: Natalie Sleeth; tr. Mary Lou Santillán-Baert
Music: Natalie Sleeth

Come and sing your praise 74

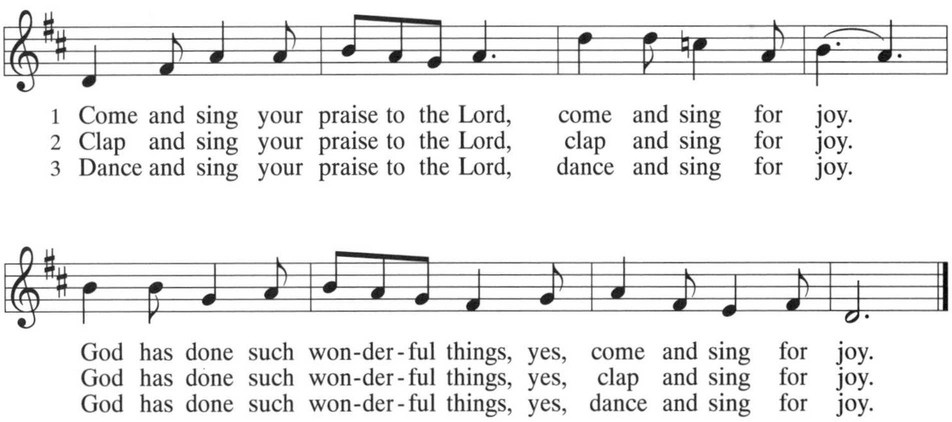

Text: Music Matters
Music: Catherine Mathia

Encourage young children to find different ways of moving to express themselves as they sing this song.

• Create additional verses with the children: *tap and sing, walk and sing, skip and sing.*

• Give each child a drum to tap the beat while they sing. Encourage each child to improvise.

• Use the child's name, singing:

_____ taps her/his praise to the Lord, _____ taps for joy.
God has done such wonderful things; yes, _____ taps for joy.

• Sing often in a class setting to focus children on the "wonderful things" God has done. How does God continue to do wonderful things in our lives today?

Come and sing together 75

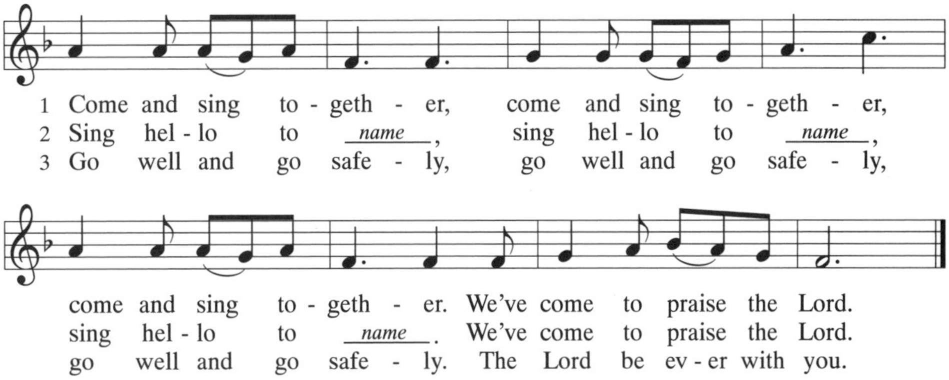

1 Come and sing to-geth-er, come and sing to-geth-er,
2 Sing hel-lo to name, sing hel-lo to name,
3 Go well and go safe-ly, go well and go safe-ly,
come and sing to-geth-er. We've come to praise the Lord.
sing hel-lo to name. We've come to praise the Lord.
go well and go safe-ly. The Lord be ev-er with you.

Text: Music Matters
Music: traditional

Here we have a greeting song that calls children to gather in community.

• Insert a child's name into stanza 2. Use one name for the entire stanza or several names in a stanza, depending on the size of the class.

• Change the beat motion frequently (such as tap, clap, nod, etc.). Use the word in the stanza.

• After several weeks of singing this song, invite children to listen to the notes that accompany their names. Set up an Orff instrument.

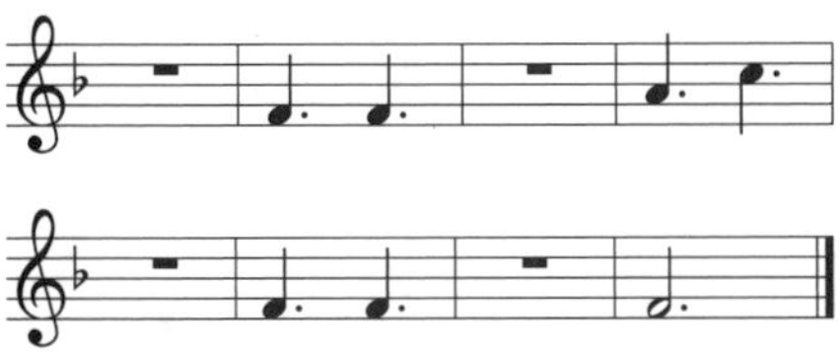

Give each child an opportunity to play the beats as their name is sung. Teach them to listen!

Sing with lower elementary school children as an opening and a closing whenever they gather.

76 Hello, everybody

Refrain
Hel-lo, ev-'ry-bod-y! How do you do? How do you do? How do you do?
Hel-lo, ev-'ry-bod-y! How do you do? God loves you to-day.
1 If your name is ____, stand up. If your name is ____, stand up.
2 If you have red on, stand up. If you have blue on, stand up.
3 If you like sun-shine, stand up. If you like rain-drops, stand up.
4 If God loves boys, . . stand up. If God loves girls, . . stand up.
If your name is ____, stand up. If your name is ____, stand up.
If you have yel-low on, stand up. If you have green on, stand up.
If you like snow-flakes, stand up. If you like rain-bows, stand up.
If God loves me, . . . stand up. If God loves you, . . stand up.
Refrain

Text: traditional
Music: traditional

Come into God's presence

77

As a community of faith, we take seriously the call to invite people to gather for worship, study, and service. How do we gather? Through the voices of children we hear the invitation to come, singing praise at any time during the church year.

- Play the ascending melodic pattern (*Come into God's presence*) on an Orff instrument—D, E, F♯, G, A. Allow each child an opportunity to play the pattern on the instrument.
- Sing the song through once, then invite the children to join in.
- Sign the words *come, alleluia, lamb, Jesus,* and *glory* (see p. 212).

Sing to open Sunday school, class sessions, or choir rehearsals, changing the stanzas by seasons.

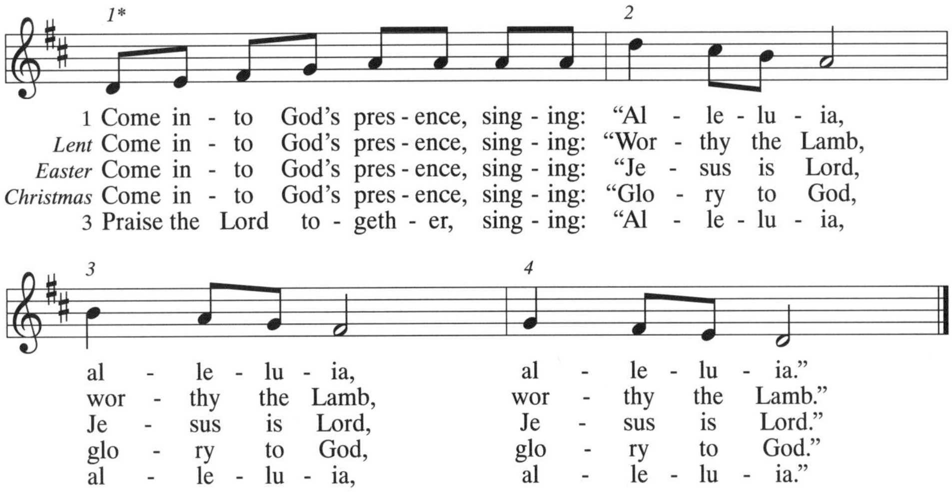
1* 2 3 4
1 Come in - to God's pres - ence, sing - ing: "Al - le - lu - ia, al - le - lu - ia, al - le - lu - ia."
Lent Come in - to God's pres - ence, sing - ing: "Wor - thy the Lamb, wor - thy the Lamb, wor - thy the Lamb."
Easter Come in - to God's pres - ence, sing - ing: "Je - sus is Lord, Je - sus is Lord, Je - sus is Lord."
Christmas Come in - to God's pres - ence, sing - ing: "Glo - ry to God, glo - ry to God, glo - ry to God."
3 Praise the Lord to - geth - er, sing - ing: "Al - le - lu - ia, al - le - lu - ia, al - le - lu - ia."

**may be sung as a round*

Text: Music Matters
Music: Russian folk song

Won't you come and sit with me

78

What does the word *welcome* mean to a very young child? Invite the children to share what they think *welcome* means.

- After singing stanza 3, teach the children to say a prayer such as, "Lord, have mercy on those who are homeless; Lord, have mercy on those who are hungry; Lord, have mercy on those who need work."
- With the children think of other people who would be welcome to come, sit, and pray.

Use the song in class as an invitation to a prayer time.

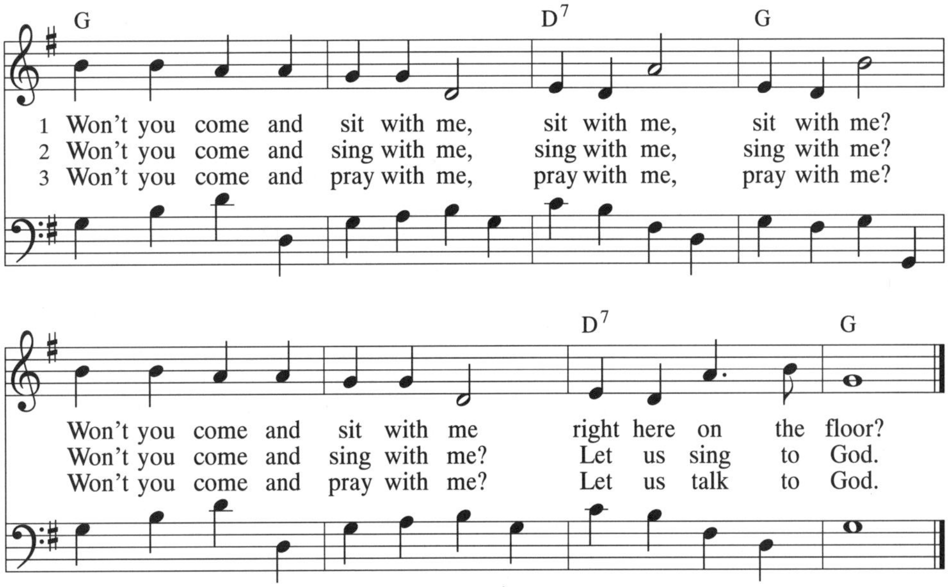
G D7 G
1 Won't you come and sit with me, sit with me, sit with me? Won't you come and sit with me right here on the floor?
2 Won't you come and sing with me, sing with me, sing with me? Won't you come and sing with me? Let us sing to God.
3 Won't you come and pray with me, pray with me, pray with me? Won't you come and pray with me? Let us talk to God.
D7 G

Text: anonymous, st. 1; Jane Haas, sts. 2-3
Music: anonymous

79 Listen, God is calling

Listen! Here is a word for children and adults alike. Open up your ears, O faithful people, and hear the word. God is calling us to share the good news, not just with some, but with all people. This call-and-response song from Tanzania reaches across the ocean to remind us of our mission.

Howard Olson, the author of this text, was a missionary in Tanzania for 43 years. He served as a parish pastor, a Bible translator, a language teacher, and as a professor at Lutheran Theological College at Makumira.

• Locate Tanzania on a map for the children and talk with them about what it means to be global partners. Why is this important?

• Clap the rhythm, adding the words. An older child can sing the part of the leader.

• Add a basic drum beat to the refrain, playing the rim with the flat part of the fingers (♩) and the palm in the center of the drum (♫). Begin on the first beat of the *All* part.

Sing in worship when Matthew 28:16-20 is read. Consider including on Reformation Sunday or when there is an emphasis on serving others through the word.

Refrain
Leader
All
G D G
Lis - ten, lis - ten, God is call - ing, through the Word in - vit - ing,
Em Am G Em D 1 G 2 G
of - fer - ing for - give - ness, com - fort, and joy. joy.
Leader
All
G D Em
1 Je - sus gave his man - date: share the good news
2 Let none be for - got - ten through - out the world.
3 Help us to be faith - ful, stand - ing stead - fast,
Leader
All
G Em D G Refrain
that he came to save us and set us free.
In the tri - une name of God go and bap - tize.
walk - ing in your pre - cepts, led by your Word.

Text: Tanzanian traditional; tr. Howard S. Olson
Music: Tanzanian tune; arr. Austin C. Lovelace

How firm a foundation

This hymn, a sermon in verse, is set to an early North American melody.

- The melody consists of only five notes, do-re-mi-sol-la, the pentatonic scale. The key is G.

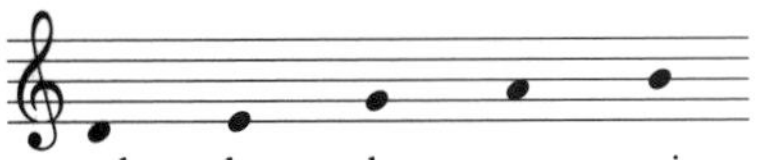

- With music in hand invite children to find melodic phrases that are identical (phrases 2 and 4). Match the syllables with the notes of this phrase and sing.
- Finish teaching the other phrases.
- Speaking voices may precede the singing of the hymn:

All: *As saints of the Lord, our faith is in God's word!*
Speaker 1: *We have no promise of escaping trials;*
Speaker 2: *but we do not need to be afraid!*
Speaker 3: *For God is our strength!*
Speaker 4: *God has promised to defend us!*
Speaker 5: *God's love never changes!*
Speaker 6: *God's grace will be sufficient through all our days!*
All: *What more can we say?*
Speaker 7: *What more can God say?*

1* 2
G C G C Bm Am D
1 How firm a foun - da - tion, O saints of the Lord,
2 Fear not, I am with you, oh, be not dis - mayed,
G C Bm Em Bm D G
is laid for your faith in his ex - cel - lent Word!
for I am your God and will still give you aid;
D G D Em C G Am D
What more can he say than to you he has said
I'll strength - en you, help you, and cause you to stand,
D7 G Am7 D Em G D G
who un - to the Sav - ior for ref - uge have fled?
up - held by my righ - teous, om - nip - o - tent hand.

* *may be sung as a round*

Text: J. Rippon, *A Selection of Hymns*, alt.
Music: North American traditional

81 A mighty fortress is our God

C G Am D G Am Em C
1 A might - y for - tress is our God, a sword and shield vic -
2 No strength of ours can match his might! We would be lost, re -
3 Though hordes of dev - ils fill the land all threat - 'ning to de -
4 God's Word for - ev - er shall a - bide, no thanks to foes, who
Dm G C G Am D G Am
to - rious; he breaks the cruel op - pres - sor's rod and
ject - ed. But now a cham - pion comes to fight, whom
vour us, we trem - ble not, un - moved we stand; they
fear it; for God him - self fights by our side with
Em F C Dm G C Am D G
wins sal - va - tion glo - rious. The old sa - tan - ic foe
God him - self e - lect - ed. You ask who this may be?
can - not o - ver - pow'r us. Let this world's ty - rant rage;
weap - ons of the Spir - it. Were they to take our house,
Am G C F C Em Am D G
has sworn to work us woe! With craft and dread - ful might
The Lord of hosts is he! Christ Je - sus, might - y Lord,
in bat - tle we'll en - gage! His might is doomed to fail;
goods, hon - or, child, or spouse, though life be wrenched a - way,

This hymn by Martin Luther (1483–1546), often called the "battle hymn" of the Reformation, has been translated into more than sixty languages. Luther wrote it not to express his own feelings but to interpret and apply Psalm 46 to the church of his own time and its struggles.

In many Lutheran churches the last Sunday in October is celebrated as Reformation Sunday. "A mighty fortress is our God" is often sung, Psalm 46 is read or sung, and these words from the Gospel of John are proclaimed: "So if the Son makes you free, you will be free indeed" (John 8:36).

- Clap the rhythm of the first phrase. Children echo. Clap the second phrase. Is it the same as the first phrase or different?
- Write the scale in the key of C with syllables on poster board.

A

do re mi fa sol la ti do

On another card write the melodic line of the first phrase (see below).

Invite children to match the syllables from card A with card B.

- Sing with syllables.
- Add the words. Discuss terms such as *fortress, oppressor's rod,* and *satanic foe*, impressing upon the children that the words testify to the greatness of God and the ultimate triumph of God's truth.
- Finish teaching stanza 1. Do the children recognize the last three measures as being familiar?

B

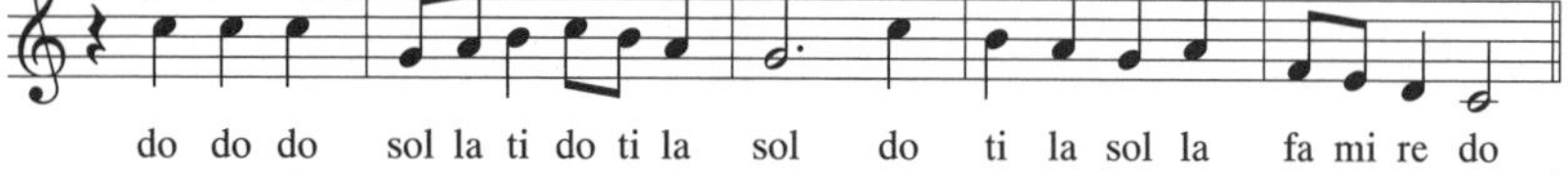
do do do sol la ti do ti la sol do ti la sol la fa mi re do

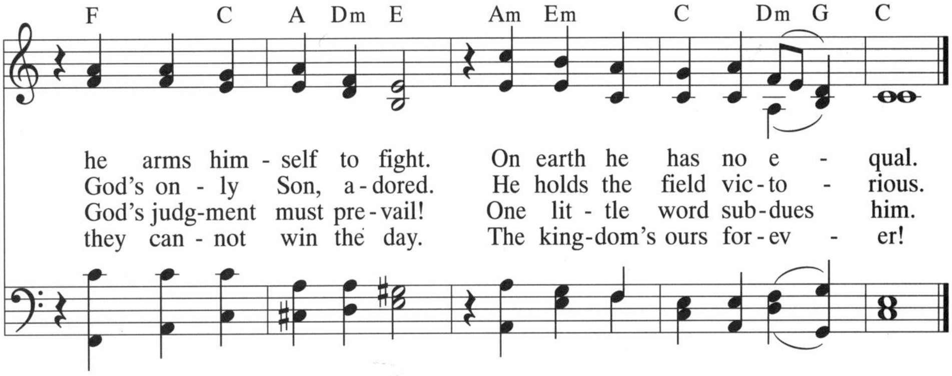

F C A Dm E Am Em C Dm G C
he arms him - self to fight. On earth he has no e - qual.
God's on - ly Son, a - dored. He holds the field vic - to - rious.
God's judg - ment must pre - vail! One lit - tle word sub - dues him.
they can - not win the day. The king - dom's ours for - ev - er!
8

Text: Martin Luther; tr. *Lutheran Book of Worship*
Music: Martin Luther

Alleluia. Lord to whom shall we go? 82

words of e - ter - nal life. Al - le - lu - ia, al - le - lu - ia.

Text: John 6:68, adapt. *Lutheran Book of Worship*
Music: Richard W. Hillert

In the liturgy people welcome the reading of the gospel with *Alleluia*. This is one of many possible alleluias people might stand and sing as they prepare to listen to the good news of their Lord. Because it is an Easter word, it is not used in Lent.

On the last Sunday after Epiphany, the Transfiguration of Our Lord, bury the alleluia. Print the word *alleluia* in large letters on chart paper or cloth. Fold it and place it in a box or container. There it will remain hidden away for the six weeks of Lent. On Easter morning invite the children to help take the alleluia out of the box and unfold it. Ask them when they last saw it and how it felt to pack it away. Talk about the joy of Jesus' resurrection. Alleluia! Christ is risen!

- Clap the rhythm of *alleluia* (𝄽 ♫ ♩ ♩). Add a gentle *sh* to feel the rest. Invite children to echo. Repeat several times.
- Teach the melody to the first alleluia and the final two alleluias; a solo voice can sing *Lord, to whom shall we go?* When the children feel more secure, finish teaching the entire response.
- Encourage children to be prepared to stand and sing with the congregation in worship. Also, sing this response in a class setting when scripture is read from one of the gospels.

83 Lord, let my heart be good soil

When one lives in the country, in a rural area, the ranchers and farmers may gather for some early-morning chitchat over coffee. The topic of conversation often is the weather and the planting season—seeds and soil. What most of them know is that what happens to seed and soil depends on God and not on them.

And so it is with us. The seed is a vital image of faith. God brings new life out of what appears to be cold, dormant—even dead. Let us pray to be open to the seed of God's word, to grow in faith, hope, and love.

- With older children, read the text together. Talk about the images portrayed in the text.
- Ask them to find and name words that appear often *(Lord, heart, soil)*.
- Assign a rhythm instrument to sound each time the word is spoken or sung:

Lord: drum, played once lightly on the word
Heart: finger cymbals
Soil: maracas, shaken to complete the note value in the measure

- Teach the melody by phrases. Are there any identical phrases? (First and second, *Lord, let my heart*. Third and fourth, *When my heart is hard/cold*.)

Sing in worship when the emphasis is on planting the seeds of faith: Matthew 13:1-23, Mark 4:1-20, and Luke 8:4-15, the parable of the sower; and Matthew 13:31-32, Mark 4:30-32, and Luke 13:18-19, the parable of the mustard seed.

E G♯m7 A E F♯m7 B
Lord, let my heart be good soil, o-pen to the seed of your
E7 B7sus E G♯m7 A E
word. Lord, let my heart be good soil, where
F♯m7 A B7 E A E
love can grow and peace is un-der-stood. When my heart is hard,
F♯m7 A B A E F♯m7 A B
break the stone a-way. When my heart is cold, warm it with the day.
Cdim7 C♯m A Am E A
When my heart is lost, lead me on your way. Lord, let my heart,
E A E A F♯m E
Lord, let my heart, Lord, let my heart be good soil.

Text: Handt Hanson
Music: Handt Hanson

Open your ears, O faithful people

See LifeSongs *recording Volume 2*

All of us, children and adults, could improve our listening skills. What we hear too often goes in one ear and out the other. We hear, but we forget.

In the parable of the sower (Matthew 13:1-9), Jesus said to the crowds, "Let anyone with ears listen!" Those who gathered around to hear him didn't always understand what he said. When Jesus spoke in parables they often missed the point because parables have a hidden meaning. Let us open our ears to welcome the gospel and hear the message.

• This Hasidic melody is energetic and strongly rhythmic. Teach the refrain first, as it is most easily learned. Sing *Torah ora* (the Law is light), for measures 1–8 and the English words for the repeat.

• Add movement to the refrain. Form a circle with hands on the shoulders of the person to each side.

Measures 1–4: Step the beat going to the right and stopping on the first beat of measure 4.
Measures 5–8: Reverse direction to the left, again stopping on the first beat of measure 8.
Add a shout of *Hey!* on the second beat.
Repeat the pattern for the remaining phrases.
Add a tambourine, playing the beats.

• Introduce the sixteenth-note pattern of the first stanza. Sing or play on the piano asking them to echo on *la*. There are four sixteenth-note patterns. How many are identical? (Three, only one is different.) Encourage children to listen carefully to the last two notes, G♯ to F♮.

Sing in a service around the hearing of the word, or when the parable of the sower is included in the readings.

E
1 O - pen your ears, O faith - ful peo - ple,
2 They who have ears to hear the mes - sage,
3 Is - ra - el comes to greet the Sav - ior,
o - pen your ears and hear God's Word. O - pen your hearts, O
they who have ears, now let them hear; they who would learn the
Ju - dah is glad to see his day, from east and west the
Dm
E
roy - al priest - hood, God has come to you.
way of wis - dom, let them hear God's Word.
peo - ples trav - el, God will show the way.
Refrain
Am
E
God has spo - ken to the peo - ple, hal - le - lu - jah!
To - rah o - ra, To - rah o - ra, hal - le - lu - jah!
Am
God has spo - ken words of wis - dom, hal - le - lu - jah!
To - rah o - ra, To - rah o - ra, hal - le - lu - jah!

Text: Hasidic traditional; English text, Willard F. Jabusch
Music: Hasidic tune; arr. Robert Hobby

85 You have put on Christ

See LifeSongs *recording Volume 1*

In baptism we claim a new future for the baptized. Their future is now one with Christ and that future changes the present and all that is to come. The baptized are grafted into a new story: the story of Jesus and the mystery of his death and resurrection, of John and the Jordan, of deliverance from bondage, of rescue from the flood, of creation created good. Now that story becomes the baptized's story, that history is our history.

• This simple refrain can be learned by even the youngest child.

• For older children, feel the two pulses in each measure by patting thighs on beat 1 and clapping on beat 2.

• Instrumentation for finger cymbals, tambourine, and handbells is available in a unison anthem by Howard Hughes (GIA G-2283).

Sing for the Baptism of Our Lord or as an acclamation after each baptism.

1*
2
3
F Bb F Bb F Bb F Bb
You have put on Christ, in him you have been bap - tized.
F Bb F Bb F Bb F Bb
Last time
F
Al - le - lu - ia! Al - le - lu - ia!

*may be sung as a round

Text: Galatians 3:27, adapt. International Commission on English in the Liturgy
Music: Howard Hughes

86 I was baptized, happy day!

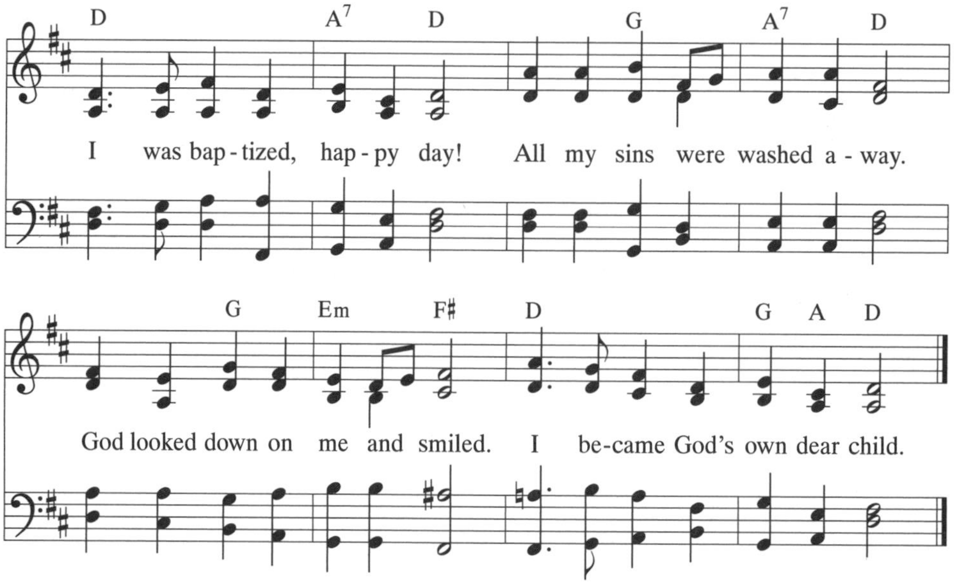
D A7 D G A7 D
I was bap - tized, hap - py day! All my sins were washed a - way.
G Em F♯ D G A D
God looked down on me and smiled. I be-came God's own dear child.

Text: Arnold Mueller
Music: French traditional

Baptized in water

This Gaelic melody is also sung with the hymns "Morning is broken" and "Praise and thanksgiving."

A baptismal theme runs throughout this hymn. Stanza 1 tells us that we are cleansed in baptism and given the gift of God's promise. In stanza 2 the old sinful way of life has been buried. A new way of life through Christ frees us from sin. Stanza 3 affirms that we have been sealed by the Holy Spirit and marked with the cross of Christ forever. We are God's children.

- Keep the melody moving by feeling three beats per measure. Teach by phrases.
- Make a card (11" x 17") of the first four notes.

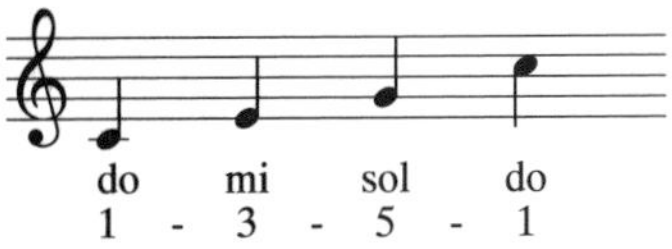
do mi sol do
1 - 3 - 5 - 1

- Play on an Orff instrument each time a new stanza is begun.
- Notice the words common to all three stanzas: *Spirit, Christ, God.* Teach the children to sign these words (see pp. 212–213).

Sing for a service of baptism, for the second Sunday after the Epiphany (the Baptism of Our Lord), or for an affirmation of baptism.

C Am Dm G Dm7 G Am
1 Bap-tized in wa - ter, sealed by the Spir - it, cleansed by the
2 Bap-tized in wa - ter, sealed by the Spir - it, dead in the
3 Bap-tized in wa - ter, sealed by the Spir - it, marked with the
Em Am C Dm7 G Em C F C
blood of Christ our king: heirs of sal - va - tion, trust-ing his
tomb with Christ our king: one with his ris - ing, freed and for -
sign of Christ our king: born of the Spir - it, we are God's
Am G C Em Am G C
prom - ise, faith-ful - ly now God's praise we sing.
giv - en, thank-ful - ly now God's praise we sing.
chil - dren; joy - ful - ly now God's praise we sing.

Text: Michael Saward
Music: Gaelic traditional; arr. B. Wayne Bisbee

88 Lift high the cross

This processional hymn was first sung for a festival occasion at Westminster Cathedral in England. As the title suggests, a cross was carried high above the heads of the worshiping assembly by an acolyte who, when serving in this role, is called a crucifer.

- Hymns can be named for places or cities (DUKE STREET), psalm numbers (OLD HUNDREDTH), saints (ST. CHRISTOPHER), countries (AUSTRIAN HYMN), and more. The tune name can also describe its use, as with "Lift high the cross" for which the tune name is CRUCIFER.

- Teach the refrain and movement:

Lift high: Begin at waist with both hands, palms down, fingers spread, moving upward slowly.
Cross: Make a fist with both hands crossing right wrist over left wrist above head.
Love: Bring arms crossed to rest on chest.
Christ: Make a *C* with right hand moving from left shoulder ending at right waist.
Proclaim: Both arms extended forward and outward at waist.
World: Bring arms up over head, fingertips touching.
Adore: Fold right hand over left fist, chest high, displaying an attitude of reverence.
Sacred name: With the index and middle fingers of each hand, make an *X* waist-high. Tap right fingers over left fingers one time for *sacred*, one time for *name*.

- Invite children to sign the refrain when the hymn is sung in worship.

Refrain
Lift high the cross, the love of Christ proclaim till all the world adore his sacred name.
1 Come, Christians, follow where our captain trod, our king victorious, Christ, the Son of God.
2 Led on their way by this triumphant sign, the hosts of God in conqu'ring ranks combine.
3 All newborn soldiers of the Crucified bear on their brows the seal of him who died.
4 O Lord, once lifted on the glorious tree, as thou hast promised, draw us all to thee.
5 So shall our song of triumph ever be: praise to the Crucified for victory!
Refrain

Text: George W. Kitchin and Michael R. Newbolt
Music: Sydney H. Nicholson

I've just come from the fountain

Water is the central theme of this African American spiritual—a fountain of water. It calls to mind the water poured over us as we were baptized into Christ. We came from the water with the gift of grace that seals our lives with the Spirit's abiding presence. We became the bearers of Christ to the world. This servant life began with water and the word.

The tune is easy, singable, and full of joyful energy.

- Teach the refrain to the children, adding a tambourine to the two pulses in each measure.
- A soloist can sing the question; children can respond with the answer.

Use in any service that has a baptismal theme. Also, sing on the Baptism of Our Lord as a sending hymn.

Refrain
Capo 1 D E♭ G A♭ D E♭ Bm Cm D E♭ G A♭ A B♭
I've just come from the foun-tain, I've just come from the foun-tain, Lord, I've
D E♭ G A♭ D E♭ E7 F7 A7 B♭7 1 D E♭ 2 D E♭
just come from the foun-tain, his name's so sweet. O Lord, I've sweet.
Leader
All
Bm Cm D E♭ G A♭ A B♭
1 O broth-er, do you love Je-sus? Yes, yes, I do love my Je-sus.
2 O sis-ter, do you love Je-sus? Yes, yes, I do love my Je-sus.
3 O sin-ner, do you love Je-sus? Yes, yes, I do love my Je-sus.
Leader
All
E7 F7 A7 B♭7 D E♭
Refrain
Broth-er, do you love Je-sus? His name's so sweet. O Lord, I've
Sis-ter, do you love Je-sus? His name's so sweet. O Lord, I've
Sin-ner, do you love Je-sus? His name's so sweet. O Lord, I've

Text: African American spiritual
Music: African American spiritual; arr. James Capers

90 Seek ye first

We all have a list of things we want, but few of us think about only those things we need. Give older children a piece of paper. Draw a line down the middle. Invite them to list on one side the things they want, and on the other side the things they need. Without mentioning names, read from the lists. Did anyone include God on their needs list?

We need God's kingdom to come among us, God's will to be done, daily food, clothing, friends, laughter, tears, God's forgiveness, help to forgive others, rescue from danger, and protection from evil. Name other needs, keeping in mind the words of the Lord's Prayer.

- This simple melody is composed of two identical phrases. There is only one note that is different. Can the children find it? The last note of each phrase is different.
- Teach the melody and the descant.

Include in a service when Luke 11:1-13 is one of the appointed readings. Have children sing the descant on stanza 2 as the congregation sings the hymn.

Descant
Al - le - lu - ia, al - le - lu - ia, al - le - lu - ia, al - le - lu - ia.
D F♯m G D G
1 Seek ye first the king - dom of God and its
2 Ask and it shall be giv - en un - to you; seek and
D Em7 A7 D F♯m
righ - teous - ness, and all these things shall be
you shall find; knock and the door shall be
G D G D Em7 A D
add - ed un - to you. Al - le - lu, al - le - lu - ia.
o - pened un - to you. Al - le - lu, al - le - lu - ia.

Text: Matt. 6:33, 7:7, adapt. Karen Lafferty
Music: Karen Lafferty

Every time I feel the spirit

Refrain
D G D
Ev - 'ry time I feel the spir - it mov - ing
A7 Bm A D G
in my heart, I will pray. Ev - 'ry time I feel the
D A7 Bm A7 D
spir - it mov - ing in my heart, I will pray.

Text: African American spiritual
Music: African American spiritual

92 Jesus listens when I pray

D A7 D A7 D
Je - sus lis - tens when I pray, when I pray, when I pray.
D G D A7 D
Je - sus lis - tens when I pray, ev - 'ry night, ev - 'ry day.

Text: Clara Ketelhut
Music: Arthur W. Gross

Prayer begins before a child is born. An expectant mother prays for the child she is carrying. Prayers continue as the infant grows and develops. Praying with children "every night, every day" will help them in developing a trusting relationship with God.

• Discuss prayer asking such questions as, Why do we pray? What do we pray for? When do we pray?

• Young children will learn this song very quickly.

• Sign key words: *Jesus, pray, night, day* (see pp. 212–213). Cup one hand to one ear for the word *listen*.

• Encourage children to sing this song before saying prayers at bedtime. Change the *I* to *we* and sing in class or in a Sunday school opening. Sing before the prayer time begins, inviting children to offer petitions. Sing the song after each petition.

It's me, O Lord

Refrain
G D7 G D G
It's me, it's me, O Lord, stand-in' in the need of prayer;
it's me,
D7 Em G D7 G
it's me, it's me, O Lord, stand-in' in the need of prayer.
it's me,
1 Not my broth - er, not my sis - ter, but it's me, O Lord,
2 Not the preach - er, not the dea - con, but it's me, O Lord,
3 Not my fa - ther, not my moth - er, but it's me, O Lord,
4 Not the strang - er, not my neigh - bor, but it's me, O Lord,
G D G
stand-in' in the need of prayer; not my broth - er, not my sis - ter, but it's
stand-in' in the need of prayer; not the preach-er, not the dea-con, but it's
stand-in' in the need of prayer; not my fa - ther, not my moth-er, but it's
stand-in' in the need of prayer; not the strang - er, not my neigh-bor, but it's
G D G Refrain
me, O Lord, stand - in' in the need of prayer.
me, O Lord, stand - in' in the need of prayer.
me, O Lord, stand - in' in the need of prayer.
me, O Lord, stand - in' in the need of prayer.

Text: African American spiritual
Music: African American spiritual

94 Lord, listen to your children praying

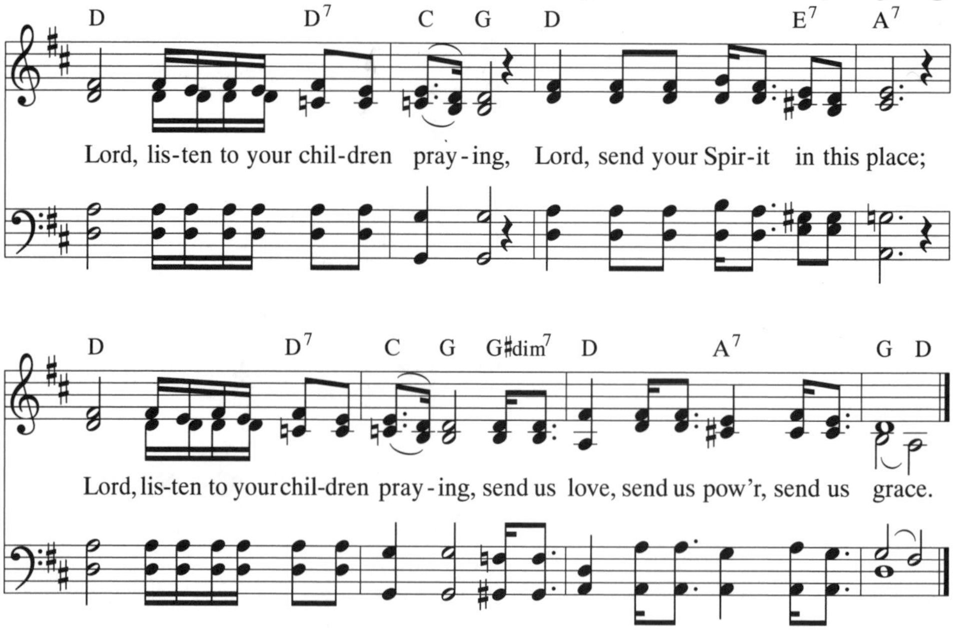
D D7 C G D E7 A7
Lord, lis-ten to your chil-dren pray-ing, Lord, send your Spir-it in this place;
D D7 C G G♯dim7 D A7 G D
Lord, lis-ten to your chil-dren pray-ing, send us love, send us pow'r, send us grace.

Text: Ken Medema
Music: Ken Medema

95 Let my prayer rise

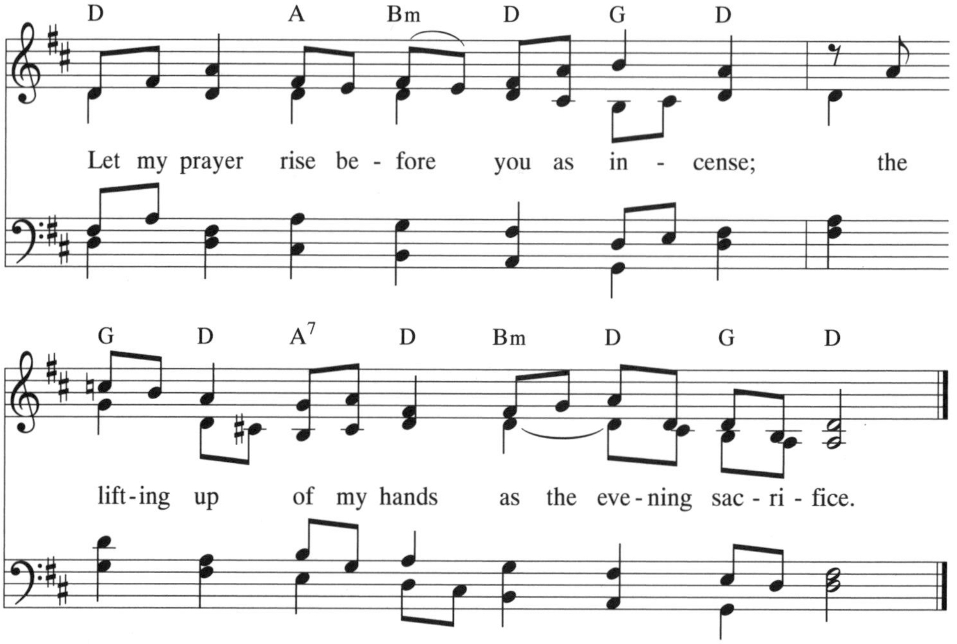
D A Bm D G D
Let my prayer rise be - fore you as in - cense; the
G D A7 D Bm D G D
lift-ing up of my hands as the eve-ning sac - ri - fice.

Text: Psalm 141:1, adapt. *Lutheran Book of Worship*
Music: David Schack

Our Father in heaven

96

Our Fa - ther in heav - en, hal - lowed be your name,
your king - dom come, your will be done,
on earth as in heav - en. Give us to - day our
dai - ly bread. For - give us our sins as
we for - give those who sin a - gainst us. Save us from the
time of tri - al and de - liv - er us from e - vil.
For the king - dom, the pow'r, and the glo - ry are
yours, now and for - ev - er. A - men

Text: Lord's Prayer, tr. International Consultation on English Texts
Music: plainsong

97 Come, Lord Jesus

The melody of this hymn has a special name. It's called TALLIS' CANON, meaning that it can be sung as a round. It was composed by Thomas Tallis (1505–1585). Even as a boy he was very musical and served as chorister at St. Paul's Cathedral in London. Later he became a well-known composer and organist.

• Experience the phrases with movement patterns. Patterns change with each new phrase, which includes the upbeat. Children are in a standing position.

Drum:

Tap both thighs
Tap both hips
Tap both shoulders
Clap hands

• Explain that the drum will tell them when a new phrase begins. In the beginning encourage children to count, later to mouth the words while they feel the beat.

• Speak the words in rhythm by phrases. Have the children echo. Continue to use the drum to indicate a new phrase.

• Teach the melody and sing the stanzas. Now try adding the words of the doxology.

Praise God, from whom all blessings flow;
Praise God, all creatures here below;
Praise God above, ye heavenly host;
Praise Father, Son, and Holy Ghost.

• Make the sign of the cross for the Trinity. With the right hand touch forehead (Father), middle of waist (Son), left shoulder (Holy) right shoulder (Ghost).

1* 2
Am D G Am D G
1 Oh, come, Lord Je - sus, be our guest, and let your gifts to us be blest. Keep us for - ev - er in your sight, and be our joy, our hearts' de - light.
2 Oh, come, Lord Je - sus, be our guest, and let your gifts to us be blest. Oh, may there be a good - ly share on ev - 'ry ta - ble ev - 'ry - where.
3 Oh, come, Lord Je - sus, be our guest, and let your gifts to us be blest. Guide us a - long the ser - vant's way, and lead us to your dawn - ing day.
4 Oh, come, Lord Je - sus, be our guest, and let your gifts to us be blest. Come deep with - in our hearts to dwell, that we may all your good - ness tell.

*may be sung as a round

Text: traditional table prayer, adapt. Susan Briehl
Music: Thomas Tallis; arr. Donald Busarow

God gave to me a life to live

See LifeSongs *recording Volume 1*

The earliest known source of this tune, PUER NOBIS, is a fifteenth-century manuscript from the library in Trier (now in Germany). It was adapted by a German-born organist and composer, Michael Praetorius.

Many texts have been coupled with this tune. This setting helps children to understand that God is the creator of all that we are. In turn we give thanks for opportunities to use our whole selves to go forth into the world to serve.

- In a standing position encourage children to feel two pulses in each measue (***1***-2-3-***4***-5-6). On the first pulse clap low, on the second pulse clap above the head.
- Teach the melody by phrases. Encourage a light tone.
- Emphasize certain words—*hands, heart, love, share*—and encourage the children to use their imaginations to create motions.

Sing in worship around the themes of creation and baptism.

Bm D G D A D G
1 God gave to me a life to live; God
2 When I am helped to see what's good, and
D A7 D G D D A7 D
gave me hands with which to give; God gave a heart with
led to do the things I should, I thank you, car - ing
G D Em A7 D A7 G A7 D
which to care; God gave me love that I might share.
God a - bove, for life and hands and heart and love.

Text: anonymous
Music: European tune, adapt. Michael Praetorius

99 The Lord is good to me

F C7
The Lord is good to me, and
F C7 F
so I thank the Lord for giv - ing me the
F7 B♭
things I need, the sun and rain and the ap - ple seed; the
F Gm C F B♭ F
Lord is good to me.

Text: Kim Gannon and Walter Kent
Music: Kim Gannon and Walter Kent

Let the vineyards be fruitful 100

Capo 3
C A G Em C Dm
E♭ C B♭ Gm E♭ Fm
Let the vine-yards be fruit-ful, Lord, and fill to the brim our cup of
G C Am C Dm C
B♭ E♭ Cm E♭ Fm E♭
bless-ing. Gath-er a har-vest from the seeds that were sown, that
Am G C Am G
Cm B♭ E♭ Cm B♭
we may be fed with the bread of life. Gath-er the hopes and
Em C Dm G C
Gm E♭ Fm B♭ E♭
dreams of all; u - nite them with the prayers we of - fer.
Am C Am G Am G C
Cm E♭ Cm B♭ Cm B♭ E♭
Grace our ta-ble with your pres-ence, and give us a fore-taste of the feast to come.

Text: John W. Arthur
Music: Ronald A. Nelson

101 I am thanking Jesus

F Gm7 B♭ F
English I am thank-ing Je-sus, I am thank-ing Je-sus, I am thank-ing
Swahili A-san-te sa-na Ye-su, a-san-te sa-na Ye-su, a-san-te sa-na
Otji-vambo Tan-di tan-ga Ye-sus, tan-di tan-ga Ye-sus, tan-di tan-ga
G C F
Je-sus from my heart. I am thank-ing Je-sus,
Ye-su mo-yo-ni. A-san-te sa-na Ye-su, a-
Ye-sus mo-mu-ti-ma. Tan-di tan-ga Ye-sus,
Gm7 C7 Dm G7 F C7 F
I am thank-ing Je-sus, I am thank-ing Je-sus from my heart.
san-te sa-na Ye-su, a-san-te sa-na Ye-su mo-yo-ni.
tan-di tan-ga Ye-sus, tan-di tan-ga Ye-sus mo-mu-ti-ma.

Text: Namibian and Tanzanian traditional
Music: African traditional, arr. *This Far by Faith*

We come to worship with thanksgiving in our hearts. From our hearts we pray this prayer: Merciful God, we offer with joy and thanksgiving what you have first given us—our selves, our time, and our possessions, signs of your gracious love. Receive them for the sake of him who offered himself for us, Jesus Christ our Lord. Amen (*With One Voice*, p. 21).

- Teach this prayer to children.
- Prepare three large posters with one set of words on each: *our selves, our time,* and *our possessions*. Have magazines and scissors on hand. Invite children to find pictures that express the meaning of selves, time, and possessions. As they find a picture ask them to place it on the corresponding poster. Have paper and markers available for those who wish to create their own.
- Talk about the pictures and how they are all signs of God's gracious love. Stress the importance of giving thanks every day for all of God's gifts.
- Teach the song to children by phrases. Also teach the African words (a = ah, e = eh, i = ee, o = oh, u = oo).
- Add rhythm instruments: drum or tambourine on *I*; finger cymbals on *Jesus*; tree chimes on *heart*. Also sign these words (see pp. 212–213; *I = me*).
- With the children, create other phrases such as *I am praising Jesus* or *I am loving Jesus*.
- Talk with children about taking this song with them during the day, in their play, at school, and at home. Sing also during the prayer time in class to express gratitude and thanks to God.

Sing for a Thanksgiving Day service while the offering is received.

All good gifts around us 102

In the book, *Every Day and Sunday, Too* by Gail Ramshaw (AFP 10-23349), there is a section with the heading, "Giving thanks." Read this to young children. Name other things for which we can show our thanks. Invite children to share their ideas. Find the reference to Psalm 92:1 in the picture. Teach them this verse: "It is good to give thanks to the Lord, to sing praises to your name, O Most High."

- Teach children the song by phrases.
- Combine hand motions with movement.

All good gifts around us: In circle formation holding hands, walk in one direction stopping on the word *us*.

Are sent from heaven above: Still holding hands, raise them in the air.

We thank you, Lord: Drop hands and touch fingertips of one hand to the mouth moving forward and down to the side.

We thank you, Lord: Touch fingertips of the other hand to the mouth moving forward and down to the side.

For all your love: Cross both arms against chest as a sign of God's love.

- Offer a prayer of thanks, then repeat the song.
- Teaching this refrain from the hymn "We plow the fields and scatter" allows the children to participate more fully in worship with the congregation. The children could sing this refrain as an antiphon when a psalm of thanksgiving is appointed, such as Psalm 92:1-4, 12-15. Sing before verse 1 and after verses 4 and 15.

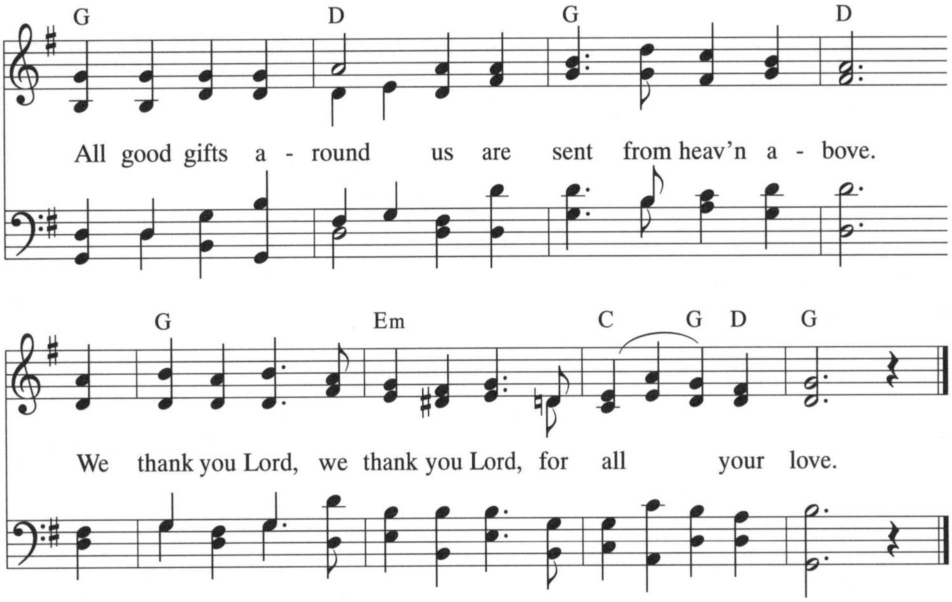
G D G D
All good gifts a - round us are sent from heav'n a - bove.
G Em C G D G
We thank you Lord, we thank you Lord, for all your love.

Text: Matthias Claudius; tr. Jane M. Campbell
Music: Johann A. P. Schulz

103 Come, let us eat

Both text and tune of this Liberian hymn are by Billema Kwillia. Born about 1925, Kwillia learned to read Loma, his own language, as a young adult, when the church's literacy program reached his town. In the early 1960s he applied for a job as literacy teacher, and worked in that capacity for a number of years.

During this time he became a Christian and was baptized. For a time he was an evangelist, conducting services and leading the Christians in his hometown. It was while Kwillia was a literacy teacher-evangelist that he sang this hymn for a meeting, and it was recorded on tape.

- Teach children the first and third phrases only. The second and fourth phrases can be sung by the congregation, thus giving children a leadership role in worship.
- Select instruments that can accompany effectively.

Sing during the distribution of communion.

F B♭ F Dm B♭
1 Come, let us eat, for now the feast is spread,
2 Come, let us drink, for now the wine is poured,
3 In . . . . . his pres - ence now we meet and rest,
4 Rise, then, to spread a - broad God's might - y word,
F B♭ C7 B♭ F Gm
come, let us eat, for now the feast is spread.
come, let us drink, for now the wine is poured.
in . . . . . his pres - ence now we meet and rest.
rise, then, to spread a - broad God's might - y word.
F B♭ Dm Gm7 B♭
Our Lord's bod - y let us take to - geth - er,
Je - sus' blood poured let us drink to - geth - er,
In the pres - ence of our Lord we gath - er,
Je - sus ris - en will bring in the king - dom,
F B♭ C B♭ F
our Lord's bod - y let us take to - geth - er.
Je - sus' blood poured let us drink to - geth - er.
in the pres - ence of our Lord we gath - er.
Je - sus ris - en will bring in the king - dom.

Text: Billema Kwillia, sts. 1-3; Gilbert E. Doan, st. 4, alt.; tr. Margaret D. Miller, sts. 1-3, alt.
Music: Billema Kwillia; arr. Leland Sateren

Feed us, Jesus

Here is a song that has as its theme the feeding of the multitudes. The feeding of the five thousand is the one miracle recorded in all four gospels: Matthew 14:13-21, Mark 6:30-44, Luke 9:10-17, and John 6:1-14. We read of the feeding of four thousand people in two of the gospels: Matthew 15:32-39 and Mark 8:1-10.

These stories bring home the importance of sharing all that we have with each other and the gift of sharing the body of Christ in communion. The two are closely linked. We are fed at the table and dismissed with the words "Go in peace. Serve the Lord." We go forth with God's love and thanksgiving in our hearts to feed others.

• Choose one of the accounts of the feeding of the multitudes to share with the children. This will make the song easier to teach. Stress the importance of sharing with others and always giving thanks (stanza 4).

• Add a tambourine to the refrain on the third and fourth beats (𝄽 𝄽 ♩ ♩).

Include in worship during the receiving of the offering when one of the gospel acounts is read, or use during a service of communion.

D A7 D D7 G A7 D
1 Je - sus spoke to man - y folk who sat up - on a hill;
2 Peo-ple heard a - bout God's word of love and peace for all;
3 Je - sus said, "Now take this bread and fish that I have blessed;
4 Ev - 'ry good and tas - ty food that gives us smiles to wear
Em A7 D Bm A E7 A
they all lis - tened hap - pi - ly, each child sat ver - y still.
when he stopped, the hun - gry peo - ple heard their stom-achs call.
pass it 'round, there's food for all, let each one be my guest."
comes to us from God's great love; our "thank you" is to share.
Refrain
D Em D Bm Em A
Feed us, Je - sus; Bread of life, from a - bove.
D Em D Em A7 D
Feed us, Je - sus! Give us your own love.

Text: John Folkening
Music: John Folkening

105 I received the living God

See LifeSongs *recording Volume 2*

Celebrations of all kinds usually feature food. Ask the children to name some of these gatherings. There are picnics, family reunions, wedding receptions, birthday parties. The list is endless. Sunday is no exception. It is a celebration of our risen Lord, and there is food for our journey.

As we approach the holy supper we see and receive bread and wine. We look beyond these elements, recognizing in the bread the food that endures for eternal life. It is our foretaste of the feast to come. We leave the table satisfied. We leave the table secure in God's love.

In these words, based on John 14:5-7, Christ shows his care for those who continue his mission in the world. This is especially important for children who receive a blessing rather than the bread and wine. Let them know that Jesus said in John 14:6, *I am the way to my Father* (stanza 2), *I am the truth, my word shall make you free* (stanza 3), *I am the life, you shall know the Spirit* (stanza 4). Encourage them to walk in the love of the Lord.

• Teach younger children the refrain and the melody to the words *Jesus said* at the beginning of each stanza. A soloist (an older child) can sing the remainder of the stanza.

• Older children can learn the entire song.

• Sign the refrain using the signs for *God, heart*, and *joy* (see p. 212).

Sing during the distribution of communion.

Refrain
C7 F B♭/C F Dm Gm C7 F
I re - ceived the liv-ing God, and my heart is full of joy.
C7 F Dm Am Dm Gm C7 F
I re - ceived the liv-ing God, and my heart is full of joy.
C Am Dm B♭ F C7 F
1 Je-sus said: I am the bread knead-ed long to give you life;
2 Je-sus said: I am the way, and my Fa-ther longs for you;
3 Je-sus said: I am the truth; if you fol-low close to me,
4 Je-sus said: I am the life far from whom no thing can grow,
Dm A Dm A Dm Gm7 C7 Refrain
you who will par-take of me need not ev - er fear to die.
so I come to bring you home to be one with us a - new.
you will know me in your heart, and my word shall make you free.
but re - ceive this liv - ing bread, and my Spir - it you shall know.

Text: anonymous
Music: anonymous; arr. David Cherwien

To the banquet, come

See LifeSongs *recording Volume 1*

The picture of a family reunion is a popular one in North America. Families today live far apart and reunions become a time to rekindle family ties. Talk with the children about such gatherings. Ask them what they remember about their travel experiences, the activities, and the location.

Every time we gather for the eucharist there is a family reunion for the children of God. There Jesus gathers us all to the one table of God's feast. It is not just for some but for all—poor and rich, healthy and sick, young and old. All are welcome at the banquet.

• Treat the words as a story before coupling with the melody. Invite the children to listen for rhyming words. Keep track of these words on a chalkboard or poster board.

• Teach by phrases inviting children to echo each time:

To the ***banquet come*** (echo)

It's not ***just for some*** (echo)

But for all, big and small, you may come (echo)

• Add clapping or rhythm instruments to the bold-face words only. Choose different instruments for each stanza. This encourages children to listen.

Sing for a service of communion.

G C Am D
1 To the ban - quet, come, it's not just for some,
2 At the ban - quet, eat, man - y friends to greet;
3 At the ban - quet, drink, with all peo - ple link,
4 To the ban - quet, come, it's not just for some,
G Am7 G
but for all, big and small: you may come.
it's a meal and it's real: you may eat.
grasp a hand, take a stand: you may drink.
but for all, big and small: you may come.

Text: Wayne L. Wold
Music: Wayne L. Wold

107 Shalom

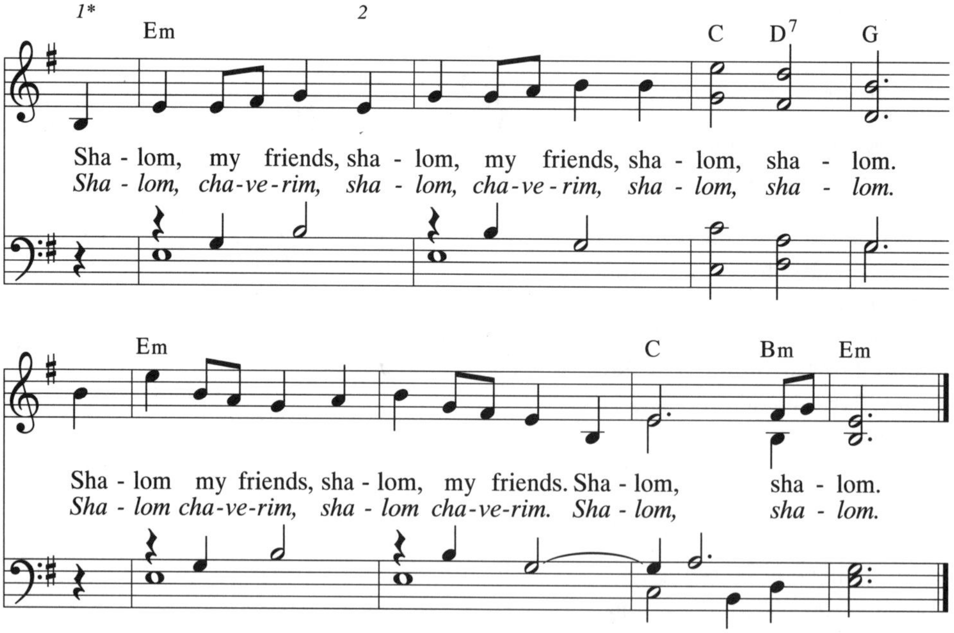
1*
2
Em
C D7 G
Sha - lom, my friends, sha - lom, my friends, sha - lom, sha - lom.
Sha - lom, cha-ve-rim, sha - lom, cha-ve-rim, sha - lom, sha - lom.
Em
C Bm Em
Sha - lom my friends, sha - lom, my friends. Sha - lom, sha - lom.
Sha - lom cha-ve-rim, sha - lom cha-ve-rim. Sha - lom, sha - lom.

**may be sung as a round*

Text: traditional
Music: Israeli traditional

Go now in peace 108

See LifeSongs *recording Volume 1*

What does the word *peace* mean to a child? Draw children into a discussion. Teach them to sign *peace* (see p. 213). How does this sign help us to understand the gift of peace? The gospel reminds us that the first gift the risen Lord gave his disciples following his resurrection was the gift of peace (John 20:19).

We share this peace in the Sunday assembly with one another. In knowing God's love we are able to center our hearts on forgiveness and our oneness with God. We are dismissed from the assembly with the words "Go in peace," and we carry with us that peace which passes all understanding. Refreshed and energized, we go in love to serve.

• Clap the rhythm, two measures at a time, inviting children to echo.

• Teach the melody showing children that the commas help them know when to take a breath. The text is clearest when sung in this way.

• Sign the words *go, peace, love, God, surround,* and *you* (see pp. 212-213).

• Invite children to be a part of worship on the second Sunday of Easter when John 20:19-31 is appointed. Teach the children three phrases from the reading:

Verse 19: "Peace be with you."
Verse 21: "Peace be with you. As the Father has sent me, so I send you."
Verse 26: "Peace be with you."

Before each of these verses the lector pauses, finger cymbals are played once, the children speak the verse, and the lector continues with the reading.

Sing as a closing song in class or choir rehearsals, or in worship following the benediction and before the dismissal.

1*
C G
Go now in peace,
go now in peace;
2
may the love of God sur - round you
3
ev - 'ry-where, ev - 'ry - where you may go.

*may be sung as a round

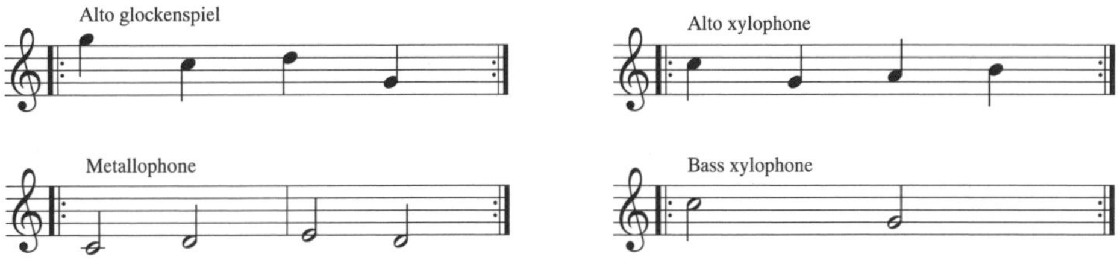
Alto glockenspiel
Alto xylophone
Metallophone
Bass xylophone

Text: Natalie Sleeth
Music: Natalie Sleeth

109 The trees of the field

Em
You shall go out with joy and be led forth with peace,
D G C G D B7
and the moun-tains and the hills will break forth be - fore you.
Em
There'll be shouts of joy and all the trees of the field
B7 Em B Em
will clap, will clap their hands.

D7 G C G D
And all the trees of the field will clap their hands.
G
The trees of the field will clap their hands.
C G D
The trees of the field will clap their hands,
B Am C♯dim B Em
while you go out with joy.

Text: Steffi Geiser Rubin
Music: Stuart Dauermann

110 Go into the world

Optional descant
3 Go ye now and
G Am D
1 Go ye, go ye in - to the world, and
2 Go ye, go ye in - to the world, and
3 Go ye, go ye in - to the world, and
tell the sto - ry to all be - liev - ers. Go ye
G Am D G
make dis - ci - ples of all the na - tions.
take the gos - pel to all the peo - ple. Go ye, go ye
tell the sto - ry to all be - liev - ers.
now, and I will be with you there!
Am D G D G
in - to the world, and I will be with you there!

Text: Natalie Sleeth
Music: Natalie Sleeth

111 Go in peace and serve the Lord

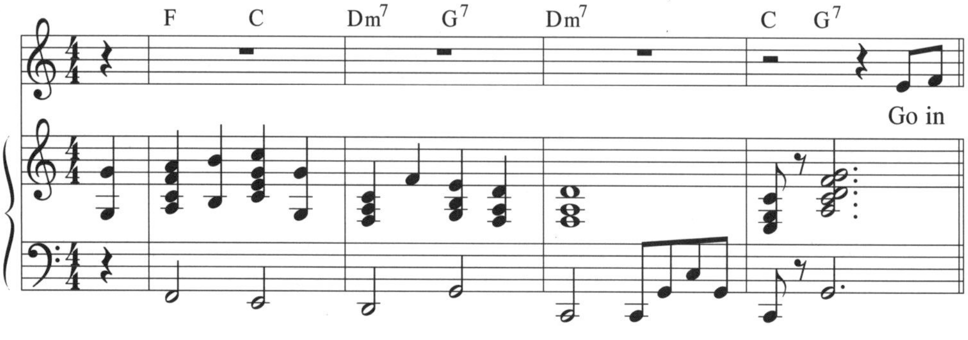
F C Dm7 G7 Dm7 C G7
Go in

C Dm7 C F G
peace and serve the Lord. God is call-ing you to-day. Go and
C Dm7 C F G F/G
tell gos-pel news ev-'ry-where. Go in
C Dm7 C F
peace and serve the Lord. God is call-ing you to-
G F C Dm7 G7
day to bring truth and love to ev-'ry
1 Dm7 C G7
na-tion. Go in
2 Dm7 C
na-tion.

Text: Handt Hanson
Music: Handt Hanson and Henry Wiens

112 God be with you

There are many ways to say good-bye. To conclude a meeting, a prayer is offered or a hymn is sung. In worship the benediction is followed by a dismissal. When we gather as Christians we encourage one another to go forth in peace, sometimes saying "May God go with you." A word we use every day, *good-bye*, actually comes from the phrase *God be with ye*. Teach children joy in singing good-bye to their classmates each week.

- Can the children find two phrases that have the same melodic line? (First and last)
- Teach the melody by phrases.
- Sign the word *God* each time it is sung. Point to another person on the word *you* with the index finger (see pp. 212–213).
- Add these movements to the third phrase:

Stanza 1:
In the morning: hands together, palms touching, fingers straight, place hands against left cheek;
when you wake: sweep right hand in front of face;
and with every breath you take: bring four fingers of right hand toward lips without touching lips, moving forward slowly.

Stanza 3:
And wherever you may go: swing index finger forward;
as the spirit winds: sign the word *spirit*;
will blow: with right hand, palm left, move from left to right to symbolize the wind blowing.

- Create with the children movement for the remaining stanzas.

Sing each week at the end of class as a parting song.

D G A7 Bm D7 G D
1 God be with you. God be with
2 God be with you. God be with
3 God be with you. God be with
4 God be with you. God be with
5 God be with you. God be with
A7 D D7
you. In the morn-ing when you wake, and with
you. When you trav-el far a-way, in your
you. And wher-ev-er you may go, as the
you. As you lis-ten, teach, and learn, and then
you. When the moon and stars shine light as you
G Em D G A7 D
ev-'ry breath you take, God be with you.
dai-ly work and play, God be with you.
spir-it winds will blow, God be with you.
safe-ly home re-turn, God be with you.
slum-ber through the night, God be with you.

Text: Rusty Edwards
Music: Rusty Edwards

The Lord is great!

Psalm 8

G Am7 G Am7 G Am7 G C
The Lord is great! Ev-'ry-bod-y sing: la, la, la, al-le-lu-ia! The
Praise the Lord
G Am7 G Am7 G Am7 G C
Lord made us! Ev-'ry-bod-y sing: la, la, la, al-le-lu-ia! God
Praise the Lord
G Am7 G Am7 G Am7 G C
made the beasts, the birds in the tree, the fish in the wat-er, and God made me! The
G Am7 G Am7 G Am7 G C
Lord is great! Ev-'ry-bod-y sing: la, la, la, al-le-lu-ia! The
Praise the Lord
G Am7 G Am7 G Am7 G
Lord is great! Ev-'ry-bod-y sing: la, la, la, al-le-lu-ia!
Praise the Lord

Text: John Erickson
Music: John Erickson

See LifeSongs *recording Volume 1*

This simple, joyful psalm sings in praise of the Creator. Listen to who is giving praise. Read Psalm 8:2, "Out of the mouths of infants and children your majesty is praised above the heavens." Affirm the children as the ones preparing to sing God's praise with their voices.

- Teach the first eight measures by phrases.
- Tell the children that we praise God's greatness and all that was created, "even the wild beasts of the field, the birds of the air, the fish of the sea, and whatsoever walks in the paths of the sea" (Psalm 8:8b-9). Who does the psalmist say is walking the paths?
- Teach the next section adding the following motions to the text:

Beasts: Place the fingertips of both hands on the chest. Rock the hands back and forth still resting on the chest. This represents the breathing motion of the animal.

Bird: Place the index finger and thumb in front of the mouth. Open and close them. This represents both the bill and the wings.

Fish: Point the right open hand forward with the palm facing left and touch the left fingertips to the right arm near the elbow. Move the right hand back and forth from the wrist. This represents the movement of the fish's tail in the water.

Me: Point the right index finger at yourself.

- Invite them to name other beasts, birds, or fish to sing in the song. Share the book, *Who Taught Frogs to Hop?* by R. D. Ingram (AFP 9-2457). This will stimulate their thinking and give them all kinds of ideas.
- Add rhythm sticks or drum on the words, *Praise the Lord, alleluia!*

Using the first eight measures, create an antiphon for Psalm 8 and sing in worship when the psalm appears in the lectionary. Or sing the entire song around the theme of creation.

114 The butterfly song

D
G
1 If I were a but-ter - fly, I'd thank you, Lord, for
2 If I were an el - e - phant, I'd thank you, Lord, by
3 If I were a wig-gly worm, I'd thank you, Lord, that
D
giv - ing me wings. And if I were a rob-in in a tree, I'd
rais - ing my trunk. And if I were a kan - ga - roo, you
I . . . could squirm. And if I were a croc - o - dile, I'd
A
A7
D
thank you, Lord, that I could sing. And if I were a
know I'd hop right up to you. And if I were an
thank you, Lord, for my big smile. And if I were a
G
fish in the sea, I'd wig-gle my tail and I'd gig-gle with glee. But
oc - to - pus, I'd thank you, Lord, for . . . my . . . fine looks. But
fuz-zy-wuz-zy bear, I'd thank you, Lord, for my fuz-zy-wuz-zy hair. But

A
D G D
I just thank you, Fa-ther, for mak-ing me me.
I just thank you, Fa-ther, for mak-ing me me.
I just thank you, Fa-ther, for mak-ing me me.
Refrain
D
For you gave me a heart and you gave me a smile. You
G
A
gave me Je-sus and you made me your child. And I just thank you,
D G D
Fa-ther, for mak-ing me me.

Text: Brian Howard
Music: Brian Howard

115 You made every part of me

See LifeSongs *recording Volume 1*

It takes the whole body to praise the Lord. Young children will enjoy singing this easily learned song.

• Introduce the actions slowly. Ask children to watch and name the parts of the body. Touch chest, mouth, hands, eyes, ears, chest. Which action was repeated?

• Sing the opening phrase. Children are to echo. Teach them to sign the word *belong* (see p. 212). Show them how the hands come together to join as one while the words *I belong to you* are sung.

• Show this sequence of actions, adding three claps after each.

Point to mouth: *sing for you.*
Hands outstretched: *work for you.*
Point to eyes: *see your world.*
Point to ears: *hear your word.*

• Now teach the melody to each phrase with actions and claps. Add the final phrase, which is the same as the beginning.

• Sing in class to help children understand that it is God who created us. Let everything that has breath praise the Lord every day!

F Gm C Gm F C7 F
You made ev - 'ry part of me, and I be - long to you. I'll
C7 F
lift my voice to sing for you, lift my hands to work for you,
C7 F
use my eyes to see your world, use my ears to hear your word.
Gm C Gm F C7 F
You made ev - 'ry part of me, and I be - long to you.

Text: Marie Pooler, alt. Helen Kemp
Music: Marie Pooler, alt. Helen Kemp

Like a tree

116

Learning the difference between right and wrong is a crucial part of a young child's life. Psalm 1 calls to mind that those who seek guidance and follow Christ will grow fruitful and strong; those who take the path of wrongdoing as a way of life will find no place.

We are invited to be like trees. Trees stand firm against the harsh winds and grow to be blessings to animals and birds with gifts of unfailing fruit and shade. Visualize this image with children. Make a connection to their lives. God has created each person and helps us grow, like a tree, into being a blessing in all that we do.

- The response can be easily taught with the leader singing the first half, the children responding with the second half.
- At the words, *You will be like a tree*, extend arm branches slowly upward in a gesture of growth. At *Come and grow with me*, sway arms like branches from side to side.
- The descant can be played by handbells or flute on the response.

Use when Psalm 1 is the appointed psalm in worship. Sing the response before the psalm verses are read or sung by the congregation and after verses 3 and 6. Or replace the psalm with the entire piece, and have a soloist sing the verses.

Refrain
G
I You will be like a tree. Come and grow with me.
II You will be like a tree. Come and grow with me.
G
Am
1 Blessed are those who delight in God's law. They are like trees planted near
2 How different for the wicked ones. They are like straw blown by the
G
Am7
D7
Refrain
G
streams. They will bear fruit in season. Their leaves will nev - er die.
wind. The path of the wicked is doomed. The good are protect - ed by God.
Handbells or flute
Refrain

Text: Psalm 1, adapt.
Music: Julie Howard; arr. Vera Lyons

117 Love is never-ending

Based on Psalm 136, this text is a responsive song of praise to the Lord as creator and as Israel's redeemer. In ancient Israel the psalm was likely led by a song leader while the choir or worshipers responded with the refrain, "God's mercy endures forever."

This setting by Marty Haugen follows the same structure, with the response proclaiming that God's love is never-ending. The part of the leader takes on a narrative form by recalling the deliverance of Israel from Egypt in stanzas 2–4 (Psalm 136:10-15).

Introduce the text of this song by reading or telling the story of Israel's deliverance at the Red Sea (Exodus 14:1—15:21). A good reference for this purpose is the *Augsburg Story Bible* (AFP 9-2607), pp. 73–74.

- Teach younger children the response with older children or a soloist singing the part of the leader.
- Add tambourine to beats 1 and 3.
- Sign the words *love* and *never-ending* (see pp. 212–213; *never-ending = ever*).

Sing in worship when the Exodus story is included (the Vigil of Easter) or when the theme emphasizes the never-ending love of God.

Leader
Em
Am7
B7
1 We give thanks un - to you, O God of might,
2 From of old you have led your peo - ple in faith,
3 You de - liv - ered the ones who called un - to you,
4 You have o - pened the sea and brought your peo - ple through,
5 You re - mem - ber your prom - ise age to age,
All
Em
B
for your love is nev - er - end - ing;
Leader
Em
we give thanks un - to you, the God of gods,
you have shown your com - pas - sion, strength, and love,
from . . . . bond - age to free - dom, you brought them forth,
brought them in - to a land that flows with life,
you show mer - cy on those of low de - gree,
All
G
Am
B7
Em
for your love is nev - er - end - ing.

Text: Psalm 136, adapt. Marty Haugen
Music: Marty Haugen

Two little eyes 118

This joyful song tells children that it takes the whole body to sing and rejoice.

• Draw the parts of the body on a large piece of poster board. Before teaching the song invite children to discuss how each part reflects our willingness to listen and serve. Use the illustrations to teach the song.

• With both hands touch the parts mentioned; sign the word *heart* (see p. 212).

Include in worship when the final hymn is "The Spirit sends us forth to serve" (WOV 723). The children may sing "Two little eyes" following stanza 3. The congregation responds with the final stanza of the hymn.

F
1 Two lit - tle eyes to look to God,
2 One lit - tle tongue to speak his truth,
U - nos o - ji - tos que mi - ran a Dios,
C
two lit - tle ears to hear his word,
one lit - tle heart for him in youth.
u - nos o - í - dos que o - yen su voz,
F
two lit - tle feet to walk his ways,
Take them, O Je - sus, let them be
dos pu - ros la - bios que ha - blan Deo_a - mor:
B♭ F C7 F
hands to serve him all my days.
al - ways will - ing, true to thee.
dos ma - ne - ci - tas doy al Se - ñor.

Text: anonymous
Music: S. V. R. Ford

119 Earth and all stars!

G C G D Em Bm
1 Earth and all stars! Loud rush - ing plan - ets!
2 Hail, wind, and rain! Loud blow - ing snow - storm!
3 Trum - pet and pipes! Loud clash - ing cym - bals!
4 En - gines and steel! Loud pound - ing ham - mers!
5 Class-rooms and labs! Loud boil - ing test tubes!
C Am7 G C D G
Sing to the Lord a new song!
Sing to the Lord a new song!
Sing to the Lord a new song!
Sing to the Lord a new song!
Sing to the Lord a new song!
Am G D G D A D
Oh, vic - to - ry! Loud shout - ing ar - my!
Flow - ers and trees! Loud rus - tling dry leaves!
Harp, lute, and lyre! Loud hum - ming cel - los!
Lime - stone and beams! Loud build - ing work - ers!
Ath - lete and band! Loud cheer - ing peo - ple!
C Am7 G C D G
Sing to the Lord a new song!
Sing to the Lord a new song!
Sing to the Lord a new song!
Sing to the Lord a new song!
Sing to the Lord a new song!

Refrain
D
C
D
G
D
God has done mar - vel - ous things.
Em
Am7
G
Am
D
G
I too sing prais - es with a new song!

Text: Herbert F. Brokering
Music: David N. Johnson

120 How majestic is your name

C F Dm7 C G7 C
O Lord, our Lord, how ma - jes - tic is your name in all the earth!
F Dm7 C G7 C
O Lord, our Lord, how ma - jes - tic is your name in all the earth!
F Dm7 G Am7 G7 C
O Lord, we praise your name. O
F Dm7 G Am7 G7 C B
Lord, we mag - ni - fy your name, Prince of
Em D G G7 C F G7 C
Peace, might - y God, O Lord God Al - might - y.

Text: Michael W. Smith
Music: Michael W. Smith

I'm so glad Jesus lifted me

G C G D
1 I'm so glad
2 Satan had me bound, Je - sus lift - ed me.
3 When I was in trouble,
D A7 D G
I'm so glad
Satan had me bound, Je - sus lift - ed me.
When I was in trouble,
G7 C G7 C
I'm so glad
Satan had me bound, Je - sus lift - ed me,
When I was in trouble,
A G B7 Em A7 G D7 G
sing - ing glo - ry, hal - le - lu - jah! Je - sus lift - ed me.

Text: African American spiritual
Music: African American spiritual; arr. *With One Voice*, 1995

122 Jesus, you help

From a very young age children need to hear the stories of Jesus healing others. Jesus loved all people, and when they hurt in any way he was there to help them. During his ministry he often encountered people who were sick, sad, and mad.

Here are examples from scripture to use with the children in helping them to understand more about Jesus' ministry. For sick, Luke 4:38-39, the healing of Simon's mother-in-law; for sad, Mark 5:22-24, 35-43, compassion for others; for mad, Mark 7:23-30, concern for those not of sound mind. Know the text well enough to be able to tell each in story form.

• Plan for children to choose one of these expressions to draw on a paper plate: *sick*, *sad*, or *mad*. Invite each child to talk about the expression they drew. Ask, "Are there times when you feel sad (glad, mad)? What was the story we heard about Jesus helping someone who was sad (glad, mad)?"

• Teach this simple melody. Ask children to hold up their plate when they hear the expression they drew.

• Display the plates as a reminder of how Jesus continues to touch each one of us with his love.

Sing often as a response to prayer, especially when praying for the sick.

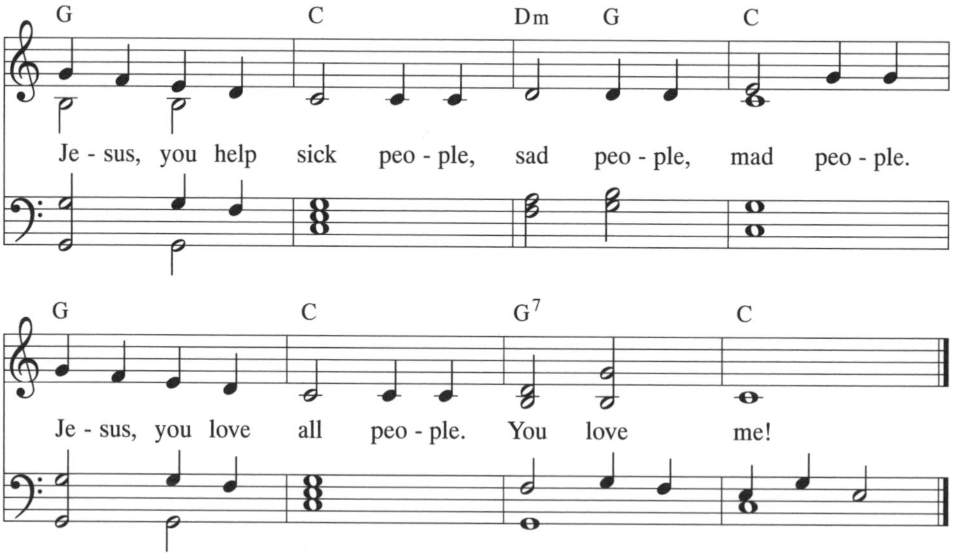
G C Dm G C
Je - sus, you help sick peo - ple, sad peo - ple, mad peo - ple.
G C G7 C
Je - sus, you love all peo - ple. You love me!

Text: Nancy Carlson
Music: Nancy Carlson

When Jesus the healer

In this hymn we meet Jesus as a person who is keenly alive, in tune with his surroundings, and aware of people, feelings, and sensations. Each of the stanzas calls us to a deeper consideration of Jesus' ministry. The response invites prayers for his healing power today.

Stanza 1: Luke 4:31-41
Stanza 2: Mark 2:3-12
Stanza 3: Mark 5:22-24, 35-43
Stanza 4: Mark 10:46-52
Stanza 5: Matthew 11:4-6
Stanza 6: Mark 6:6-13

- Each stanza can be sung as a call and response.
- Add instruments. A glockenspiel can play the melody with the leader. Tree chimes can sound each time the *All* part is sung.

Sing for a service of healing or when the theme focuses on any of the above readings.

Leader
F B♭ C
1 When Je - sus the heal - er passed through Gal - i - lee,
2 A par - a - lyzed man was let down through a roof.
3 The death of his daugh - ter caused Jai - rus to weep.
4 When blind Bar - ti - mae - us cried out to the Lord,
All
Am Dm C7 F
Heal us, heal us to - day!
Leader
Am Dm
the deaf came to hear and the
His sins were for - giv - en, his
The Lord took her hand, and he
his faith made him whole and his
C7 F
blind came to see.
walk - ing the proof.
raised her from sleep.
sight was re - stored.
All
Am Dm C7 F
Heal us, Lord Je - sus!

5 The lepers were healed and the demons cast out. Heal us, heal us today!
A bent woman straightened to laugh and to shout. Heal us, Lord Jesus.

6 The twelve were commissioned and sent out in twos, Heal us, heal us today!
to make the sick whole and to spread the good news. Heal us, Lord Jesus.

7 There's still so much sickness and suffering today. Heal us, heal us today!
We gather together for healing and pray: Heal us, Lord Jesus.

Text: Peter Smith
Music: Peter Smith

124 Jesus' hands were kind hands

When we think about hands, we can recall hymns that talk about our hands, such as "Lord, take my hand and lead me" and "Take my hands and let them move." With the first stanza of this song we are drawn immediately into singing about the hands of Jesus, hands that are kind and caring. Jesus is the master servant. We are the Master's servants. In the second stanza we ask prayerfully that our hands be made strong and gentle as we open our hands in service as Christ to one another.

- Sing the first phrase with syllables, encouraging children to read the notation by sight and by sound. Write the syllables in the key of G on poster board (11" x 17") encouraging them to play a matching game with the syllables and the notes. Ask them to find how many times this phrase

sol la ti do re mi

appears in the song (three times).

- Sing the third phrase with syllables. It is sung only once; the song's form is AABA.
- Sing the melody with syllables, then add the words. Encourage the children to use good posture when singing and to think of taking a breath only at the end of each phrase.

Sing in any service focusing on the ministry of Christ and our call to follow and serve others.

G D Em D7 G
1 Je - sus' hands were kind hands, do - ing good to all,
2 Take my hands, Lord Je - sus, let them work for you;
Em C G Am Em D7 G
heal - ing pain and sick - ness, bless - ing chil - dren small,
make them strong and gen - tle, kind in all I do.
Am A7 D
wash - ing ti - red feet and sav - ing those who fall;
Let me watch you, Je - sus, till I'm gen - tle too,
G D Em D7 G
Je - sus' hands were kind hands, do - ing good to all.
till my hands are kind hands, quick to work for you.

Text: Margaret Cropper
Music: French traditional

Forgive our sins as we forgive

125

We all know what weeds are like! They can take over a once beautiful garden or yard. The idea for this hymn came to the author, Rosamond Herklots, as she was digging up docks in a long-neglected garden. Docks are coarse weeds with small green flowers and large leaves. She writes, "Realizing how these deeply rooted weeds were choking the life out of the flowers in the garden, I came to feel that deeply rooted resentments in our lives could destroy every Christian virtue and all joy and peace unless, by God's grace, we learned to forgive" (P. Wezeman and A. Liechty, "The Lord's Prayer," in *Hymn Stories for Children*, Kregel Resources, p. 37).

Forgiving others is not an optional activity for Christians. It is the heart of the gospel. God forgives us and strengthens us to be a forgiving people. In the Lord's Prayer we pray, "Forgive us our sins as we forgive those who sin against us." May this hymn inspire us to be reconciled with each other so that our lives will spread God's love, peace, and joy.

- Talk with the children about making room in their lives for these gifts to grow by removing any weeds of resentment toward others.

- The tune, ST. ANNE, has been selected for this text to make the hymn more accessible to children. One syllable or a word appears with each note in this two-phrase hymn. The melody has an easy, gentle flow.

Sing in a service of repentance and forgiveness.

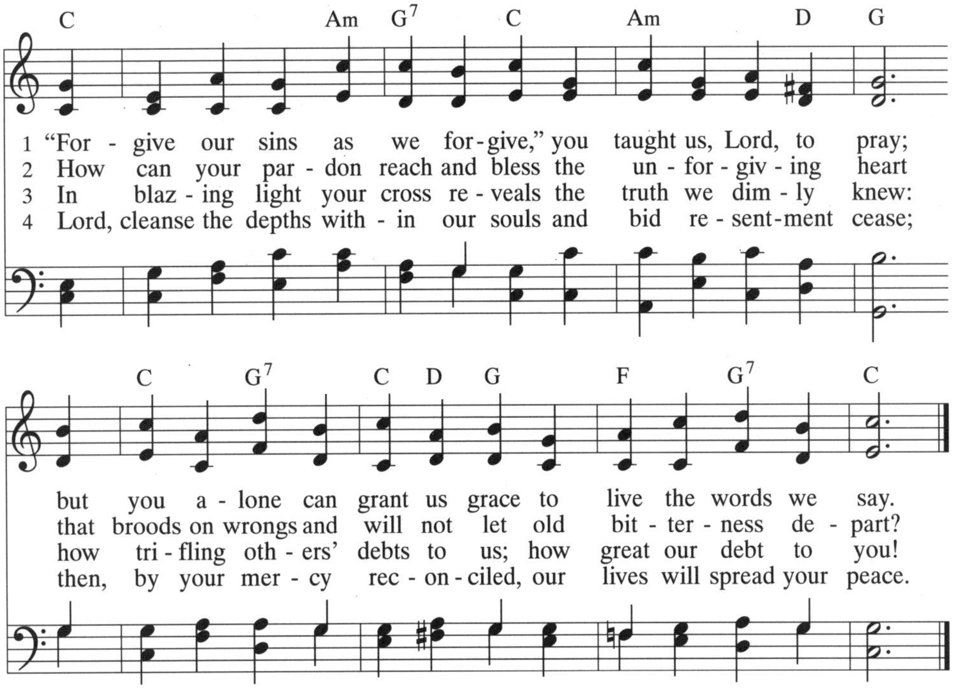
C Am G7 C Am D G
1 "For - give our sins as we for - give," you taught us, Lord, to pray;
2 How can your par - don reach and bless the un - for - giv - ing heart
3 In blaz - ing light your cross re - veals the truth we dim - ly knew:
4 Lord, cleanse the depths with - in our souls and bid re - sent - ment cease;
C G7 C D G F G7 C
but you a - lone can grant us grace to live the words we say.
that broods on wrongs and will not let old bit - ter - ness de - part?
how tri - fling oth - ers' debts to us; how great our debt to you!
then, by your mer - cy rec - on - ciled, our lives will spread your peace.

Text: Rosamond E. Herklots, alt.
Music: William Croft

126 Life together

See LifeSongs *recording Volume 1 or Volume 2*

D G A Bm Em7 D GM7 A D
Refrain
Life to-geth-er, now and for-ev-er: to-geth-er for-ev-er in
D G A Bm Em D
Je-sus' name. Life to-geth-er, now and for-ev-er: to-
G Asus A D G A Bm
To stanzas
Last time
geth-er for-ev-er, we all pro-claim. all pro-claim. To-
Em7 D GM7 A D GM7 A Bm

geth-er for-ev - er, in Je - sus' name.
Em7 D GM7 A7sus A D G A D
Stanzas
1 Gath-er in the Spir - it; come in from ev - 'ry place.
2 Cel - e-brate to - geth - er and share the liv - ing bread.
G A7 G F♯m7 Bm7 Em7 Asus A D C♯m7 F♯7
Live and learn the way of God, the sav-ing word of grace.
Go in peace to serve the Lord in ev - 'ry day a - head.
Refrain
G A7 G F♯m7 F♯ Bm E E7 Em7/A A

Text and music: Brian Pearson and Sherry Pearson

127 Bind us together, Lord

Families are a gift from God. When we think of being bound together in love our thoughts immediately turn to our own families. But when we gather as a church we are seen—and should see ourselves—in a different light. At baptism we are welcomed into the Lord's family, united there with all our fellow members of the body of Christ.

When we leave the assembly we realize we are part of an even greater community. We are connected to the world, to our global family. In Ephesians 2:13-22 we hear that Christ has created one new humanity and has reconciled both groups to God in one body through the cross.

• Use a globe or a wall map to show children where they live. Discuss how we are part of a larger community in Christ. Many churches today connect with other countries through companion synods or missionary programs. What is your church's involvement?

• Teach the refrain. A soloist can sing the two stanzas.

• Add a tambourine to the word *bind* each time it is sung. After the first person plays on the first word of the first phrase, the instrument is passed on to the neighbor. Continue passing the tambourine throughout the refrain.

Sing for any service with an emphasis on missions.

Refrain
F Dm Gm
Bind us to-geth-er, Lord, bind us to-geth-er with cords that
C7 F
can-not be bro - ken. Bind us to-geth-er, Lord,
Dm Gm C F
bind us to-geth-er, Lord; bind us to-geth-er in love.
F C7 F C7 F
1 There is on-ly one God. There is on-ly one King.
2 You are the fam-'ly of God. You are the prom-ise di-vine.
C7 F C7 F Bb/C
There is on-ly one Bod-y; that is why we can sing.
You are God's cho-sen de-sire, . . you are the glo-rious new wine.
Refrain

Text: Bob Gillman
Music: Bob Gillman

Many are the lightbeams

Jesus Christ invites us to abide in him. As members of a Christian community of faith we are many, yet we are one in Christ. Through illustration, help children understand how God protects us here on earth, in and through Christ's name, and melds us into one.

- Stanza 1: Draw a circle representing the one light. Add one line for every child. Write one name on each beam.
- Stanza 2: Draw a tree trunk, adding branches with the names of the children.
- Stanza 3: Draw a heart remembering John 3:16, God's love for all people.
- Stanza 4: Draw a cross and invite the children to share how they serve (loving, sharing, being kind, helping). Write each on a circle of construction paper and add to the cross.
- Stanza 5: Draw a church and add their names inside it.
- Teach one stanza each week until completed. Illustrations could be drawn and added week-by-week to a large piece of poster board, one drawing for each learned stanza.

Sing during the Easter season or when there is an emphasis on our oneness in Christ.

Em Am B7 Em Am7
1 Man - y are the light - beams from the one light. Our one
2 Man - y are the branch - es of the one tree. Our one
3 Man - y are the gifts giv'n, love is all one. Love's the
4 Man - y ways to serve God, the spir - it is one; ser - vant
5 Man - y are the mem - bers, the bod - y is one; mem - bers
D7 G Am D7
light is Je - sus. Man - y are the light - beams
tree is Je - sus. Man - y are the branch - es
gift of Je - sus. Man - y are the gifts giv'n,
spir - it of Je - sus. Man - y ways to serve God, the
all of Je - sus. Man - y are the mem - bers, the
G C Em B7 Em
from the one light; we are one in Christ.
of the one tree; we are one in Christ.
love is all one; we are one in Christ.
spir - it is one; we are one in Christ.
bod - y is one; we are one in Christ.

Text: Cyprian of Carthage; tr. Andres Frostenson
Music: Olle Widestrand; arr. Marty Haugen

129 If anybody asks you who I am

We are welcomed into Christ's community through baptism. Through water and the word we are named God's beloved children, for this is who we are. Stanza 2 speaks of the washing away of our sins at baptism. In stanza 3 the water also symbolizes our dying and rising with Christ. Stanza 4 looks to God's ultimate goal for each of us as the final chapter of baptism. Stanza 5 expresses our desire that God's love remain with us through Christ, our friend.

- A simple, repetitive melody shows how these words lead in each stanza: *who, how, what, where, who's*.
- Add claves to the final three beats of the text for emphasis.
- Repeat the final phrase of stanza 5 two more times to make a fitting conclusion.

Sing when the worship service has a baptismal emphasis or on Reformation Sunday around the gospel, John 8:31-36, extending stanza 2 as suggested above for stanza 5.

E
1 If an-y-bod-y asks you who I am, who I
2 If an-y-bod-y asks you how I am, how I
3 If an-y-bod-y asks you what that means, what that
4 If an-y-bod-y asks you where I'm go - ing, where I'm
5 If an-y-bod-y asks you who's my friend, who's my
A B7 E
am, who I am, if an-y-bod-y asks you
am, how I am, if an-y-bod-y asks you
means, what that means, if an-y-bod-y asks you
go - ing, where I'm go-ing, if an-y-bod-y asks you
friend, who's my friend, if an-y-bod-y asks you
B7 E
who I am, say that I'm a child of God.
how I am, say that I'm a - live and free.
what that means, say that I was born a - gain.
where I'm go - ing, say that I am going to heav'n.
who's my friend, say that Je-sus is his name.

Text: anonymous, st. 1; Jaroslav Vajda, sts. 2-5
Music: Southern folk song

We are all one in Christ

Ephesians 4:4-6 is the foundation of this hymn. By virtue of our baptism we are one body, one people out of many. Our baptismal identity provides an opportunity to see ourselves as part of a larger family—God's family—connected with the world in a variety of ways. How appropriate to sing these scriptural words to a Spanish tune.

- Teach the melody by phrases. Are there two phrases that sound alike? (The first two phrases.)
- Add bongos playing this rhythm: ♩. ♪ ♩ ♩
- Add maracas to the first two phrases only: ♫ ♫ ♫ ♫
- Create a hand pattern. Beginning with the first beat: pat thighs twice, clap hands together twice, snap fingers twice, clap hands together twice. Repeat the pattern.
- Sign key words in the last two phrases: *God, Lord, love, Spirit* (see pp. 212–213).
- Use movement for two of the words:

Faith: Bring arms above head, cross right wrist over left wrist to form a cross.
Baptism: With palms down, bring hands upward above the face and wiggle fingers in a downward movement suggesting water.

Sing when Ephesians 4:4-6 is one of the appointed readings, for a service of communion, or when the emphasis is on mission and our baptismal call.

Em
We are all one in Christ, we are one bod - y, all one
So - mos u - no en Cris - to, so - mos u - no. So - mos
B7
1 Em
2 Em
peo - ple out of man - y. man - y.
u - no, u - no so - lo. so - lo.
Am
Em
There is one God, and on - ly one Lord; there is one
Un so - lo Dios, un so - lo Se - ñor, u - na so - la
B7
Em
Am
faith, one ho - ly love. There is one bap - tism; there is one
fe, un so - lo a - mor. Un so - lo bau - tis - mo, un so - lo Es-
Em
B7
Em
Spir - it, who is God the com - fort - er.
pí - ri - tu, y e - se es el con - so - la - dor.

Text: anonymous; tr. Gerhard Cartford
Music: anonymous

131 Chatter with the angels

What comes to children's minds when they hear the opening phrase, *Chatter with the angels*? Invite comments. This is a spiritual that was sung by slaves who came to the Americas from Africa. As an oppressed people they often sang of the day when they would cross over from the burdens of slavery to deliverance in a happier, heavenly place. In this song, joining a band of angels offered a freedom unknown to those who were slaves.

Spirituals commonly use the pentatonic scale of only five notes: *do-re-mi-sol-la*. The fourth (*fa*) and seventh (*ti*) steps of the scale have been avoided. Notice how easily this song is learned by children.

sol la do re mi sol la

- Teach children the sound of *mi-re-do*. Sing the song for them. Ask them to listen and to raise their hand every time they hear *mi-re-do* (the last measure of each phrase).
- Teach the song by phrases. Ask children to clap on the *mi-re-do*.
- Set up an Orff instrument with A-G-F and invite one child to play at the end of each phrase.
- Experience the actions indicated for each stanza or encourage children to create their own. To keep them actively listening have them march, skip, dance, or tiptoe for first three measures of each phrase, then stand motionless for the fourth, clapping on the *mi-re-do*.
- Sing this song with "All night, all day" (#155). Divide the group in half to experience these partner songs effectively.

Chat-ter with the an - gels soon in the morn - ing, chat-ter with the an - gels
in that land. Chat-ter with the an - gels soon in the morn - ing,
chat-ter with the an - gels, join the band. I hope to
join that band and chat-ter with the an - gels all day long!
I hope to join that band and chat-ter with the an - gels all day long!

Text: African American spiritual
Music: African American spiritual

Kids of the kingdom

C F C G
1 Kids of the king - dom, that's what we are:
2 My name is ________, I love the Lord.
3 Kids of the king - dom, that's what we are:
4 Praise to the Fa - ther, praise to the Son,
C F C G C
kids of the king - dom, that's what we are.
My name is ________, I love the Lord.
kids of the king - dom, that's what we are.
praise to the Spir - it, the Three in One.
C E Am G F C G C
We love Je - sus, we love the Lord.
They love Je - sus, they love the Lord.
We love Je - sus, we love the Lord.
We love Je - sus, we love the Lord.
C E Am G F C G C
We love Je - sus, we love the Lord.
They love Je - sus, they love the Lord.
We love Je - sus, we love the Lord.
We love Je - sus, we love the Lord.

Text: Ralph Torres
Music: Ralph Torres

133 We are the church

See LifeSongs *recording Volume 1*

A familiar finger play among young children goes like this:

Here is the church, (Hold the hands back to back with the fingers pointing down. Fold the hands with the fingers inside.)
And here is the steeple. (Extend both index fingers up.)
Open the doors, (Open the thumbs apart.)
And see all the people! (Open the hands so the fingers point up and wiggle the fingers.)

The scripture readings for the Day of Pentecost, the birthday of the church, tell us that we believers are part of a much greater church, not one confined to a building. The church is a place of rest and refreshment where people gather to worship God and from which they are sent out with good news for the whole world. We are called to be this church we cannot see. Through the power of the Holy Spirit we are set on a path toward God's message of love, freedom, and salvation for all creation. Therefore, Pentecost is a day when we strive for understanding and communion with our neighbors.

• Gather in a circle. Establish partners, by counting off by twos; one and two become partners.

continued on next page

Refrain
G C
I am the church! You are the church!
G D G Em
We are the church to - geth - er! All who fol - low Je - sus,
Am D Bm C D7 G
all a - round the world, yes, we're the church to - geth - er!
G
1 The church is not a build - ing, the
2 We're man - y kinds of peo - ple with
3 And when the peo - ple gath - er, there's
4 At Pen - te - cost some peo - ple re -

continued from previous column

- Teach the refrain adding these motions:

I am the church: Point to self.
You are the church: Point to partner.
We are the church together: Shake partner's hand, then join the larger circle.
All who follow Jesus, all around the world: Hold hands and walk to the right in a circle stopping on the word *world*.
Yes: Both hands thrust upward.
We're the church together: With arms still raised, move slowly to the center touching fingers.

- As stanzas are sung, step back slowly into circle formation until the refrain is sung again. Repeat movement.

Sing in a Sunday school opening or in a class setting when the discussion centers on the birth of the church as on the Day of Pentecost.

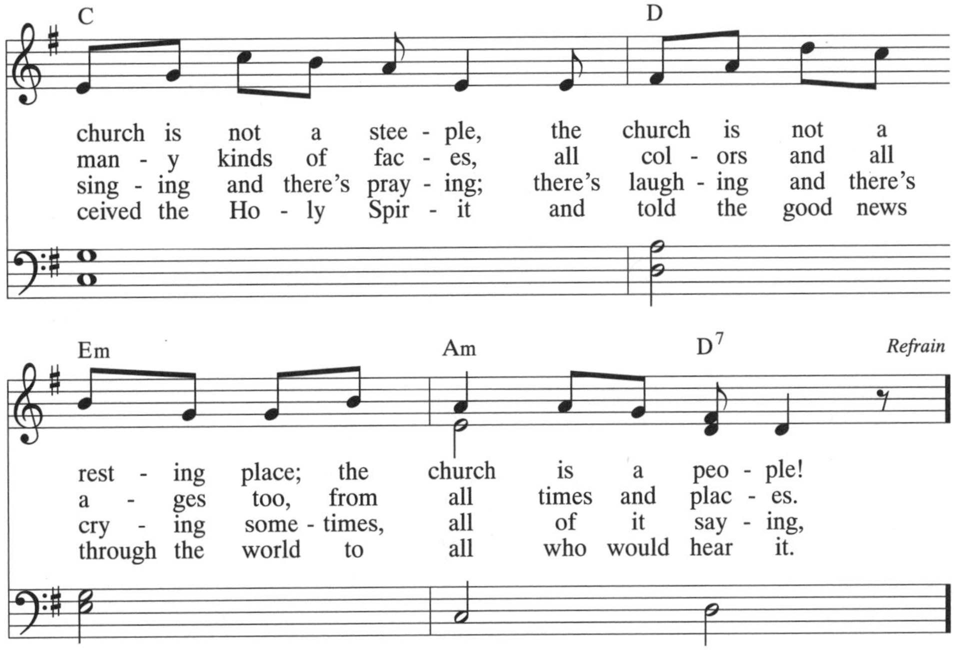
C
D
church is not a stee - ple, the church is not a
man - y kinds of fac - es, all col - ors and all
sing - ing and there's pray - ing; there's laugh - ing and there's
ceived the Ho - ly Spir - it and told the good news
Em
Am
D7
Refrain
rest - ing place; the church is a peo - ple!
a - ges too, from all times and plac - es.
cry - ing some - times, all of it say - ing,
through the world to all who would hear it.

Text: Richard Avery and Donald Marsh
Music: Richard Avery and Donald Marsh

134 Love, love, love!

The words of this song describe how we as the church live in response to God's love for us. We celebrate love, peace, and joy in and with our families, both at home and at church.

• Introduce the first three notes of the melody with this body pattern: clap, pat thighs, clap. Children repeat. Now sing the words *Love, love, love*. The body pattern follows the voice line.

• Continue teaching the song by phrases adding the body pattern each time on the words *love, love, love.*

• Sing the other stanzas pointing to self on stanza 4 and to others on stanza 5.

• Choose a different rhythm instrument for each of the stanzas to add to the body pattern: stanza 1, drum; stanza 2, wood block; stanza 3, triangle; stanza 4, cowbell; stanza 5, guiro. Add a tambourine to the words *Mother, father, sister, brother* (♩ ♩ ♩ ♩). Encourage each player to listen carefully for the words on which they play.

Sing in a Sunday school opening or in class when the emphasis is living a life of faith through our actions with others. Encourage children to sing this at home with their families.

F Bb F Gm7 C F
Love, love, love! That's what it's all a - bout! 'Cause
Gm7 C F Gm7 C F
God loves us, we love each oth - er, moth-er, fa - ther, sis - ter, broth - er.
Gm7 C F Gm7 C F C
Ev-'ry-bod-y sing and shout, 'cause that's what it's all a - bout! It's a-bout
F Bb F C F Bb F
love, love, love! It's a-bout love, love, love!

Additional stanzas ad lib:
Peace, peace, peace!
Joy, joy, joy!
Me, me, me!
You, you, you!

Text and music: Lois Brokering and Herbert F. Brokering

There's a Spirit in the air

There is a saying, "Don't put off until tomorrow what you can do today." That is easier said than done. Sometimes we put our faith on hold. But there is a Spirit—God's Spirit—telling us to take the gift that has been given to us and tell the world what God has done. Don't be afraid to live tomorrow's life today.

The author of this song text, Brian Wren, speaks of concerns facing the church and society. He has chosen words that children need to hear and sing now.

• To learn this song begin with the text. Read the words gently, in rhythm, until they flow easily. Divide into two groups, assigning two phrases to each group. Add the music, allowing this text to shine.

• "Christ the Lord is risen today!" (#64) uses this thirteenth-century French tune. Is the melody the same or different? (The melody is the same, the rhythm different.) Is the text the same? (No.) Who wrote that text? (Charles Wesley.)

• Sing stanza 1 of "Christ the Lord is risen today!" There is an energetic feeling to this Easter hymn. Now sing stanza 1 of "There's a Spirit in the air." Wren's text is set to the same melody with a different meter. The change in the rhythm helps us to feel the winds of the Spirit.

Sing on Pentecost Sunday or when the church is called to be a sign in the world.

Capo 3 D Em A D G D A D
F Gm C F B♭ F C F
1 There's a Spir - it in the air, tell - ing Chris - tians ev - 'ry - where:
2 Lose your shy - ness, find your tongue; tell the worlds what God has done.
3 When be - liev - ers break the bread, when a hun - gry child is fed,
4 Still the Spir - it leads the fight, see - ing wrong and set - ting right:
G Em7 F♯ D G A D
B♭ Gm7 A F B♭ C F
praise the love that Christ re - vealed, liv - ing, work - ing, in our world.
God in Christ has come to stay. Live to - mor - row's life to - day!
praise the love that Christ re - vealed, liv - ing, work - ing, in our world.
God in Christ has come to stay. Live to - mor - row's life to - day!

Text: Brian Wren
Music: French traditional; arr. Richard Redhead

136 On the poor

Kyrie eleison, Christe eleison, Kyrie eleison are responses that have their roots in the Jerusalem church of the fourth century. Petitions asking for God's help were offered by the deacon with the congregation responding, *Kyrie eleison* (Lord, have mercy). *Kyrie* is the Greek word for *Lord.*

This ancient liturgical prayer asks God to show us mercy. What does it mean to show mercy? The three stanzas reflect the threefold response of the early church. The stepward movement of the melody and the repetitive rhythm will make this an easy song to teach.

- In a standing position with arms resting at sides of the body, add these movements.

Stanzas 1 and 3:
Measure 1: *poor*. Raise right arm slowly extending straight above head.
Measure 2: *poor*. Raise left arm slowly extending straight above head.
Measure 3: *mercy*. Both arms burst upward slightly and out to sides returning to original position on the word *Lord*.
Measures 5–8. Repeat movement ending with palms of both hands together as if in prayer.

Stanza 2:
Measure 1: *poor*. Bring right arm straight out in front of body at the waist.
Measure 2: *poor*. Bring left arm straight out in front of body at the waist.
Measure 3: *mercy.* Both arms burst out away from body returning to the sides of the body on the word *Christ*.
Measures 5–8. Repeat movement ending with palms of both hands together as if in prayer.

C F G C
1 On the poor, on the poor, show your mer - cy, O Lord.
2 On the poor, on the poor, show your mer - cy, O Christ.
3 On the poor, on the poor, show your mer - cy, O Lord.
A Dm G C
On the poor, on the poor, show your mer - cy, O Lord.
On the poor, on the poor, show your mer - cy, O Christ.
On the poor, on the poor, show your mer - cy, O Lord.

Text: traditional liturgical text, adapt.
Music: Paraguayan traditional

- Invite children to create other petitions such as *Neighbors near, neighbors far; show your mercy, O Lord*; or *On us all, big and small, show your mercy, O Lord.*

Sing in a Sunday school opening or in worship as a response to prayer.

Make me a servant

God gives us a mission at baptism. In this covenant we are to live among God's faithful people, to hear God's word and share in the holy supper, to proclaim the good news of God in Christ through word and deed, to serve all people following the example of our Lord Jesus, and to strive for justice and peace in all the earth.

- Discuss one part of this covenant each week. Record shared ideas on a large poster entitled "Make me a servant." Remembering the promises made at baptism on our behalf, we carry within ourselves the resurrection life of the risen Christ. What does it mean to fully live among and serve God's faithful people?
- Sing the first interval using syllables *sol-do*. Sing the first eight measures with the words. How many times did they hear the interval *sol-do*? (Three times.)
- Teach the first twelve measures.
- Sing the interval in measure 13 on *sol-mi*. Sing the remaining seven measures with the words, inviting children to identify how many times the interval *sol-mi* was sung. (Three times.)
- Finish teaching the song.

Sing as a prayer petition in a Sunday school opening or as a class session closing. In worship sing around the reading of Matthew 20:20-28 or Mark 10:35-45.

F Dm7 Gm7 C7
Make me a ser - vant, hum - ble and meek.
Gm7 B♭ C7 B♭ F A
Lord, let me lift up those who are weak.
Dm G Gdim
And may the prayer of my heart al - ways be:
F Gm7 F Gm7
Make me a ser - vant, make me a ser - vant,
F C7sus F
make me a ser - vant to - day.

Text: Kelly Willard
Music: Kelly Willard

138 Here I am, Lord

1 "I, the Lord of sea and sky, I have heard my peo-ple cry.
2 "I, the Lord of snow and rain, I have borne my peo-ple's pain.
3 "I, the Lord of wind and flame, I will tend the poor and lame.
G C G C G D
All who dwell in deep-est sin my hand will save.
I have wept for love of them. They turn a-way.
I will set a feast for them. My hand will save.
G Em Am G C Am Am7 D
I, who made the stars of night, I will make their dark-ness bright.
I will break their hearts of stone, give them hearts for love a-lone.
Fin-est bread I will pro-vide till their hearts be sat-is-fied.
G C G C G D

Who will bear my light to them? Whom shall I send?"
I will speak my word to them. Whom shall I send?"
I will give my life to them. Whom shall I send?"
G Em Am7 G C Am G C D
Refrain
D G C G
Here I am, Lord. Is it I, Lord? I have heard you
Am7 G C D G
call-ing in the night. I will go, Lord, if you
C G Am7 D G
lead me. I will hold your peo-ple in my heart.

Text: Daniel Schutte
Music: Daniel Schutte; arr. Michael Pope, Daniel Schutte, and John Weissrock

139 You are the seed

Both the text and tune for this hymn were written by Cesáreo Gabarain. He is one of the finest and best-known composers of liturgical music in Spanish. He was born in the Basque region of Spain in 1936 and he died there in 1991. Locate the area on a map. Other hymns by Gabarain include "Grains of wheat" (WOV 708) and "You have come down to the lakeshore" (WOV 784).

- Clap these rhythms inviting children to echo.

- Speak stanza 1 in rhythm by phrases. Children echo each phrase.
- Design a poster to illustrate key words in the text using creative suggestions from the children.
- Teach stanza 1 and the refrain using the poster to help them memorize the hymn.
- Add maracas (♫ ♫ ♫ ♫) to accompany the refrain.

Have children sing in worship when the emphasis is on our mission to serve.

D A Bm D G
1 You are the seed that will grow a new sprout; you're a star that will
2 You are the flame that will light - en the dark, so re - splen - dent with
3 You are the life that will nur - ture the plant; you're the waves in a
A7 D A Bm G
shine in the night; you are the yeast and a small grain of salt, a
hope, faith and love; you are the shep - herds to lead the whole world to
tur - bu - lent sea; yes - ter - day's yeast is be - gin - ning to rise, a
D G A7 D A Bm D
bea - con to glow in the dark. You are the dawn that will bring a new day;
wa - ters and pas - tures of peace. "You are the friends that I chose for my - self,
new loaf of bread it will yield. There is no place for a cit - y to hide,
G A7 D A
you're the wheat that will bear gold - en grain; you are a sting and a
you're the word that I want to pro - claim. You are the new reign of
there's no moun - tain can cov - er its might; let your light shine so that

Bm G D G A7 D
soft, gen - tle touch, to wit - ness where - ev - er you go.
God built on rock, where jus - tice and truth are at home."
your lov - ing works give hon - or and glo - ry to God.
Refrain/Estribillo
A D G A7
Go, my friends, go to the world, pro - claim the great love of
Be, my friends, a loy - al wit - ness, from the dead Christ a -
Id, a - mi - gos, por el mun - do, a - nun - cian - do el a -
Sed, a - mi - gos, mis tes - ti - gos de mi re - su - rrec-
D Em7 A7 Bm
God; mes - sen - gers to tell the way of life,
rose; "Lo, I'll be with you for - ev - er - more,
mor, men - sa - je - ros de la vi - da,
ción. Id lle - van - do mi pre - sen - cia;
1 G A 2 G A7 D
peace and par - don for all.
till the end of the world."
de la paz y el per - dón.
con vo - so - tros es - toy.

Text: Cesáreo Gabarain; tr. Raquel Gutiérrez-Achon and Skinner Chávez-Melo
Music: Cesáreo Gabarain; arr. Skinner Chávez-Melo

140 Love your neighbor

We communicate with our faces. A face can say *I'm angry, I'm sad, I'm glad, I'm lonely*. So powerful are the expressions of the face that in biblical times the human face was frequently regarded as representative of the whole person. To seek someone's face meant to make an effort to be in that person's presence. We come into God's presence when we show love for God and for one another.

- Sing the refrain for the children, inviting them to feel the two beats in each measure by rocking from side to side.
- Sing the stanzas asking them to listen for emotions and feelings we have all experienced—loneliness, sadness, hurt, joy.
- Have several rhythm instruments on hand (maracas, claves, drum, tambourine, finger cymbals). Do any of these instruments express such feelings? If so, add one instrument to the word in the song.
- Create with the children a movement or facial expression for each of the key words.

Sing in worship when the emphasis is on loving others.

Refrain
G C G
Love your neigh - bor as your - self; be
C Am7 D7 G C
gen - tle, kind and true. Love your neigh - bor as your -
G C Am7 D7 G
self; for God has first loved you.

G C
1 Be a friend to those who are lone - ly. Be a
2 Je - sus was a friend to the lone - ly. Je - sus
Am D Bm
friend to those who are sad. Let your love help those who are
was a friend to the sad. Je - sus' love helped those who were
Em Am D7 Refrain
hurt - ing. Let your love make ev - 'ry - one glad!
hurt - ing. Je - sus' love still makes ev - 'ry - one glad!

Text: Susan Eltringham
Music: Susan Eltringham

141 Come now, you blessed

See LifeSongs *recording Volume 2*

Would children be surprised to know that in the faces of those who are hungry, homeless, and sick, there is Christ? The world stands in need of food and drink, care and clothing. The meal we share together in worship at the invitation of Christ is a hungry feast. Each week we are prepared and shaped for another week of service. The sending from worship is all about mission. God's word calls us to action. How are we living out this call?

- In Matthew 25:31-40, Jesus is speaking to his disciples. Divide the children into two groups. Assign one group to read stanzas 1 and 3 as words from Jesus, the other group stanza 2 as the disciples' response. Both groups can read stanza 4 as our commitment to showing and seeing God's love in all that we do.
- In teaching the melody, ask children to look for identical phrases (phrases 1 and 3).
- Keep a feeling of one beat per measure to encourage a smooth flow.

Sing in worship when Matthew 25:31-40 is appointed as the gospel reading or when the focus is on social justice.

Capo 3 G B♭ C E♭ G B♭
1 "Come now, you bless - ed, eat at my ta - ble,"
2 When did we see you hun - gry or thirst - y?
3 "When you gave bread to the earth's hun - gry chil - dren,
4 Christ, when we meet you out on life's road - ways,
D F
said Je - sus Christ to the righ - teous a - bove.
When were you home - less, a strang - er a - lone?
when you gave wel - come to war's ref - u - gees.
look - ing to us in the fac - es of need,
G B♭ C E♭ G B♭
"When I was hun - gry, thirst - y, and home - less,
When did we see you sick or in pris - on?
When you re - mem - bered those most for - got - ten,
then may we know you, wel - come and show you
C E♭ G B♭ Am Cm D F G B♭
sick and in pris - on, you showed me your love."
What have we done that you call us your own?
you cared for me in the small - est of these."
love that is faith - ful in word and in deed.

Text: Ruth Duck
Music: Emily R. Brink

Love God and your neighbor

See LifeSongs *recording Volume 1*

To love the Lord your God and your neighbor as yourself are the two greatest commandments. Matthew 22:34-40 tells us to love God with all our heart, soul, and mind; Mark 12:28-34 and Luke 10:25-28 add the word *strength*. The significance is the same. Love for neighbor is a natural outgrowth of total devotion to God. In what ways do we show our devotion to God?

• Sing in four-measure phrases, asking children to echo after each phrase.

• Sing again, clapping one beat on *heart, mind*, and *strength*.

• Add an instrument to each word: *heart*, finger cymbals; *mind*, tambourine; *strength*, guiro.

• Practice a movement for each phrase.

Phrase 1: Step to the side with right foot on first beat bringing left foot to rest next to right on third beat. Continue to end of the phrase.

Phrase 2: Step to side with left foot on first beat bringing right foot to rest next to left on third beat. Continue to end of phrase.

Phrase 3: Remaining in place, pat thighs on first beat, clap on third beat.

• Before singing as a two- or three-part canon, divide into groups and experience the movement alone, thinking the words.

• Sing in canon with instruments and movement.

Sing in a Sunday school opening or in class when learning about our love of God and our call to love and serve our neighbor.

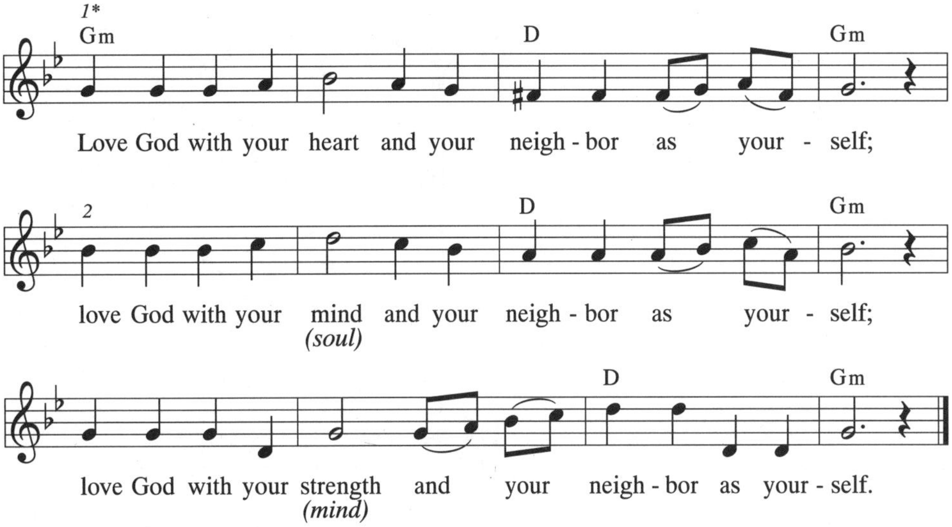
1*
Gm
D
Gm
Love God with your heart and your neigh - bor as your - self;
2
D
Gm
love God with your mind and your neigh - bor as your - self;
(soul)
D
Gm
love God with your strength and your neigh - bor as your - self.
(mind)

**may be sung as a round*

Text: from the Gospels
Music: traditional

143 Blest are they

G D C G D
1 Blest are they, the poor in spir-it; theirs is the king-dom of God.
2 Blest are they, the low-ly ones; they shall in-her-it the earth.
3 Blest are they . . . who show mer-cy; mer - cy shall . . be theirs.
4 Blest are they . . . who seek peace; they are the chil-dren of God.
5 Blest are you who suf-fer hate, all . . . be-cause. . . of me. Re-
G D C D G
Blest are they, full of sor-row; they shall be con-soled.
Blest are they who hun-ger and thirst. they shall have their fill.
Blest are they, the pure of heart; they . . . shall see God.
Blest are they who suf-fer in faith; the king-dom of God is theirs.
joice, be glad, yours is the king-dom; shine for all to see.
Refrain
C D G C G A7 D
Re - joice and be glad! Bless-ed are you; ho-ly are you!
Am D G Em C D G
Re - joice and be glad! Yours is the king-dom of God!

Text: David Haas
Music: David Haas, arr. Norma de Waal Malefyt

Jesus, Jesus, let us tell you

Jesus made a promise to his disciples that they would not be alone after his death. The Spirit that God had promised to send would be with them. We need constantly to be reminded that the Holy Spirit did not come just to be with the early disciples. The Spirit also leads and guides us today. The Spirit gives us power to witness to Christ's resurrection and to carry on his mission.

- The repetition and flowing melody make this round very accessible for children.
- Feel the rhythm of the half note. Hold left hand, palm up, to the left at waist level. With right hand, tap the left hand on the first half note (beat 1). Reverse, right hand, palm up, to the right, tap the right hand with the left hand on the second half note (beat 3). Sway gently from side to side leaning into the beat.
- Teach the song. Once the text and melody have been learned, sing as a two-part round on stanza 4, keeping stanzas 1–3 in unison.
- Add the Orff instruments, one for each stanza, beginning with the bass xylophone for a four-measure introduction and stanza 1. For stanza 2, add alto glockenspiel; stanza 3, soprano glockenspiel; and stanza 4, alto or soprano xylophone.

Sing on the Day of Pentecost or in a service where the gospel reflects the two greatest commandments, love of God and neighbor.

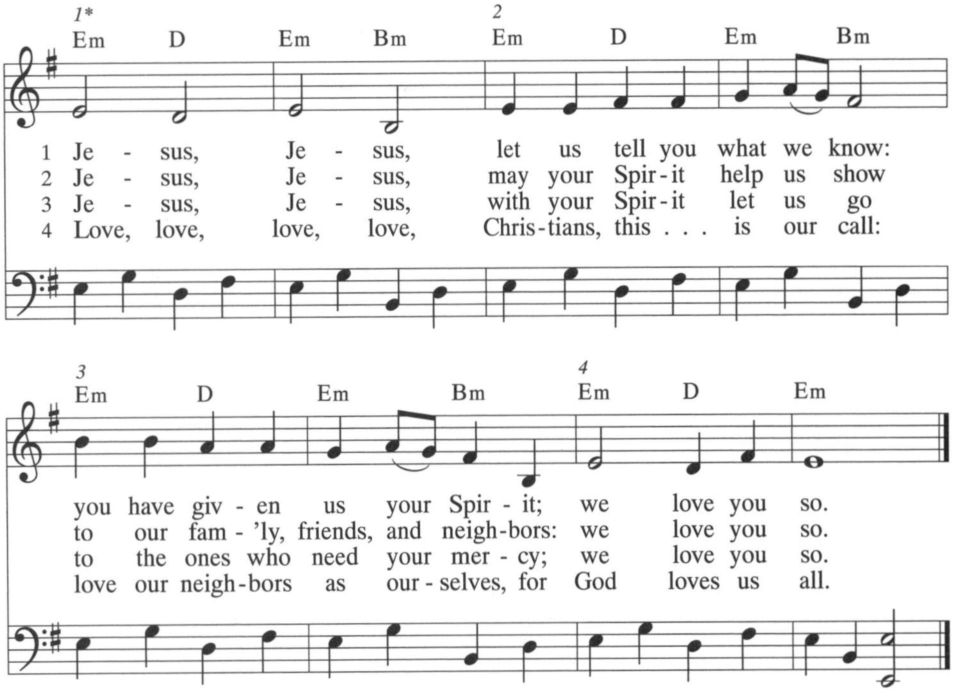
1* 2 3 4
Em D Em Bm Em D Em Bm
Em D Em Bm Em D Em
1 Je - sus, Je - sus, let us tell you what we know:
2 Je - sus, Je - sus, may your Spir-it help us show
3 Je - sus, Je - sus, with your Spir-it let us go
4 Love, love, love, love, Chris-tians, this . . . is our call:
you have giv - en us your Spir - it; we love you so.
to our fam - 'ly, friends, and neigh-bors: we love you so.
to the ones who need your mer - cy; we love you so.
love our neigh-bors as our - selves, for God loves us all.

*may be sung as a round

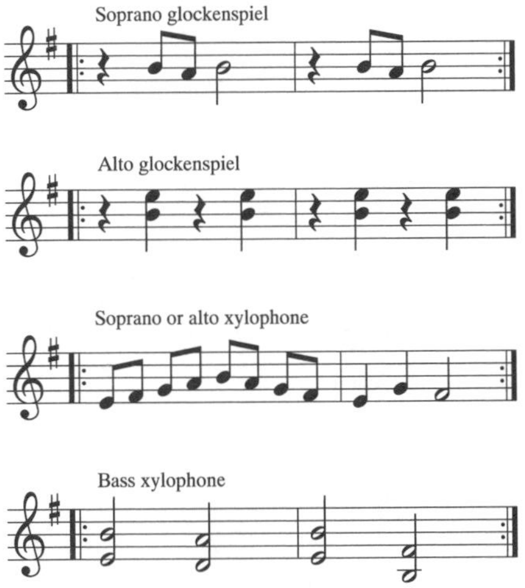
Soprano glockenspiel
Alto glockenspiel
Soprano or alto xylophone
Bass xylophone

Text: traditional, sts. 1 and 4; Bert Polman, st. 2; Joanne Hamilton, st. 3
Music: traditional; arr. Richard L. Van Oss

145 All around the world

Refrain
G C Am7 G Am
All a - round the world kids are pray - ing,
G C Am7 D
all a - round the world pray - ing to God.
G C Am7 G Am
Chil - dren, lift your hands and voic - es say - ing,
C Am7 D G C G
"Hear our prayer, O God." All a-round the world!
To stanzas
C
Last time
D G

D C G
1 Je - sus shows us how to have a con - ver - sa - tion
2 Pray for those in need and pray with - out dis - trac - tion.
D C G
with our might - y God who made the whole cre - a - tion.
Wor - ship God each day and put your prayers in ac - tion.
D C G F
We can say a prayer in ev - 'ry sit - u - a - tion. God is lis -
Share the news of Christ and start a chain re - ac - tion. Make dis - ci -
Refrain
C D G D C D
t'ning! God is there!
ples! Spread God's word!

Text: Dori Erwin Collins
Music: Dori Erwin Collins

146 Jesu, Jesu, fill us with your love

Thomas Colvin, a missionary in Africa, wrote this text about Christian love in 1963 in the village of Chereponi in northern Ghana. The tune is a folk song from Ghana and was originally a love song. Children might enjoy locating Ghana on a map or globe.

Two lessons Jesus taught are captured in the text: the parable of the good Samaritan (Luke 10:25-37), and Jesus' washing of his disciples' feet (John 13:1-20).

Children will ask, "Why wash people's feet?" Tell them that on Maundy Thursday, Jesus gave us the commandment to love one another as he has loved us. As a forgiven people, we are to be willing to kneel for people (to help mom when she is sick) and to honor the most humble tasks (taking out the garbage). What does a life of servanthood mean?

• Sing the refrain and stanza 1 for the children. Encourage them to sway gently from side to side to feel two beats per measure. They could also tap the beat lightly on their knees. (*Jesu* is pronounced *Yeh-soo.*)

• Add a hand drum to the refrain with this beat:

Play six times

The drum picks up the beat again on the last note of the stanzas. There should be no rhythmic pause between the refrain and stanzas.

Sing on Maundy Thursday and in services with a servanthood theme.

Refrain
F
C7
Je - su, Je - su, fill us with your love, show
F C7 F
us how to serve the neigh-bors we have from you.
F Dm Gm C7 F
1 Kneels at the feet of his friends, si - lent - ly wash - es their feet,
2 Neigh-bors are wealth-y and poor, var - ied in col - or and race,
3 These are the ones we will serve, these are the ones we will love;
4 Kneel at the feet of our friends, si - lent - ly wash-ing their feet:
Dm Gm C7 F Refrain
mas - ter who pours out him - self for them.
neigh-bors are near - by and far a - way.
all these are neigh-bors to us and you.
this is the way we will live with you.

Text: Tom Colvin
Music: Ghanaian folk tune, adapt. Tom Colvin; arr. Jane Marshall

If you love me

See LifeSongs *recording Volume 1*

How shall we witness? One of the best ways we can witness is by example. What does being an example mean to children? Children squabble and fight with one another at times. They know the pain of separation and anger with their friends and their family. They also know what it means to "make up." A simple word such as *sorry* along with a gesture of a handshake or a hug carries the meaning of being once divided, now reconciled. Sometimes we have to be the one to initiate the first move.

Jesus was talking with his disciples when he said, "If you love me, you will keep my commandments" (John 14:15). Share John 14:21 with the children. By living lives that are Christ-centered, like the disciples, we can more fully love, follow, serve, and witness.

- Teach stanzas 1 and 2 by phrases.
- Sing stanza 3 for the children. Ask them to listen to whether the notes step or skip. (There are no skips in this section, only notes that step.)
- Finish teaching the song. Show the contrasts between the two sections: A section, major key; B section, minor key.
- Orff instruments or handbells may be added. Accompany the song as directed with an introduction of two measures.

Sing in worship when John 14:15-21 appears in the lectionary.

F
1 If you love me, tru - ly love me, keep my com-mand-ments
2 If you love me, tru - ly love me, come now and my dis -
4 If you love me, tru - ly love me, in - to the world a -
day by day. If you love me, tru - ly love me,
ci - ple be. If you love me, tru - ly love me,
rise and go. If you love me, tru - ly love me,
Fine
fol - low for - ev - er in my way.
fol - low and so re - mem - ber me.
there ev - 'ry-where my wit - ness show.
Dm
3 Through the land my peo - ple feed, al - le - lu - ia,
C
D.C.
in their sor - row, in their need, al - le - lu - ia.
Orff instruments
Play 5 times
Fine
Play 3 times
D.C.

Text: Natalie Sleeth
Music: Natalie Sleeth

148 Let me be your servant, Jesus

In my backyard there is a large mound of dirt. When the grandchildren visit they enjoy climbing to the top. Once there, these words ring loud and clear: "I'm king of the mountain!" They often struggle with one another to retain this position. Ask children if they have had such experiences. Is the top of the mountain a safe, secure place to be?

Congregations can be like people on a hill. Christ teaches us how we should live among one another as servants. Our place is not to stand in the center—or as king of the mountain—and be served, honored, or revered. Our place is to serve so that others might see Jesus. In this song, we offer ourselves to Jesus to share in doing his work.

- The stepwise movement makes this an easy song to teach. Add simple motions, pointing to hands, feet, etc.
- On the refrain, teach by speaking the words in rhythm. Add clapping (see pattern below).
- Teach the melody line to the refrain, then the stanzas. Ask if there are two phrases that sound alike (phrases 2 and 4).
- Reinforce the claps with rhythm instruments.

Use in a service of communion alternating with the congregation singing "Let us talents and tongues employ" (WOV 754). Congregation begins with stanza 1 of "Let us talents and tongues employ," then children sing stanza 1 of "Let me be your servant, Jesus." Continue the pattern. Or, have children sing the entire song when there is an emphasis on serving others.

C
Dm7
G7
C
1 Let me be your hands, Lord Je - sus, help-ing those who come my way.
2 Let me be your voice, Lord Je - sus, tell-ing peo - ple of your love.
3 Let me be your ears, Lord Je - sus, hear-ing those who cry for help.
Dm
G7
C
Let me be your feet, Lord Je - sus, run-ning er - rands ev-'ry day.
Let me share your work, Lord Je - sus, me on earth and you a - bove.
Let me share in help - ing oth - ers and not just think of my - self.
Refrain
F C F C F C F C
Hands and feet, a voice to bring good news, great news of our King.
Dm7
Em7
G7
C
Let me be your ser-vant, Je - sus, help-ing you in ev-'ry way.

Text: Judith A. Helms
Music: Judith A. Helms

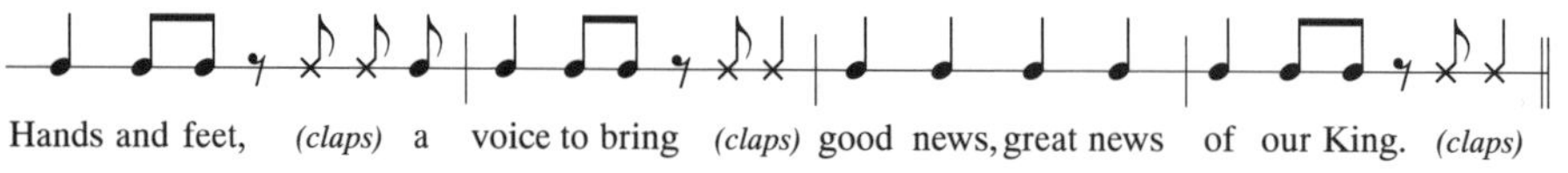

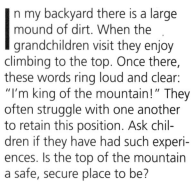

Jesus wants me for a helper 149

Young children need to know they are needed and loved. Here is one way to share that Jesus needs them, too. It is a song which answers the basic question, *What does it mean to be a Christian today?*

The book, *Every Day and Sunday, Too* by Gail Ramshaw (AFP 10-23349), provides words and images that help answer this very important question. Children will delight in learning more about living out their baptism. Look for surprising details in the artwork. Use portions of this book to teach this song.

- To introduce stanza 1 read the section on "Giving thanks." Ask how we can show our love for Jesus by giving thanks.
- For stanzas 2 and 3, read the section on "Giving." Look at the pictures and discuss other ways of giving ourselves in kind and loving deeds.
- For stanza 4, read the section on "Setting the table." Compare setting the table at home to setting the table in worship.
- Teach one stanza each week.
- Sing in class to help children "speak about the ordinary, joyful, and sad experiences of daily life and Christ's presence with them" (Gail Ramshaw; Introduction, *Every Day and Sunday, Too,* Augsburg Fortress, 1996).

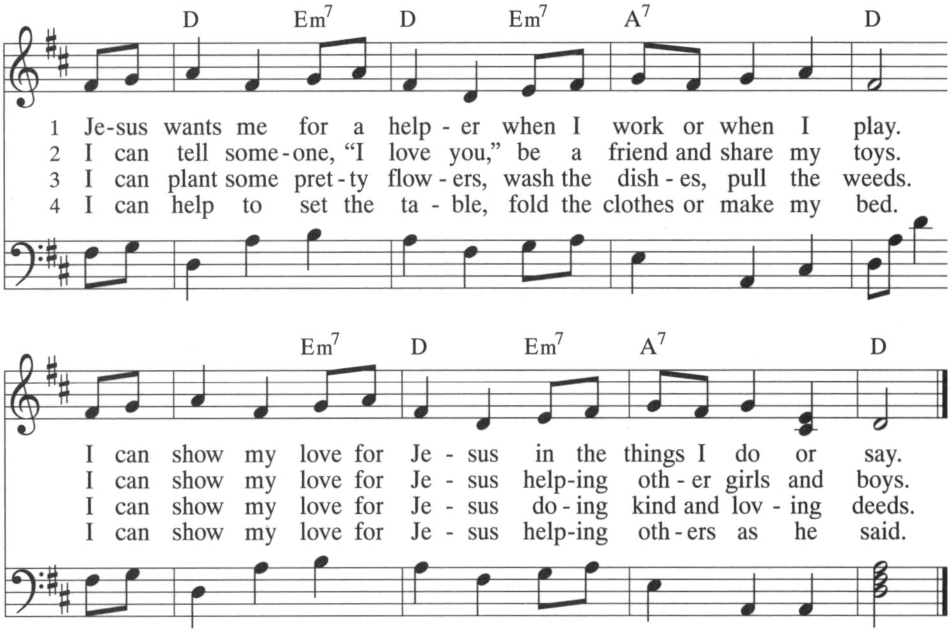
D Em7 D Em7 A7 D
1 Je-sus wants me for a help - er when I work or when I play.
2 I can tell some-one, "I love you," be a friend and share my toys.
3 I can plant some pret - ty flow - ers, wash the dish - es, pull the weeds.
4 I can help to set the ta - ble, fold the clothes or make my bed.
Em7 D Em7 A7 D
I can show my love for Je - sus in the things I do or say.
I can show my love for Je - sus help-ing oth - er girls and boys.
I can show my love for Je - sus do - ing kind and lov - ing deeds.
I can show my love for Je - sus help-ing oth - ers as he said.

Text: Dorothy N. Schultz
Music: Dorothy N. Schultz

150 The tiny seed

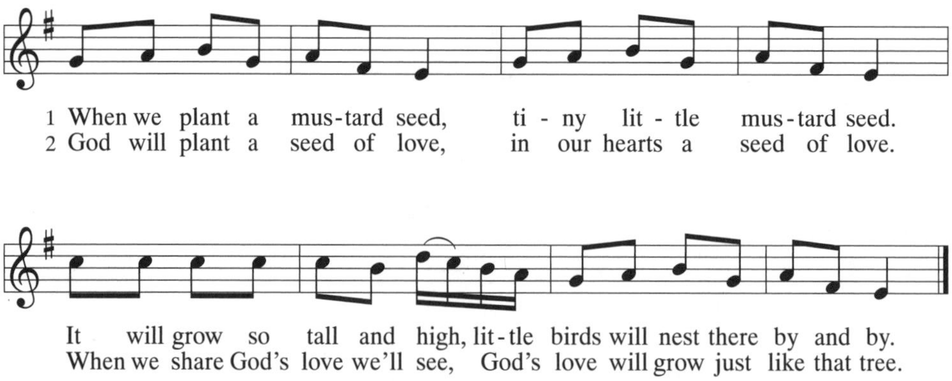

1 When we plant a mus-tard seed, ti - ny lit - tle mus-tard seed.
2 God will plant a seed of love, in our hearts a seed of love.
It will grow so tall and high, lit-tle birds will nest there by and by.
When we share God's love we'll see, God's love will grow just like that tree.

Text: Catherine Mathia and Audrey Sillick
Music: Arabic folk song

Jesus speaks of the smallest of seeds, the mustard seed, in Mark 4:30-32. The mustard seed grew in abundance in the region where Jesus taught. From such a small seed surely only a tiny shrub could be expected. Amazingly, the mustard seed grows to a height of 12 to 15 feet with branches large enough to shelter and protect nesting birds. There is much greater power in that tiny seed than meets the eye.

It is so with us. The seed of faith planted in us at baptism grows and flourishes under God's gentle care.

• Talk with the children about how a tiny seed grows into a tree. Encourage them to act out the movements from a seed to a tree with birds in its branches.

• Invite the children to show the movements as you sing the first stanza of the song.

• Talk with the children about the seed of God's love in their hearts. Improvise appropriate movements for the second stanza with the children's help.

Sing in worship when Matthew 13:31-32 or Mark 4:30-32 is read.

We love

See LifeSongs *recording Volume 1*

Martin Luther believed we need to hear the word often because it is easy to forget that God loves us. This simple yet effective song helps us to understand how it is we can love others. It reinforces our knowing that all love comes from God.

• Ask the children to tap the beat lightly on their knees with their fingertips while the song is being introduced by the leader.

• Sing by phrases inviting children to echo each phrase with claps.

• Assign rhythm instruments (claves) to be played each time the words *we love* appear, with other children continuing to clap where noted.

Sing in worship when love for others is the emphasis.

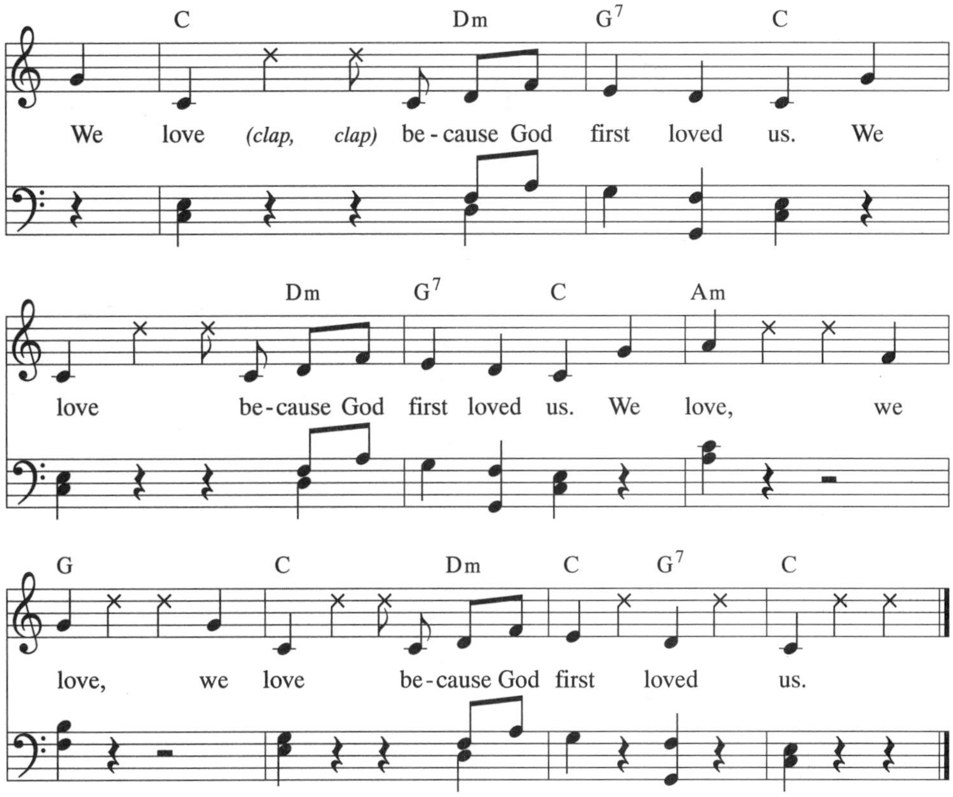
C Dm G7 C
We love (clap, clap) be-cause God first loved us. We
Dm G7 C Am
love be-cause God first loved us. We love, we
G C Dm C G7 C
love, we love be-cause God first loved us.

Text: 1 John 4:19
Music: Ann F. Price

152 This is my commandment

Joy is a word easily understood by children. Invite children to share times of joy. Christ tells us that our joy will be full in loving one another. Explore with the children how they can practice this commandment to love in their lives.

- Teach the melody two measures at a time using the echo method.
- Sing four measures and encourage the children to echo.
- Teach the signing for the words *love* and *joy* (see pp. 212-213).
- Experience the AABA form by inviting the children to walk to the beat while singing the A section, remaining still for the B section.
- Divide into two groups. One group focuses only on the signing, while the other group moves through the AABA form. Reverse the roles.
- Teach the signing for the additional stanzas, which use the words *trust, serve,* and *life* (see pp. 212–213).

Sing in any service where the commandment to love one another is included in the reading of scripture.

1*
F Bb F C7
This is my com-mand-ment, that you love one an-oth-er that your joy may be
F 2 Bb
full. This is my com-mand-ment, that you love one an-oth-er that your
F C7 F Bb F C
joy may be full, that your joy may be full, that your
F Bb C F
joy may be full. This is my com-mand-ment, that you
Bb F C7 F
love one an-oth-er that your joy may be full.

**may be sung as a round*

Additional stanzas ad lib:

This is my commandment, that you trust one another . . .
This is my commandment, that you serve one another . . .
This is my commandment, that you lay down your lives . . .

Text: John 15:11-12
Music: anonymous, arr. *LifeSongs*

When I needed a neighbor

Sydney Carter shook up the church in the 1960s with new words to hymns and catchy, pop-style tunes. This hymn is one example of his work, written in 1965. The simple folk-like quality of the melody flows gently with the text from Matthew 25:34-40. The text is shaped to present a question as if Christ himself was searching for answers.

When we gather for worship we are shaped for another week of service. God's word calls us to action, challenging us to treat all people as equals. Talk with children about how worship prepares us not only for social action, but also to see Christ in one another. What does Christ promise in stanza 4?

- Involve the children in a simple chant as Matthew 25:35-36 is read. Prepare large cards (11" x 17") on which have been written the words *hungry, thirsty, stranger, naked, sick,* and *prison* (one word per card). Begin reading, *for I was* (pause). Children chant the word *hungry* three times and then listen while the phrase is completed: *and you gave me food*. Continue this pattern with the other words.

- As verse 37 is read invite children to supply the missing word, speaking again as a chant. Encourage them to listen to Christ's answer in verse 40.

- Select rhythm instruments to give emphasis to key words of the song.

Stanza 1: *neighbor* (♫) tambourine.
Stanza 2: *hungry/thirsty* (♩) finger cymbals.
Stanza 3: *shelter* (𝅗𝅥) scrape guiro.
Stanza 4: (♩ ♩ ♩ ♩) play this beat on a hand drum as if walking. Continue into the refrain with this beat: ♫ | ♩ , for a fitting conclusion.

Em G B7 Em Bm Em
1 When I need - ed a neigh - bor, were you there, were you there? When I need - ed a neigh - bor, were you there?
2 I was hun - gry and thirst - y, were you there, were you there? I was hun - gry and thirst - y, were you there?
3 When I need - ed a shel - ter, were you there, were you there? When I need - ed a shel - ter, were you there?
4 Wher - ev - er you trav - el, I'll be there, I'll be there; wher - ev - er you trav - el, I'll be there.
Refrain
D7 G Em G B7 Em
And the creed and the col - or and the name won't mat - ter; were you there?
(4) I'll be there.

Text: Sydney Carter
Music: Sydney Carter

Refrain: *creed* (♩) triangle; *color* (♫) claves; *name* (♩) large cymbal played with a felt covered mallet.

Sing in a service when Matthew 25:31-40 is read or in any service emphasizing mission.

154 I love to tell the story

1 I love to tell the sto - ry of un - seen things a - bove,
2 I love to tell the sto - ry: how pleas - ant to re - peat
3 I love to tell the sto - ry, for those who know it best
4 I love to tell the sto - ry, of how, from heav'n a - bove
of Je - sus and his glo - ry, of Je - sus and his love.
what seems, each time I tell it, more won - der - ful - ly sweet!
seem hun - ger - ing and thirst-ing to hear it like the rest.
our Lord and Sav - ior Jes - us was sent to show God's love
I love to tell the sto - ry, be - cause I know it's true;
I love to tell the sto - ry, for some have nev - er heard
And when, in scenes of glo - ry, I sing the new, new song,
to ev - 'ry sin - ful crea - ture up - on this earth - ly place;
it sat - is - fies my long - ings as noth - ing else would do.
the mes - sage of sal - va - tion from God's own ho - ly word.
I'll sing the old, old sto - ry that I have loved so long.
how Christ, the gift from hea - ven, is God's great gift of grace.

Refrain
I love to tell the sto - ry; I'll sing this theme in glo - ry
and tell the old, old sto - ry of Je - sus and his love.

Text: Katherine Hankey, sts. 1-3; Jeffrey E. Burkart, st. 4
Music: William G. Fischer

All night, all day 155

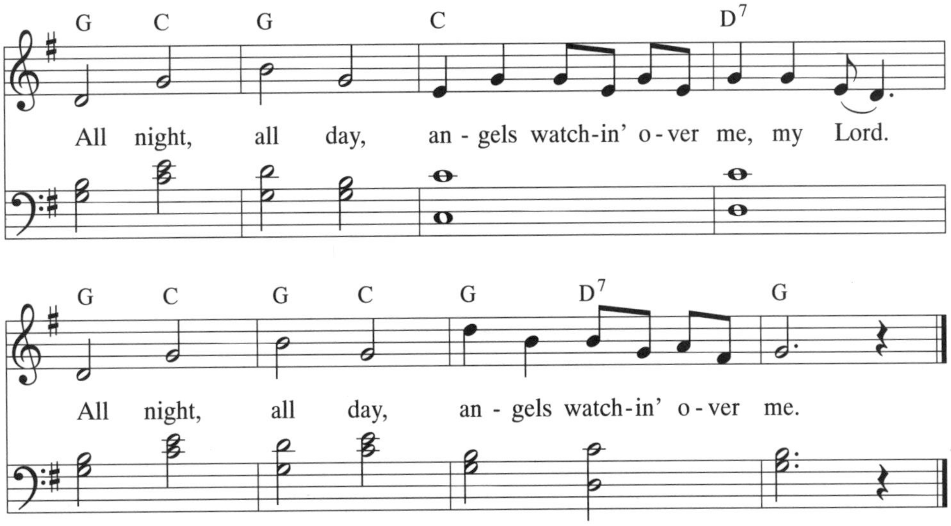
G C G C D7
All night, all day, an - gels watch-in' o - ver me, my Lord.
G C G C G D7 G
All night, all day, an - gels watch-in' o - ver me.

Text: African American spiritual
Music: African American spiritual

156 One in a hundred

F Bb F Bb
1 Have you heard a - bout the lit - tle lost sheep who was one in a
2 The good shep-herd went to res - cue that lamb, though his sup - per was
F Bb F Bb
hun - dred? He was missed by the shep - herd who knew
cook-ing; al-though man - y hun - gry an - i - mals growled,
F Bb F Bb Gm
that he of - ten had wan-dered. Since the sheep were do - ing fine,
he just kept right on look-ing. When that lamb was found at last,
Am D7 Gm A7 D7
he left the nine - ty - nine to look for the lamb he knew:
the shep-herd held him fast, so glad that his search was through:

Gm Bb C7 F
the good news is the lamb in the sto - ry is you!
Refrain
F Faug
So if you're one in a hun - dred, or one in a mil - lion, or
Bb Gm C7
if you're feel - ing lost as if you're one in a bil - lion, don't you
F D7 Gm C7 A D7
know? Je - sus loves you so! You'll
Gm C7 F
nev - er, nev - er, ev - er be a - lone.

Text: John Folkening
Music: John Folkening

157 Jesus, shepherd us

See LifeSongs *recording Volume 1*

Children may think it a bit unusual to be called sheep. Help them to understand this image by referring to scripture passages that apply the shepherd image to Jesus. Print on large card (11" x 17") the following verses omitting the word *shepherd.* Invite the children to supply the missing word as each passage is spoken.

John 10:11: I am the good *shepherd*. The good *shepherd* lays down his life for his sheep. (Who is the shepherd?)

Hebrews: 13:20: Our Lord Jesus, the great *shepherd* of the sheep.

Psalm 23:1: The Lord is my *shepherd*.

John 10:27: My sheep hear my voice. I know them, and they follow me. (Who are the sheep? Who cares for them and guides them? Yes, we are the sheep who are to obey and follow the shepherd.)

• Set up Orff instruments with two different note patterns.

A

B

Instrument A plays each time the ascending passage is sung (three times); instrument B plays the descending pattern only once.

• Teach by phrases, encouraging children to listen for the ascending (A) and descending (B) passages. Play A and B each time they are sung.

G Am7 D G
1 Je - sus, shep - herd us, your sheep, when we wake and
2 Je - sus, shep - herd us, your sheep, when the road is
3 Je - sus, shep - herd us, your sheep, when we fall and
Am7 D Em C D7
when we sleep, when we laugh and when we weep.
rough or steep, when the way is wide or deep.
when we leap, in your pas - ture, safe - ly keep,
G Am7 C G C G D
Je - sus, shep-herd us, your sheep.

Text: Wayne L. Wold
Music: Wayne L. Wold

• Ask for volunteers to play the A and B passages as they are sung.

Sing in worship on the fourth Sunday of Easter (Good Shepherd Sunday) or when the theme focuses on God's care for us.

Give me oil in my lamp

1 Give me oil in my lamp, keep me burn-ing. Give me oil in my lamp, I pray. Give me oil in my lamp, keep me burn-ing. Keep me burn-ing till the break of day.
2 Give me love in my heart, keep me shar-ing. Give me love in my heart, I pray. Give me love in my heart, keep me shar-ing. Keep me shar-ing till the break of day.
3 Give me joy in my heart, keep me sing-ing. Give me joy in my heart, I pray. Give me joy in my heart, keep me sing-ing. Keep me sing-ing till the break of day.
4 Give me faith in my heart, keep me pray-ing. Give me faith in my heart, I pray. Give me faith in my heart, keep me pray-ing. Keep me pray-ing till the break of day.
Refrain
Sing ho-san-na, sing ho-san-na, sing ho-san-na to the King of kings!
Sing ho-san-na, sing ho-san-na, sing ho-san-na to the King!

Text: traditional
Music: traditional

159 I've got peace like a river

G G7 C D7
1 I've got peace like a river, I've got peace like a river,
2 I've got joy like a fountain, I've got joy like a fountain,
3 I've got love like an ocean, I've got love like an ocean,
G Em A7 Am7 D
I've got peace like a river in my soul;
I've got joy like a fountain in my soul;
I've got love like an ocean in my soul;
G G7 C D7
I've got peace like a river, I've got peace like a river,
I've got joy like a fountain, I've got joy like a fountain,
I've got love like an ocean, I've got love like an ocean,
G Em A7 G
I've got peace like a river in my soul.
I've got joy like a fountain in my soul.
I've got love like an ocean in my soul.

Text: Traditional
Music: African American spiritual

Jesus loves me!

This song's message has been carried all over the world. Translated into many foreign languages, missionaries have taught it to new Christians in the countries they served. It first appeared as a poem in a story written by Anna Warner and her sister, Susan Warner, in 1859. In their book, *Say and Seal*, the poem was spoken to a sick child.

- Experience the beat with young children. Sing a stanza for children while they tap on their bodies with both hands.

  Pattern: ♫ ♫ | ♫ ♩
  Phrase 1: Tap head with both hands
  Phrase 2: Tap shoulders
  Phrase 3: Clap hands
  Phrase 4: Pat thighs

- Refrain: For each of the phrases make a large rainbow with one hand and arm in front of the body moving from one side to the other in a large half circle. Using the other hand and arm, repeat the pattern for the next phrase. Invite children to feel the smooth flow of the phrases.

- Teach the song by phrases. Add the signs for *yes, Jesus, loves*, and *me* to the refrain (see pp. 212–213).

Sing in worship when the congregation sings the hymn "Children of the heavenly Father" (#167). Have the children sing stanzas 1 and 2 of "Jesus loves me" between stanzas 2 and 3 of "Children of the heavenly Father." Or sing for a service of baptism.

D G D
1 Je - sus loves me! this I know, for the Bi - ble tells me so;
2 Je - sus loves me! he who died heav - en's gates to o - pen wide;
3 Je - sus loves me! loves me still, though I'm ver - y weak and ill;
4 Je - sus loves me! he will stay close be - side me all the way;
D G D A7 D
lit - tle ones to him be - long, they are weak, but he is strong.
he will wash a - way my sin, let his lit - tle child come in.
from his shin - ing throne on high, comes to watch me where I lie.
when at last I come to die, he will take me home on high.
Refrain
D G D A7
Yes, Je - sus loves me, yes, Je - sus loves me,
D G D A7 D
yes, Je - sus loves me, the Bi - ble tells me so.

Text: Anna B. Warner
Music: William B. Bradbury

161 Fear not for tomorrow

See LifeSongs *recording Volume 2*

In this adaptation of one of Natalie Sleeth's anthems, we hear the call to not be afraid but to put all our trust in God. The flowing melody with the words of reassurance remind us of God's continuing care each and every day.

- Read Matthew 6:25-34.
- Write verse 34 on poster board (11" x 17"), underlining the words *tomorrow* and *today*. Relate these two words to the scripture reading.
- On the reverse side of the poster board, write the verse omitting such words as *worry, tomorrow, trouble*, and *today*. This will encourage the children to commit the verse to memory.
- Emphasize the feeling of two pulses in each measure when teaching the stanzas.

Sing in worship when the emphasis is on trust or when the focus is on doubt and faith.

F Bb F C7
1 Fear not for to - mor - row and what it may bring, but
2 Fear not for to - mor - row and what lies a - head, though
3 Fear not for to - mor - row, but lift up your voice in
F Bb F Bb F Bb
trust in the Lord and o - bey. In joy or in sor - row, in
fu - ture e - vents be un - known; but wel - come the morn - ing with
an - thems of glo - ri - ous praise. Give thanks for your bless - ings and
F C7 Dm C7 F
ev - 'ry good thing, the Lord will not lead you a - stray.
cour - age in - stead, for you will not face it a - lone.
tru - ly re - joice, for God will be with you al - ways.
Refrain
Bb C7 Am Dm Gm7
God will take care of you, go ev' - ry - where with you, al - ways be

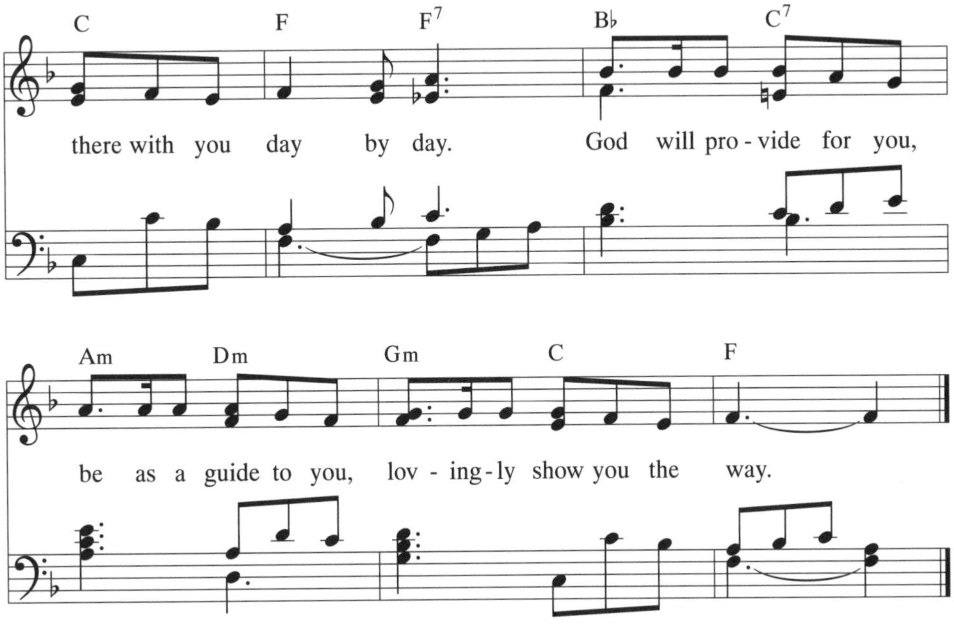
C F F7 B♭ C7
there with you day by day. God will pro - vide for you,
Am Dm Gm C F
be as a guide to you, lov - ing - ly show you the way.

Text: Natalie Sleeth
Music: Natalie Sleeth

In our work and in our play 162

Growing up in today's world is not easy. To a young child, frightening times can be overwhelming and unsettling. Teach the importance of knowing and recognizing that God is with them in work, play, and all of life.

- Teach two measures at a time, tapping on each beat:

In our work and in our play:
Tap shoulders.
God is with us every day:
Pat thighs.
Therefore we will never fear:
Clap hands.
For our loving God is near:
Hug self.

- Ask the children to mouth the words while they tap shoulders, pat thighs, etc.
- Sing one time with words and rhythm patterns, one time mouthing the words with rhythm patterns, and one time with words only.

Sing as a Sunday school gathering.

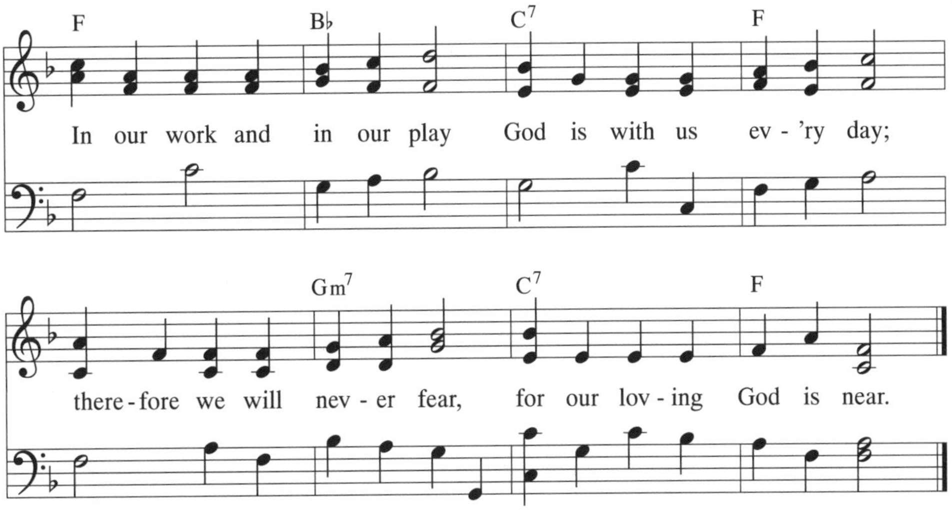
F B♭ C7 F
In our work and in our play God is with us ev - 'ry day;
Gm7 C7 F
there - fore we will nev - er fear, for our lov - ing God is near.

Text: William A. Kramer
Music: Franz Schubert, adapt.

163 On eagle's wings

Refrain
A D Em
"And I will raise you up on ea - gle's wings, bear you on the
A7 D D7 G Em A
breath of dawn, make you to shine like the sun, and
Bm F♯m Em A7 D
hold you in the palm of my hand."

Text: Michael Joncas
Music: Michael Joncas

Come, we that love the Lord

Stanzas of this hymn were written by Isaac Watts (1674–1748), who turned his talent for poetry to the service of the church at age fifteen. He told his father that "the singing of God's praise is the part of worship next to heaven, and its performance among us is the worst on earth." His father challenged him to "give us something better." Watts accepted the challenge and wrote over 600 hymns.

Believing that our songs are a human offering of praise to God, he wanted singers to be involved with the text, responding with adoration. If psalms were to be used, he felt they should speak the common-sense language of a Christian.

This joyful hymn is based on Psalm 48. Watts didn't write the refrain, but he did write the stanzas. In the psalm, Zion, with its temple and city, had been chosen as God's mountain. Children will enjoy marching up the mountain to Zion.

- Teach the refrain. Invite younger children to create other actions such as walking, running and skipping. They will have many ideas.
- Read Psalm 48:1-3 with older children.
- Talk about a citadel being a fortress of considerable height for defending the city of Zion. The presence of God was Zion's defense, not the fortress wall.
- Teach stanza 1, relating the text to the psalm verses (Psalm 48:1-3).

F C7 F C F C
1 Come, we that love the Lord, and let our joys be known;
2 Let those re - fuse to sing who nev - er knew our God;
3 The hill of Zi - on yields a thou-sand sa - cred sweets
4 Then let our songs a-bound, and ev - 'ry tear be dry;
F B♭ F B♭ C F
join in a song with sweet ac - cord, join in a song with
but chil - dren of the heav'n - ly King, but chil - dren of the
be - fore we reach the heav'n - ly fields, be - fore we reach the
we're march - ing through Em - man - uel's ground, we're march - ing through Em -
G7 C F C F7 Gm F C7 F
sweet ac - cord and thus sur - round the throne, and thus sur-round the throne.
heav'n-ly King may speak their joys a-broad, may speak their joys a - broad.
heav'n-ly fields, or walk the gold - en streets, or walk the gold - en streets.
man - uel's ground, to fair - er worlds on high, to fair - er worlds on high.
Refrain
F C
We're march - ing to Zi - on, beau - ti-ful, beau - ti-ful Zi - on:
F B♭ F C7 F
we're march - ing up-ward to Zi - on, the beau - ti-ful cit-y of God.

Text: Isaac Watts, stanzas; Robert Lowry, refrain
Music: Robert Lowry

165 What does it mean to follow Jesus?

What does it mean to follow Jesus? The question is simply asked, but the answer is more difficult, for we live in an anxious and troubled world where it is easier to be fearful than courageous and more common to look out for oneself than to care for the neighbor in need.

In God's eyes we are all worthy messengers who can share the good news through lives that model Christ's life. Children may ask how we do this. (Because God loves us we can love others.) We can treat others with kindness and respect. (Because we are forgiven we can forgive others.) We can learn to apologize. (Jesus invited people from all walks of life to come. We can accept those who are not like us.) Allow the text of this song to show children how to live life every day as a child of God.

- Chant the words of the refrain in rhythm. Divide the children into three groups. Group 1 begins chanting, *What does it mean to follow Jesus?* Group 1 continues chanting as group 2 enters with, *What does it mean to go his way?* Groups 1 and 2 continue chanting as group 3 enters with, *What does it mean to do what he wants me to?* All three groups chant together:

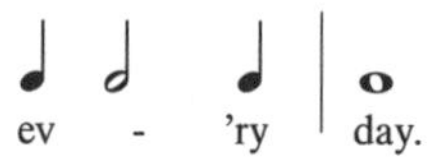
ev - 'ry day.

Rotate sections until everyone has chanted each of the questions.

- Teach the melody of the refrain. Add claves to the first beat and a guiro to the third beat.
- Teach the stanzas.

Have the children sing in worship around the gospel readings when the emphasis is on following Christ.

Refrain
Capo 3
What does it mean to fol - low Je - sus? What does it mean to go his way? What does it mean to do what he wants me to,
To stanzas
ev - 'ry day?
Last time
ev - 'ry day?
1 I can love my neigh - bor, just as Je - sus said.
2 I can say I'm sor - ry when I've done some wrong.
I can help my broth - er, see that he is fed.
I can sing his prais - es in both words and song.

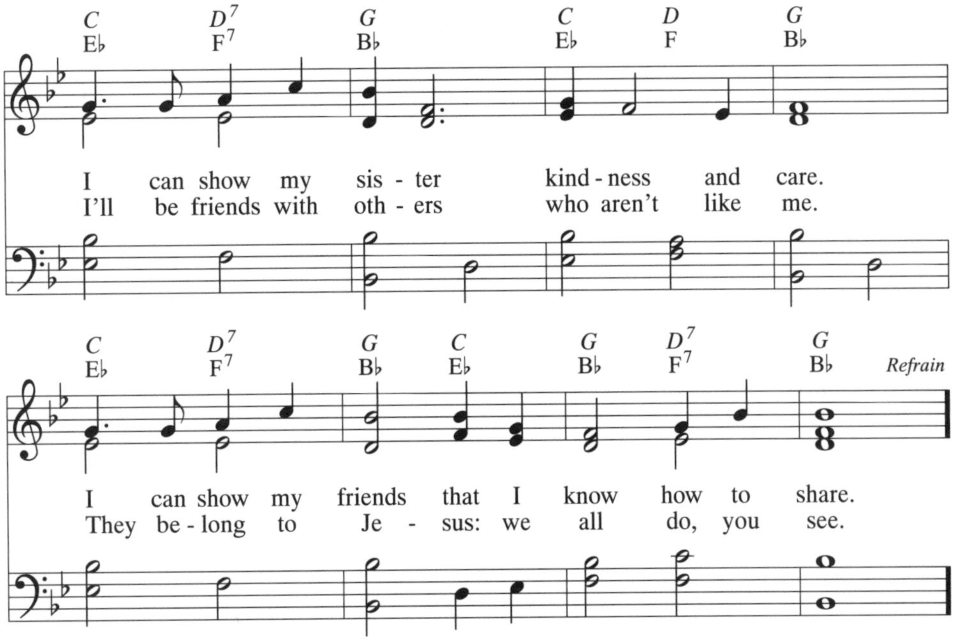

I can show my sis - ter kind - ness and care.
I'll be friends with oth - ers who aren't like me.

I can show my friends that I know how to share.
They be - long to Je - sus: we all do, you see.

Text: Lois Brokering
Music: Lois Brokering

Walk! Walk! 166

Listen to the fruit of the Spirit as named in Galatians 5:22-23. Talk with the children about what it means to write these things in our hearts. Notice how the words are grouped according to the number of syllables. This will make them easier to learn.

• Draw a bare tree branch on a large piece of poster board with the title "Fruit of the Spirit." Make nine good-sized leaves on which have been written each of the fruits.

• Take time to discuss each characteristic with the children, placing the leaves on the tree in the order they appear in the chant. Teach the chant for group 3 to all the children.

• Assign group 1 and group 2 to only a few children since these groups provide an accompaniment for group 3.

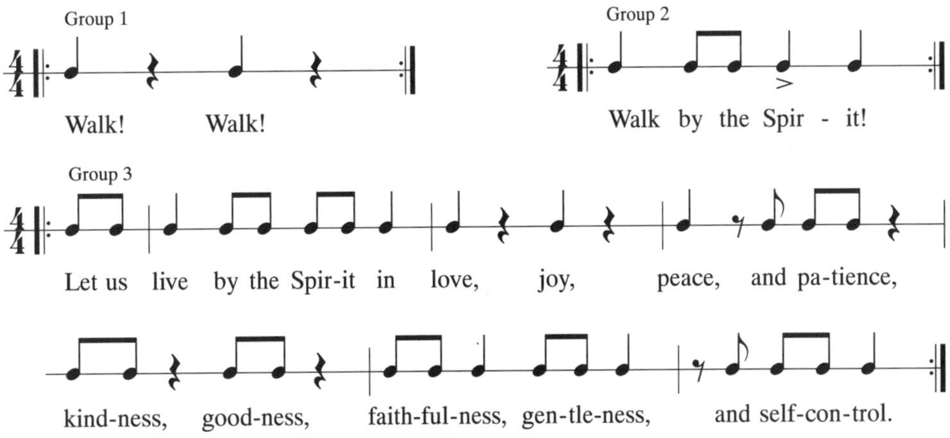

Group 1
Walk! Walk!
Group 2
Walk by the Spir - it!
Group 3
Let us live by the Spir-it in love, joy, peace, and pa-tience,
kind-ness, good-ness, faith-ful-ness, gen-tle-ness, and self-con-trol.

Text: Galatians 5:22-23, 25
Music: Betty Ann Ramseth

Use as a processional when the second reading is from Galatians 5, or in any service that stresses we are to be instruments of God's redeeming love.

167 Children of the heavenly Father

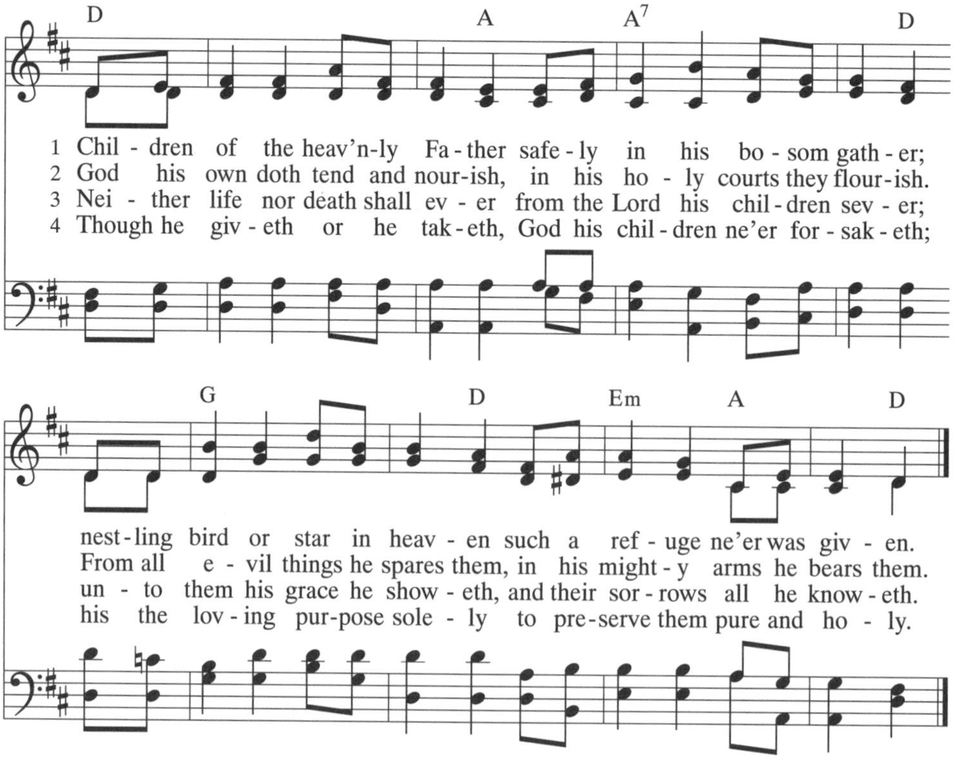
D A A7 D
1 Chil - dren of the heav'n-ly Fa - ther safe - ly in his bo - som gath - er;
2 God his own doth tend and nour-ish, in his ho - ly courts they flour-ish.
3 Nei - ther life nor death shall ev - er from the Lord his chil - dren sev - er;
4 Though he giv - eth or he tak - eth, God his chil - dren ne'er for - sak - eth;
G D Em A D
nest - ling bird or star in heav - en such a ref - uge ne'er was giv - en.
From all e - vil things he spares them, in his might - y arms he bears them.
un - to them his grace he show - eth, and their sor - rows all he know - eth.
his the lov - ing pur-pose sole - ly to pre-serve them pure and ho - ly.

Text: Caroline V. Sandell Berg; tr. Ernst W. Olson
Music: Swedish folk tune

Caroline V. Sandell Berg, a Swedish-born author, began writing hymns at an early age as a result of seeing her father drown. She wrote some 1,650 poems in a warm, personal, evangelical style.

This well-known hymn owes much of its popularity to the simple, child-like folk melody. Caroline Sandell, called Lina, did not use this melody originally. The hymn was first associated with the tune in 1873 and has remained wedded to it ever since.

The images in stanza 1 draw children into the text. The word *bosom*, however, is strange to their ears. It is actually the space that is formed when arms reach out to pull us close, as in a hug. Invite comments about times they have received big hugs from parents or grandparents. Not even a bird who receives shelter in a tree or a star in the heavens has been given such a place of safety. In God's mighty arms we are protected and comforted. Wherever we go we are in God's embrace.

• This rhythm (♫ ♩ ♩) forms the basis of this hymn, occuring four times in each phrase. Clap the first phrase, holding left hand palm up, with the right hand tapping the left palm. Reverse for the second phrase, right hand, palm up, with left hand tapping the right palm.

• Ask children to identify how many beats there are in each measure. How many beats are in the very first measure? (One, the other two beats are in the last measure to make a three beat measure.) An unaccented beat, 3-***1***-2-3, added to the beginning where normally there would be an accented beat, ***1***-2-3, is called "anacrusis."

• Teach stanza 1, encouraging a good breath to support the whole phrase.

As a hymn sung by the congregation, children can sing stanza 1. Use in worship when these scriptures are read: Matthew 6:25-34, Luke 18:15-17, or Romans 8:35-39.

God is our refuge and strength

168

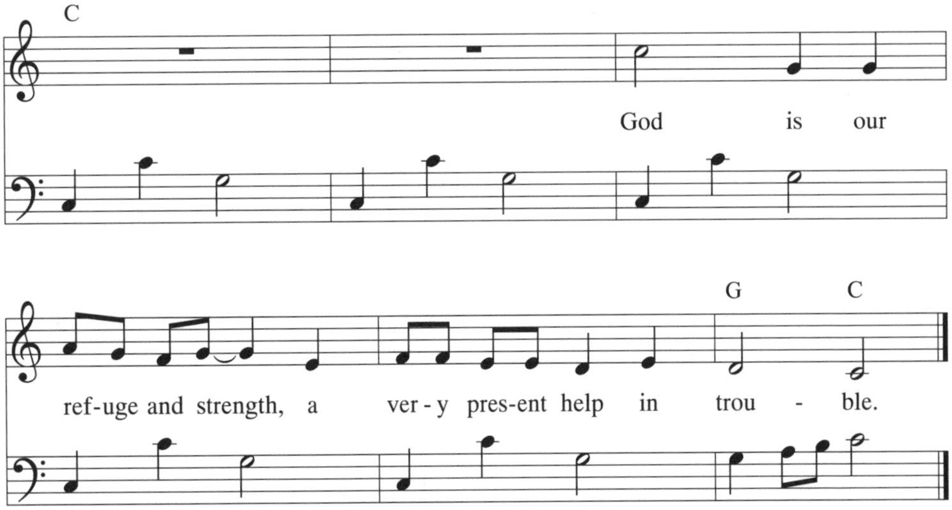
C
God is our
G C
ref-uge and strength, a ver-y pres-ent help in trou - ble.

Text: Psalm 46:1
Music: Marilyn Comer

Even though the continents break up and sink beneath the waters of the seas, a fearless trust in God prevails in Psalm 46. We hear in 46:1 that God breaks through in spite of the turmoil of this life. We can take comfort in the promise that the God who makes "wars to cease" remains a constant presence today and will bring all fighting and trouble to an end. Share with the children that in those troubling times there is a verse (46:10) we need to repeat often, even daily.

•Teach these chants from Psalm 46:10.

A
Be still and know that I am God.

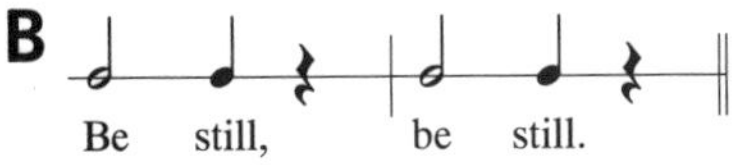
B
Be still, be still.

Psalm 46:10 from *That I May Speak* (AFP 11-9490) by Betty Ann Ramseth, p. 8.

• Assign B to half of the group of children who begin with a hushed, articulate chant. After four measures the other group chants A several times. Phase out A with B, quietly concluding after four more measures.

• Teach the melody to "God is our refuge and strength." Accompany with an Orff instrument (or keyboard) adding finger cymbals or triangle to the words *God* and *trouble*.

Sing as an antiphon to Psalm 46 before verse 1 and after verses 4, 8, and 12, with the congregation speaking or chanting the verses.

169 Lord of all hopefulness

Every day is a little life, and our whole life is but a day repeated. Therefore live every day as if it would be the last." This quote from an English bishop named Joseph Hall (1574–1656) finds meaning in the text of this hymn. God knows our every need even before we ask. Nevertheless, we petition God to be with us in all that we do and to fill our hearts with bliss, strength, love, and peace. It is a prayer to carry with us throughout a day or a lifetime.

- Each musical phrase of this Irish folk tune is different. Teach one stanza each week and keep reviewing the stanzas previously learned.
- Use handbells, playing the melody as an introduction and coda. If possible, use with organ accompanying the voices.

In worship sing this hymn as a response of trust and hope in God's promise to be with us.

Capo 1 D G D A D A
E♭ A♭ E♭ B♭ E♭ B♭
1 Lord of all hope-ful-ness, Lord of all joy, whose trust, ev - er
2 Lord of all ea - ger-ness, Lord of all faith, whose strong hands were
3 Lord of all kind - li - ness, Lord of all grace, your hands swift to
4 Lord of all gen - tle - ness, Lord of all calm, whose voice is con -
D G A G D
E♭ A♭ B♭ A♭ E♭
child - like, no cares could de - stroy: be there at our wak - ing, and
skilled at the plane and the lathe: be there at our la - bors, and
wel - come, your arms to em - brace: be there at our hom - ing, and
tent - ment, whose pres - ence is balm: be there at our sleep - ing, and
Bm G Bm G Em7 D
Cm A♭ Cm A♭ Fm7 E♭
give us, we pray, your bliss in our hearts, Lord, at the break of the day.
give us, we pray, your strength in our hearts, Lord, at the noon of the day.
give us, we pray, your love in our hearts, Lord, at the eve of the day.
give us, we pray, your peace in our hearts, Lord, at the end of the day.

Text: Jan Struther
Music: Irish folk tune, arr. Carlton R. Young

I am trusting you, Lord Jesus

170

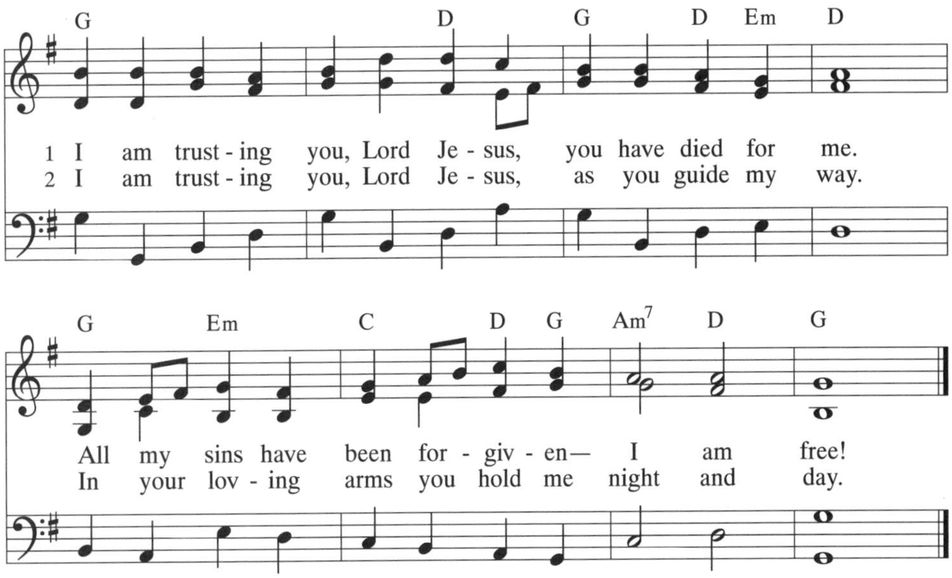
G D G D Em D
1 I am trust - ing you, Lord Je - sus, you have died for me.
2 I am trust - ing you, Lord Je - sus, as you guide my way.
G Em C D G Am7 D G
All my sins have been for - giv - en— I am free!
In your lov - ing arms you hold me night and day.

Text: Dorothy N. Schultz
Music: Henry W. Baker

New words set to this familiar hymn tune will help children understand the importance of placing their trust in the Lord Jesus. We hear about disasters striking close to home. The world news often turns our attention to civil wars, new rivalries, and ancient feuds. These things trouble us, and yet we need to realize that God will stay with us until the earth as we know it is no more. Children of all ages need this reassurance.

- Talk with the children about trust, using the text of each stanza to lead the discussion. Stanza 1, we are forgiven and free because of Christ's death on the cross; stanza 2, we can trust Jesus to guide our path and to hold us tightly in his loving arms.
- Teach two measures at a time.
- Combine signing and movement to reinforce the text. Sign the words *trust, Jesus, died, me, way*, and *day* (see pp. 212–213).

Sins: With both arms, make a sweeping motion away from body as if letting go.
Free: Turn around one time in place.
Arms: Hug self.
Night: Flick fingers in air showing stars.

- Encourage children to sing this as a bedtime prayer or anytime they are feeling afraid.

171 Have no fear, little flock

This singable hymn can easily become a favorite with children. Based on Luke 12:32, Jesus is speaking to believers and encouraging them to seek the spiritual benefits of the kingdom rather than the material goods of the world. How does Jesus address the flock?

- For younger children teach the first two measures of each stanza.
- Clap the words of this rhythm: ♫. ♩ Add wood block.
- Sing the entire song with children singing the first two measures. A soloist sings measures three and four.
- Older children can learn all stanzas, adding the available instruments as suggested.

Sing on a Sunday when Luke 12:32 is included in the reading of scripture. Stanza 1 can be sung as the gospel acclamation and stanza 4 at the conclusion of the reading of the gospel. The hymn can also be sung when the focus is on the shepherd protecting and guiding the flock, as in Psalm 23.

Capo 1 G D DM7 G D
A♭ E♭ E♭M7 A♭ E♭
1 Have no fear, lit - tle flock; have no fear, lit - tle
2 Have good cheer, lit - tle flock; have good cheer, lit - tle
3 Praise the Lord high a - bove; praise the Lord high a -
4 Thank-ful hearts raise to God; thank - ful hearts raise to
A D Bm7
B♭ E♭ Cm7
flock, for the Fa - ther has cho - sen to
flock, for the Fa - ther will keep you in
bove, for he stoops down to heal you, up -
God, for he stays close be - side you, in
G D Bm Em A7 D
A♭ E♭ Cm Fm B♭7 E♭
give you the king-dom; have no fear, lit - tle flock!
his love for - ev - er; have good cheer, lit - tle flock!
lift and re - store you; praise the Lord high a - bove!
all things works with you; thank - ful hearts raise to God!

Text: Luke 12:32, st. 1; Marjorie Jillson, sts. 2-4
Music: Heinz Werner Zimmerman

The great commandments

See LifeSongs *recording Volume 1*

In just two commandments Jesus sums up the whole of the scriptures. We are to love the Lord with heart, soul, and mind, and love neighbor as self. As God's chosen ones how do we respond to these two commands?

- Practice the signs for *love, heart,* and *yes* with the children (see pp. 212–213).
- Learn movements for these additional words:

Soul: Touch thumbs and index fingers to each other, right hand over left. Draw hands apart, lifting right hand upward and pulling left hand downward.
Mind: Tap forehead with index finger.
Yourself: Tap chest with index finger.

- Add an instrument on the final word of each phrase with the rhythm: 𝄽 ♫ | ♩

Stanza 1: claves
Response: hand drums
Stanza 2: tambourine
Response: maracas

Sing in a Sunday school opening or in class when the theme focuses on the two great commandments.

F
C7
1 You shall love the Lord with all your heart; you shall
2 You shall love your neigh-bor as your-self; you shall
F
love the Lord with all your soul; you shall love the
love your neigh-bor as your-self; you shall love your
B♭ F C7 F
Lord with all your mind; yes, heart, soul and mind.
neigh-bor as your-self; yes, you shall . . . love.
Optional responses to stanzas 1 & 2
1 Yes, I want to love the Lord with all my heart; and I
2 Yes, I want to love my neigh-bor as my-self; yes, I
want to love the Lord with all my soul; and I want to love the
want to love my neigh-bor as my-self; yes, I want to love my
Lord with all my mind; yes, heart, soul and mind.
neigh-bor as my-self; yes, I want to love.

Text: Pauline Palmer Meek
Music: Pauline Palmer Meek; arr. H. Myron Braun

173 Faith that's sure

See LifeSongs *recording Volume 2*

"Increase our faith!" the apostles said to the Lord. Feeling somewhat inadequate they wanted greater faith to lay hold of the power to live up to Jesus' standards. The reply came as a surprise: "If you had faith the size of a mustard seed . . ." (Luke 17:5-10). The planting of the smallest seed may seem like an insignificant beginning, but under favorable conditions the plant can grow to great heights. The kingdom of heaven can expand and grow in much the same way through our service to others.

• Talk with the children about giving attention to the greatest seed of all, the mighty word of God. Planted in us the seed of God's word bears new life that grows in faith, hope, and love.

• Teach the refrain two measures at a time. Encourage the children to listen carefully and to think the beginning note each time before singing. Ask them to think the first note, hum it softly, then sing.

• Add rhythm instruments on certain words.

Faith, own: finger cymbals
Rock: cowbell
Planted in the soil: maracas

• Claves follow a rhythm pattern:

• Use a bass xylophone for the introduction and refrain. Keyboard accompanies the stanzas. Play three times.

Sing in worship around a theme of growing in God's love.

Refrain
G
F
Faith that's sure is a rock un-shak-a-ble, plant-ed in the soil where God's
G
love is sown. Faith that's sure is a rock un - shak-a - ble.
F
G
Fine
F
Je-sus is my Lord. I'm his ver - y own!

C
G
1 Com - pli - cat - ed ways con-fuse me. I praise my God in the
2 Come and join the cel - e - bra - tion, new in the Lord by the
C
sim - ple ways. Sing and dance and shout for Je - sus,
Spir - it's pow'r. Come on, friend, the Lord's a - wait - ing,
G
D
Refrain
pray - ing to the Lord each and ev - 'ry day!
wait - ing for your heart this . . . ver - y hour!

Text: Suzanne Lord
Music: Suzanne Lord

174 Beautiful Savior

Capo 1
D E♭ A B♭ D E♭ A B♭ D E♭
1 Beau - ti - ful Sav - ior, King of cre - a - tion,
2 Fair are the mead - ows, fair are the wood - lands,
3 Fair is the sun - shine, fair is the moon - light,
4 Beau - ti - ful Sav - ior, Lord of the na - tions,
G A♭ D E♭ A7 B♭7 D E♭ A B♭
Son of God and Son of Man!
robed in flow'rs of bloom - ing spring;
bright the spar - kling stars on high;
Son of God and Son of Man!
D E♭ B7 C7 Em Fm A7 B♭7 D E♭
Tru - ly I'd love thee, tru - ly I'd serve thee,
Je - sus is fair - er, Je - sus is pur - er,
Je - sus shines bright - er, Je - sus shines pur - er
Glo - ry and hon - or, praise, ad - o - ra - tion,
G A♭ D E♭ A7 B♭7 D E♭
light of my soul, my joy, my crown.
he makes our sor - rowing spir - it sing.
than all the an - gels in the sky.
now and for - ev - er - more be thine!

Text: *Gesangbuch*, Münster; tr. Joseph A. Seiss
Music: Silesian folk tune

Heleluyan

Passed from one generation to another, this Native American alleluia is a tribal song of the Creek Indians. Muscogee was the language of the Creek people. In 1838 and 1839 the Creek, along with the Cherokee, were forced westward to Indian Territory (now Oklahoma). Their bitter trek during the dead of winter has become known as the Trail of Tears. This song may have originated during that forced thousand-mile march.

- With younger children, sing accompanied only by a hand drum playing a quarter note pulse.
- Give each child an opportunity to play the drum. The group sings the song to the tempo set by each child.
- Older, more experienced children will enjoy playing drums together to accompany this song.

Use in worship as a gospel acclamation.

1*
2
He - le - lu - yan, he - le - lu - yan. He - le, he - le - lu - yan.
Hal-le - lu - jah, hal - le - lu - jah. Hal - le, hal - le - lu - jah.
He - le - lu - yan, he - le - lu - yan. He - le, he - le - lu - yan.
Hal-le - lu - jah, hal - le - lu - jah. Hal - le, hal - le - lu - jah.

**may be sung as a round*
pronounced: Hay-lay-loo-yahn

Music: traditional Muscogee (Creek) Indian; transc. Charles Webb

176 Praise God, from whom all blessings flow

Written by Thomas Ken (1637–1711), this hymn has come to be known as the Doxology. A doxology is a hymn of praise to God. Ken was chaplain of Winchester College. In an effort to encourage worship among the boys he wrote a manual of prayers. In the manual he admonished the boys to be sure to sing early in the morning and in the night. His morning hymn, "Awake, my soul, and with the sun" (LBW 269) and his evening hymn, "All praise to thee, my God, this night" (LBW 278) both conclude with this doxology.

The melody is OLD HUNDREDTH. "Old" refers to the so-called "old" version since this tune was originally associated with Psalm 100.

- Invite children to find the tune index in their church hymnal or worship resource. Locate OLD HUNDREDTH to see how many times it appears.
- Now find the index that lists authors, composers, and sources of hymns. Check to see how many texts by Thomas Ken are listed.

Sing in worship when the hymn, "All people that on earth do dwell" (LBW 245) is sung. In place of stanza 5, children can sing the doxology. Also, sing in Sunday school as the offering is received.

G Em D G
Praise God, from whom all bless - ings flow. Praise
C G D Em D
God, all crea-tures here be - low. Praise God a - bove, you
Am7 D G D G D7 G D G
heav'n - ly host. Praise Fa-ther, Son, and Ho - ly Ghost.

Text: Thomas Ken, alt.
Music: Louis Bourgeois

Halle, halle, hallelujah!

G D7 G
Hal - le, hal - le, hal - le - lu - jah!
C Am D
Hal - le, hal - le, hal - le - lu - jah!
Hal - le - lu - jah!
G B7 Em
Hal - le, hal - le, hal - le - lu - jah!
Am G D G
Hal - le - lu - jah! Hal - le - lu - jah!

Music: Caribbean traditional; arr. Mark Sedio

178 Oh, sing to the Lord

Em Am
1 Oh, sing to the Lord, oh, sing God a new song.
2 For God is the Lord, and God has done won - ders.
3 So dance for our God and blow all the trum - pets.
4 Oh, shout to our God, who gave us the Spir - it.
5 For Je - sus is Lord! A - men! Al - le - lu - ia!
B7 Em
Oh, sing to the Lord, oh, sing God a new song.
For God is the Lord, and God has done won - ders.
So dance for our God and blow all the trum - pets.
Oh, shout to our God, who gave us the Spir - it.
For Je - sus is Lord! A - men! Al - le - lu - ia!
E7 Am
Oh, sing to the Lord, oh, sing God a new song.
For God is the Lord, and God has done won - ders.
So dance for our God and blow all the trum - pets,
Oh, shout to our God, who gave us the Spir - it.
For Je - sus is Lord! A - men! Al - le - lu - ia!
Em B7 Em
Oh, sing to our God, oh, sing to our God.
Oh, sing to our God, oh, sing to our God.
and sing to our God, and sing to our God.
Oh, sing to our God, oh, sing to our God.
Oh, sing to our God, oh, — sing to our God.

1 Cantad al Señor un cántico nuevo.
Cantad al Señor un cántico nuevo.
Cantad al Señor un cántico nuevo.
¡Cantad al Señor, cantad al Señor!

2 Pues nuestro Señor ha hecho prodigios.
Pues nuestro Señor ha hecho prodigios.
Pues nuestro Señor ha hecho prodigios.
¡Cantad al Señor, cantad al Señor!

Text: Brazilian folk song; tr. Gerhard Cartford
Music: Brazilian folk tune; arr. Gerhard Cartford

Hallelujah! Praise ye the Lord!

G G7 C Am7 G D7 G
Hal-le - lu, hal-le-lu, hal-le - lu, hal-le-lu-jah! Praise ye the Lord! Hal-le-
G7 C Am7 G D7 G
lu, hal-le-lu, hal-le - lu, hal-le-lu - jah! Praise ye the Lord!
D D7 G
Praise ye the Lord! Hal-le-lu - jah! Praise ye the Lord! Hal-le-lu - jah!
G7 Am D D7 G
Praise ye the Lord! Hal-le - lu - jah! Praise ye the Lord!

Text: traditional
Music: traditional

180 I will sing, I will sing

This bright, energetic song of praise will appeal to children of all ages. Scripture references for three of the stanzas include John 8:36 (stanza 3), Psalm 126:5 (stanza 4), and Philippians 2:9-10 (stanza 5).

• Teaching the syncopation will be challenging. Begin by speaking stanza 1, accenting the word *sing*. Add a tambourine and hand claps every time it appears.

• Accompany with autoharp in the key of D (D, A^7) using a rhythmic strum. Guitar could also be used.

Sing in a service that includes one of the above scripture references, or use as a response (stanza 1 only) following the reading of Psalm 13.

E
1 I will sing, I will sing a song un - to the Lord.
2 We will come, we will come as one be - fore the Lord.
3 If the Son, if the Son shall make . . . you . . . free,
4 They that sow in tears . . . . shall reap . . . . in . . . joy.
5 Ev - 'ry knee shall bow . . . and ev - 'ry tongue con - fess,
6 In his name, in his name we have the vic - to - ry.
B
E
I will sing, I will sing a song un - to the Lord.
We will come, we will come as one be - fore the Lord.
if the Son, if the Son shall make . . . . you . . . free,
They that sow in tears . . . . shall reap . . . . . in . . . joy.
ev - 'ry knee shall bow . . . and ev - 'ry tongue con - fess,
In his name, in his name we have the vic - to - ry.
I will sing, I will sing a song un - to the Lord.
We will come, we will come as one be - fore the Lord.
if the Son, if the Son shall make . . . . you . . . free,
They that sow in tears . . . . shall reap . . . . . in . . . joy.
ev - 'ry knee shall bow . . . and ev - 'ry tongue con - fess,
In his name, in his name we have the vic - to - ry.

B
E
Al - le - lu - ia, glo - ry to the Lord.
Al - le - lu - ia, glo - ry to the Lord.
you . . . shall be free . . . . . in - deed.
Al - le - lu - ia, glo - ry to the Lord.
that . . . Je - sus Christ . . . . is . . . Lord.
Al - le - lu - ia, glo - ry to the Lord.
Refrain
E
Al - le - lu, al - le - lu - ia, glo - ry to the Lord. Al - le -
B
E
lu, al - le - lu - ia, glo - ry to the Lord. Al - le - lu, al - le - lu - ia, glo-
B
E
- ry to the Lord. Al - le - lu - ia, glo - ry to the Lord.

Text: Max Dyer
Music: Max Dyer

181 I've got the joy, joy, joy

C Am
1 I've got the joy, joy, joy, joy,
2 I've got the peace that pass - es un - der - stand - ing,
3 I've got the love of Je - sus, love of Je - sus,
G7 C G7 C
down in my heart, down in my heart, down in my heart;
down in my heart, down in my heart, down in my heart;
down in my heart, down in my heart, down in my heart;
I've got the joy, joy, joy, joy,
I've got the peace that pass - es un - der - stand - ing,
I've got the love of Je - sus, love of Je - sus,
G7 C G7 C
down in my heart, down in my heart to stay.
down in my heart, down in my heart to stay.
down in my heart, down in my heart to stay.

Text: George W. Cooke
Music: George W. Cooke

Clap your hands, all you people

See LifeSongs *recording Volume 2*

Children will enjoy singing this song reflecting the words of Psalm 47:1. Read this verse from different translations of the Bible. Are there words common to each translation? The psalmist calls us to rejoice in God, who is Lord over all the earth.

- Introduce by phrases, speaking the words as a rhythm chant. Feel the energy of the text. Articulate the words clearly.
- Teach the melody by phrases.
- Accompany with autoharp or guitar. Give an introduction of four C-chords while children clap on the four beats. They will then clap only on the words *Clap your hands*. Add a tambourine on the words *Hosanna* and *Praise him*.

Sing in worship on the Ascension of Our Lord in place of Psalm 47; or use as an antiphon, singing the first four measures (ending on beat 4) before verse 1 and after verses 4 and 7. After verse 9, sing all eight measures.

1*
C
G7
C
Clap your hands, all you peo-ple, shout un-to God with a voice of tri-umph.
2
C
G7
C
Clap your hands, all you peo-ple, shout un-to God with a voice of praise! Ho -
G7
C
san - na, ho - san - na, shout un-to God with a voice of tri-umph.
G7
C
Praise him, praise him, shout un-to God with a voice of praise!

may be sung as a round

Text: Psalm 47:1, adapt.
Music: Jimmy Owens; arr. David Peacock

183 Sing alleluia

The word *alleluia* is a bright and joyful response all ages can sing with enthusiasm. It is a word based on the Hebrew *hallelujah*, which means "all of you praise the Lord." Because God dwells in each of us, we sing praises (stanza 1). As children of God, we know the love of God and can share it with others (stanza 2). Because all that we receive in life is a gift from God, we can give thanks (stanza 3). Yes, we can sing praise through our alleluias.

• The melody of the stanzas is composed of two identical musical phrases in D minor, which makes for ease in teaching. The refrain, written in D major, is more challenging. Teach only one measure at a time.

• Add the instruments with a keyboard. Consider using tambourine and hand drum with unison voices and keyboard, or alto glockenspiel, soprano metallophone, and finger cymbals with voices and keyboard.

Sing as an offering piece during the Easter or Pentecost seasons.

Dm Gm A Dm
1 Peo-ple, all, come sing and shout; God is in us dwell - ing.
2 Ev - 'ry one a child of God, sis - ter or a broth - er.
3 For the gifts that we re - ceive, come with thank-ful giv - ing.
Gm A Dm
Spread the joy - ful news a - bout; sing with voic - es swell - ing.
All who know the love of God, share with one an - oth - er.
Let the prom - ise we be - lieve light the life we're liv - ing.
Refrain
D G A D
Sing al - le - lu - ia, sing al - le - lu - ia;
D G Em A D
raise your voic - es, shout with joy; sing praise to God, the Sav - ior.
Tambourine
Alto glockenspiel
Hand drum
Soprano metallophone and finger cymbals

Text: Sue Ellen Page; adapt. Eric D. Johnson
Music: Sue Ellen Page

One, two, three

What's in a name? Ask children if they know how they got their names (some will have a response). Tell the children, "If you have been baptized, you have another name."

All those who are baptized share the name "Christian." We have been claimed by God, washed in water, and marked with the cross of Christ. All this was received in the name of the triune God, Father, Son, and Holy Spirit. We call this relationship between God, Jesus, and the Holy Spirit, the Trinity. *Trinity* means the "unity of three beings as one."

Show an illustration of the Trinity, if one is available. Explain that God the Father is the creator who gives us the gift of life, God the Son gives us the gift of salvation, and God the Spirit helps us to know and understand these gifts.

• Teach the song by phrases.

• Add one or more rhythm instruments (claves, wood block, etc.) to the numbers *one, two, three* and to *three in one, one in three*.

• Add tree chimes (or wind chimes) to *it's part of God's mystery*.

• There is a simple trinitarian blessing which comes to us from early Christians in Ireland. Teach this blessing to children to use in the morning when they rise and at bedtime when the day is over. *The sacred Three be over me, the blessing of the Trinity.*

Sing in a Sunday school opening or use in class to reinforce learning on the Trinity.

E B7 E B7 E B7 E
One, two, three, the Ho-ly Trin-i-ty. It shall be for
B7 E B7 E
all e-ter-ni-ty. Three in one and one in three,
B7 C♯m E B7 E B7 E
it's part of God's mys-ter-y. One, two, three, the Ho-ly Trin-i-ty.

Text: Pamela L. Hughes
Music: Pamela L. Hughes

185 Oh, for a thousand tongues to sing

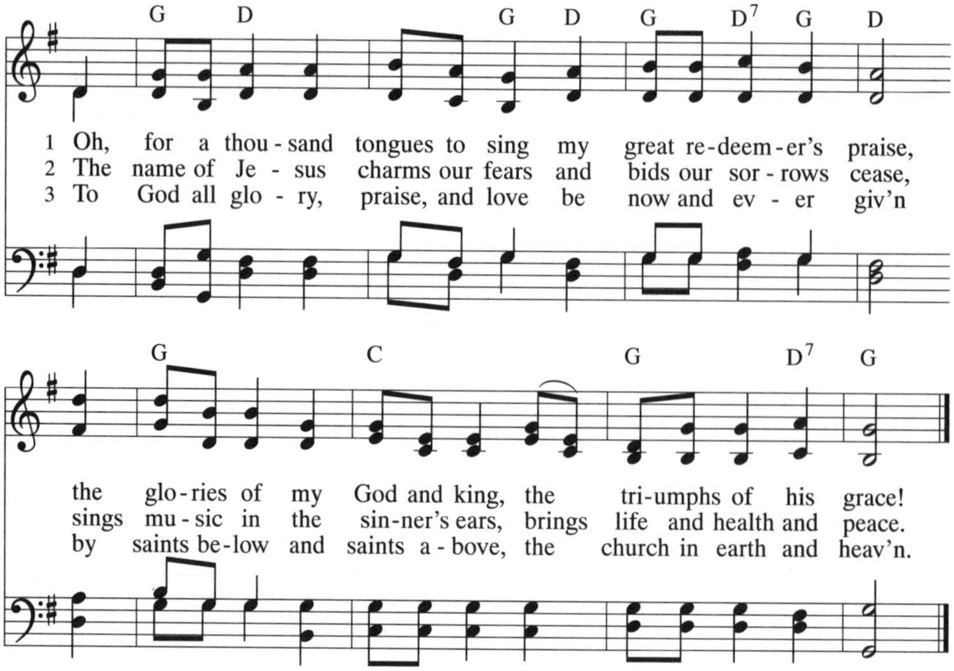
G D G D G D7 G D
1 Oh, for a thou - sand tongues to sing my great re-deem-er's praise,
2 The name of Je - sus charms our fears and bids our sor - rows cease,
3 To God all glo - ry, praise, and love be now and ev - er giv'n
G C G D7 G
the glo-ries of my God and king, the tri-umphs of his grace!
sings mu-sic in the sin-ner's ears, brings life and health and peace.
by saints be-low and saints a - bove, the church in earth and heav'n.

Text: Charles Wesley
Music: Carl G. Gläser; arr. Lowell Mason

Charles Wesley (1707–1788) was a clergyman of the Church of England who wrote hymns morning, noon, and night. With 6,500 hymns, he is the most prolific hymn writer in the history of English hymnody. Invite older children to look in the back of a hymnal for his name. How many hymns are included?

Wesley wrote this hymn to commemorate the first anniversary of his conversion: a day when he felt his own heart warmed by God's love. The word *tongue* means "language." The idea to use this expression came from his mentor and friend who said, "If I had a thousand tongues, I would praise Christ with them all." A hymn of deep personal experience for Wesley, it is also a shout of exultation for us to sing God's praise (P. Wezeman and A. Liechty, "Special Days and Holidays," *Hymn Stories for Children*, Kregel Resources: Grand Rapids, Mich., p. 43).

• Experience the rhythmic flow of this hymn by chanting. Divide the children into three groups.

A

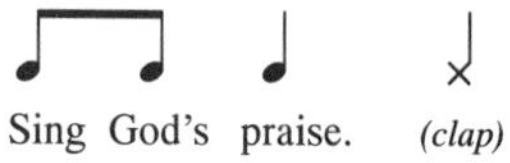
Sing God's praise. (clap)

B

Thou - sand tongues

C

chants the words of stanza 1 in rhythm.

• Try this: A begins, after two measures B enters, after two more measures C enters on a pickup note (beat 3). As C finishes, A and B continue for two measures, then B drops out while A continues for two measures and concludes with the final clap. Rotate parts until all have participated as group C.

• Teach everyone the melody to stanza 1.

Sing in a service where there is a strong sense of evangelical concern for the world. Assign one of the stanzas to the children.

Make a glad noise to the Lord 186

A joyful psalm of praise and thanksgiving, this psalm allows us to call out to God together as a community of faith with whatever talents we bring. God accepts us as we are. The psalm serves to remind us that we are created by God and to God we belong. Enter then into worship with thanksgiving in your heart and praise on your lips.

- In the song, the first two phrases share an identical rhythm pattern. Clap this pattern, inviting children to echo. Be clear about the syncopation.
- For the third and fourth phrases, chant the words in rhythm using the echo method. Ask for good diction.
- Teach the song, adding large cymbals or finger cymbals on the fourth beat of measures 2, 4, and 8.
- Sing in unison or as a two-part canon when Psalm 100 appears in the lectionary. Use Psalm 100:2 as a spoken introduction to the psalm. A solo voice or the whole group could be used. Assign an Orff instrument to play a C while the verse is spoken. This will establish the pitch for the singing immediately following verse 2. Verse 5 may be spoken following the song, ending with a C from the Orff instrument.

Use as an entrance psalm in a Thanksgiving service.

Make a glad noise to the Lord, all earth. Know that God made us; we
are God's own. We are God's peo - ple, and God is our shep - herd.
En - ter the gates with thanks - giv - ing and praise. We are God's peo - ple, and
God is our shep - herd. En - ter the gates with thanks - giv - ing and praise.

Text: based on Psalm 100:1, 3, 4
Music: Czechoslovakian folk song

187

Alleluia

G C Am7 D C G
1 Al - le - lu - ia, al - le - lu - ia, al - le - lu - ia, al - le - lu - ia;
2 He's my Sav - ior, al - le - lu - ia, he's my Sav - ior, al - le - lu - ia;
3 He is wor - thy, al - le - lu - ia, he is wor - thy, al - le - lu - ia;
4 I will praise him, al - le - lu - ia, I will praise him, al - le - lu - ia;
G C Am7 D7 C G
al - le - lu - ia, al - le - lu - ia, al - le - lu - ia, al - le - lu - ia.
he's my Sav - ior, al - le - lu - ia, he's my Sav - ior, al - le - lu - ia.
he is wor - thy, al - le - lu - ia, he is wor - thy, al - le - lu - ia.
I will praise him, al - le - lu - ia, I will praise him, al - le - lu - ia.

Text: Jerry Sinclair
Music: Jerry Sinclair

188

Alleluia

G A D Em7 A Bm E A
Al - le - lu - ia, al - le - lu - ia! Al - le - lu - ia,
Bm D Em A D
al - le - lu - ia, al - le - lu - ia!

Text: traditional
Music: *Geistliche Kirchengesäng*, Köln

Rejoice in the Lord always

1*
F
C7
F
Re - joice in the Lord al - ways, and a - gain I say, re - joice! (clap, clap)
2
C7
F
Re - joice in the Lord al - ways, and a - gain I say, re - joice!
3
C7
F
Re - joice! Re - joice! And a - gain I say, re - joice!
4
C7
F
Re - joice! Re - joice! And a - gain I say, re - joice!

*may be sung as a round

Text: Philippians 4:4
Music: traditional

Paul's letter to the Philippians was written from prison at a time when the apostle faced possible martyrdom. Nevertheless, his words reveal a real concern for others. In Philippians 4:4 his call is to rejoice in the Lord always. In the verses that follow he conveys an attitude of joy, hope, gratitude, and peace.

• Use a tambourine each time the word *rejoice* (♩ ♩) is sung.

• With older children sing in canon. Reinforce the canon form with movement. Teach this movement or create one of your own:

First phrase: In circle formation, walk to the right for seven beats, stopping to add the claps as shown in the music.
Second phrase: Reverse.
Third phrase: Remain in place for this pattern: pat thighs, clap, snap, clap, pat thighs, clap, snap, then add the claps from the music.
Fourth phrase: Repeat pattern of the third phrase.

• Divide the children into the number of groups desired for the canon. Each group forms a circle. Group 1 begins with movement and singing. The other groups remain in place until their entrance.

• Sing without movement one time, with movement only (no singing) one time, and finally sing with movement one time.

Use in worship when the congregation sings "Now thank we all our God" (LBW 533, 534). Have children sing before or after the hymn. Also, consider singing on a Sunday when Philippians 4:4-7 is one of the readings.

190 Sleep, baby Jesus

Tune: Rock-a-bye baby

Sleep, baby Jesus,
sleep on the hay.
Mary is singing,
little lambs play.
Joseph is watching,
stars shine so bright.
So sleep, baby Jesus,
sleep through the night.

Text: Daphna Flegal and Linda Ray Miller

191 Jesus, Jesus

Tune: Jesus in the morning

Jesus, Jesus
Baby Jesus sleeping
Mother Mary keeping
Jesus, Jesus
Jesus in a manger bed.

Jesus, Jesus
Holy angels winging
Mother Mary singing
Jesus, Jesus
Jesus in a manger bed.

Jesus, Jesus
Little shepherds kneeling
Mother Mary feeling
Jesus, Jesus
Jesus in a manger bed.

Jesus, Jesus
Everyone receiving
Everyone believing
Jesus, Jesus
Jesus in a manger bed.

Text: Herbert F. Brokering

192 Twinkle, twinkle

Tune: Twinkle, twinkle little star

Twinkle, twinkle, little star
How I wonder what you are
Hanging near a tiny place
Shining on a baby's face
Twinkle, twinkle, little star
How I wonder what you are.

Twinkle, twinkle, little light
How I wonder, why so bright
Wise ones coming from afar
Guided by a bursting star
Twinkle, twinkle, little light
How I wonder, why so bright.

Twinkle, twinkle, little Lamb
How I wonder who I am
You know all the stars above
You gave me the world to love
Twinkle, twinkle, little Lamb
How I wonder who I am.

Text: Herbert F. Brokering

Peter, Andrew, James, and John

193

Tune: Ten little Indians

Peter, Andrew, James and John,
Peter, Andrew, James and John,
Peter, Andrew, James and John,
by Lake Galilee.

Jesus walked to them and called them,
Jesus walked to them and called them,
Jesus walked to them and called them,
"Come and go with me."

Text: Virginia Williams

Jesus called

194

Tune: This is the way

Jesus called men to follow him,
follow him, follow him.
Jesus called men to follow him,
like Peter, James, and John.

Jesus called women to follow him,
follow him, follow him.
Jesus called women to follow him,
like Susanna, Joanna, and Mary.

Jesus calls us to follow him,
follow him, follow him.
Jesus calls us to follow him,
like (*name each child in your class*).

Text: based on Matthew 4:18-22 and Luke 8:1-3

Jesus told a story

195

Tune: She'll be coming 'round the mountain

Oh, Jesus told a story about love.
Oh, Jesus told a story about love.
Give your friend a helping hand,
love God all you can.
Oh, Jesus told a story about love.

Speak: Happy are those who know
how to love.

Oh, Jesus told his people to forgive.
Oh, Jesus told his people to forgive
Listen and forgive,
that's how God wants us to live
Oh, Jesus told his people to forgive

Speak: Happy are those who know
how to forgive.

Oh, Jesus told of helping one another.
Oh, Jesus told of helping one another.
If God's helpers we would be,
we'll help those we see in need.
Oh, Jesus told of helping one another.

Speak: Happy are those who know
how to help each other.

Oh, Jesus told a story about prayer.
Oh, Jesus told a story about prayer.
Take time every day
To turn to God and pray.
Oh, Jesus told a story about prayer.

Speak: Happy are those who know
how to pray.

Text: Jenni Douglas, based on Luke 15:11-32 and Matthew 6:9

196 This is the way we sing our praise

Tune: This is the way

This is the way we sing our praise,
Cup hands around mouth.
sing our praise, sing our praise.
This is the way we sing our praise,
la, la, la!

This is the way we clap our praise,
Clap hands.
clap our praise, clap our praise.
This is the way we clap our praise,
clap, clap, clap!

This is the way we dance our praise,
Tap toes.
dance our praise, dance our praise.
This is the way we dance our praise,
tap, tap, tap!

Text: based on Psalm 47

197 The creation

Tune: This is the way

God made the sun and moon and stars, moon and stars, moon and stars.	*Hold arms in circle over head for sun and moon. Hold arms over head and wiggle fingers for stars.*
God made the sun and moon and stars, and saw that it was good.	*Touch fingers of right hand to lips. Move hand forward. Drop it to the open palm of the left hand.*
God made the earth and sky and seas, sky and seas, sky and seas.	*Touch the floor for earth. Reach arms up for sky. Wave arms in front of you for seas.*
God made the earth and sky and seas, and saw that it was good.	*Repeat sign for good.*
God made the seeds and plants and trees, plants and trees, plants and trees,	*Crouch down and slowly stand with arms above head.*
God made the seeds and plants and trees, and saw that it was good.	*Repeat sign for good.*
God made the fish and birds and bees, birds and bees, birds and bees.	*Put palms together and wiggle hands for fish. Flap arms for birds and bees.*
God made the fish and birds and bees, and saw that it was good.	*Repeat sign for good.*
God made cows and creeping things, creeping things, creeping things.	*Take small, creeping steps.*
God made cows and creeping things, and saw that it was good.	*Repeat sign for good.*
God made people like you and me, you and me, you and me.	*Point to others. Point to self.*
God made people like you and me, and saw that it was good.	*Repeat sign for good.*
God rested on the seventh day, seventh day, seventh day.	*Hold hands under head as if sleeping.*
God rested on the seventh day, for it was very good.	*Repeat sign for good.*

Text: Daphna Flegal

Sing a song of mercy

198

Tune: Sing a song of sixpence

Sing a song of mercy:
fish and loaves of bread!
Many thousand hungry
waited to be fed.
When the crowd was seated
down at Jesus' feet,
five loaves and two little fish
were all they had to eat.

Sing a song of mercy:
fish and loaves of bread!
Many thousand hungry
waited to be fed.

When the crowd was ready,
Jesus blessed the food.
Five loaves and two little fish
would taste so very good.

Sing a song of mercy:
fish and loaves of bread!
Many thousand hungry
ate till they were fed.
When the meal was over—
wasn't it a treat—
baskets full of leftovers,
twelve more than they could eat!

Text: Herbert F. Brokering

Come, come, come to me

199

Tune: Row, row, row your boat

Come, come, come to me
On the raging sea
Jesus, Jesus, still the storm
Deep inside of me.

See, see, see the pain
Far as eye can see
Jesus, Jesus, heal the hurt
Deep inside of me.

Hear, hear, hear the cry
From the greenwood tree
Jesus, Jesus, hear the sigh
Deep inside of me.

See, see, see the way
God leads me to be
Jesus, Jesus, be the way
Deep inside of me.

Calm, calm, calm the storm
On the raging sea
Jesus, Jesus, I have peace
Deep inside of me.

Text: Herbert F. Brokering

Can you listen

200

Tune: Are you sleeping?

Can you listen? Can you listen? — *Cup hand around one ear, then the other.*
Girls and boys, girls and boys, — *Point to children.*
listen to the Bible, listen to the Bible. — *Cup hand around one ear, then the other.*
God is love. God is love. — *Cross hands over heart*

Repeat motions for remaining stanzas

Can you listen? Can you listen?
Girls and boys, girls and boys,
listen to the Bible, listen to the Bible.
Love is kind. Love is kind.

Can you listen? Can you listen?
Girls and boys, girls and boys,
listen to the Bible, listen to the Bible.
Live in love. Live in love

Text: based on 1 John 4:8, 1 Corinthians 13:4, and Ephesians 5:2

American sign language

Alleluia

Belong

Born

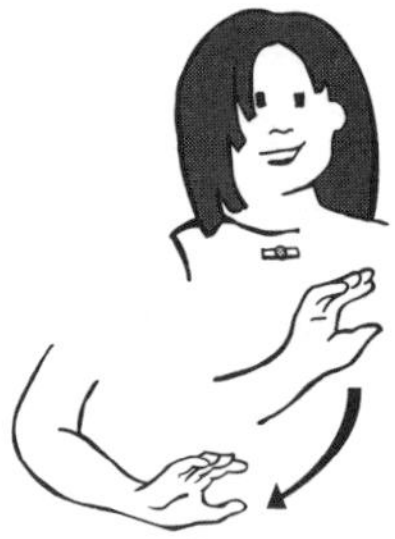

Christ

Come

Day

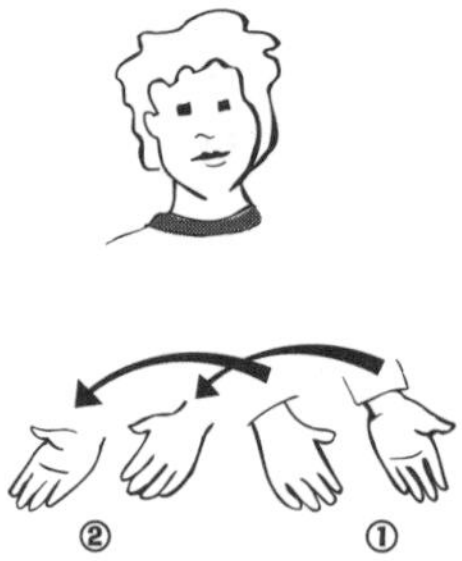

Died

Ever

Forgive

Glory

Go

God

Heart

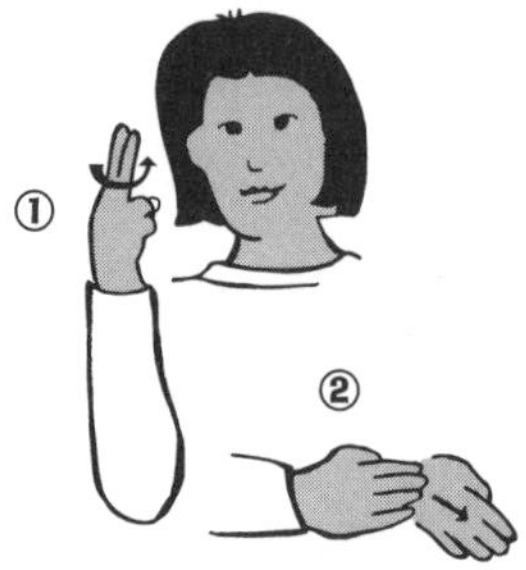

Holy

Jesus

Joy

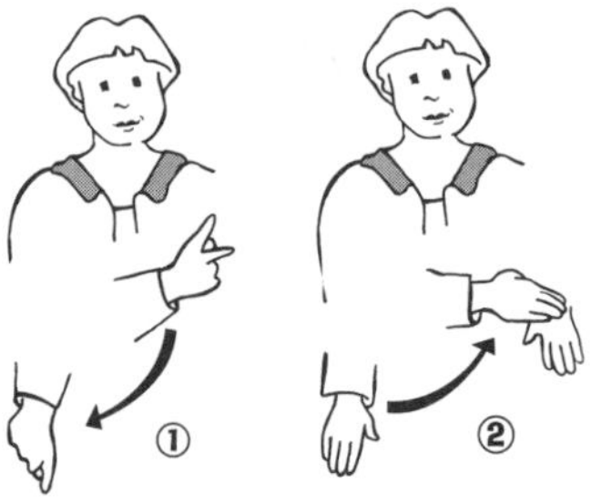

Kingdom

Know

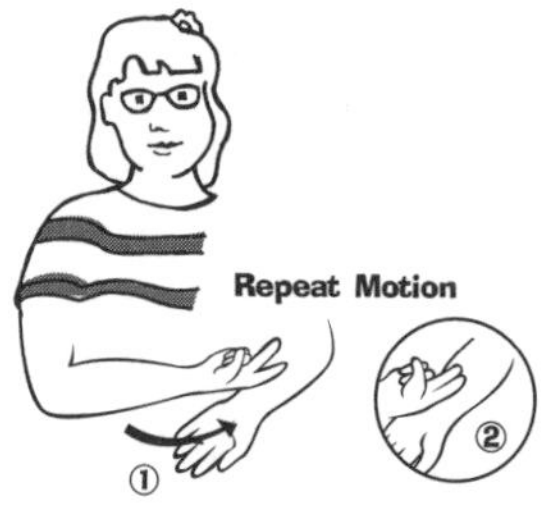

Lamb

Life

Light

Lord

Love

Me

Night

Peace

Power

Pray

Remember

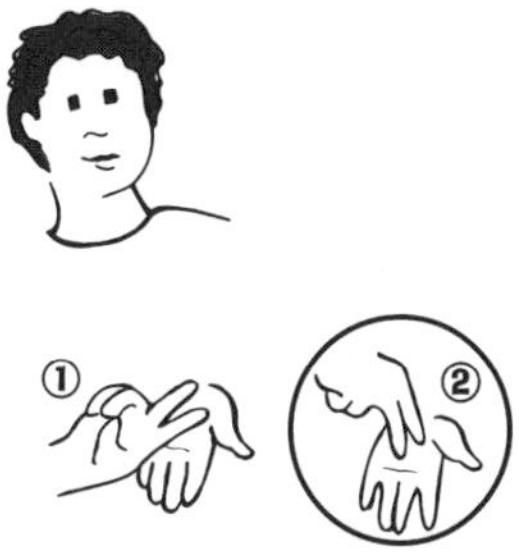
Rise

Serve

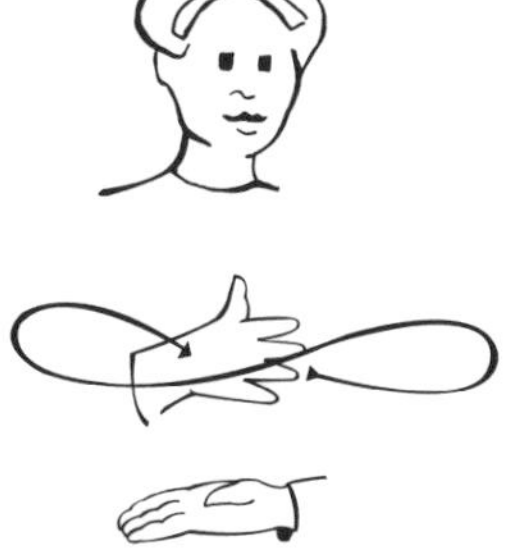
Song

Sorry

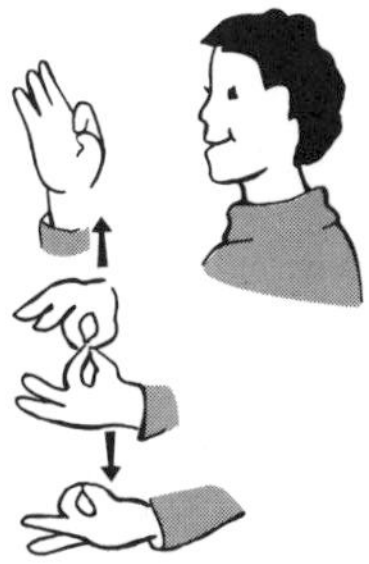
Spirit

Surround

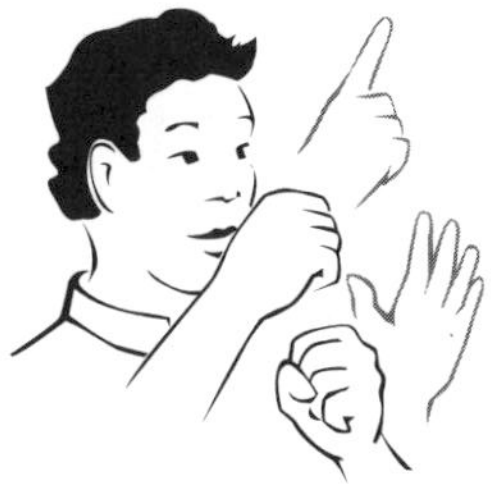
Trust

Way

Worship

Yes

You

Guitar chords

Am	A7	Am7	AM7	Am7(♭5)	Adim7	Asus	A7sus	A2	B♭	B♭m
B♭7	B♭m7	B♭m7(♭5)	B♭dim7	B♭sus	B♭7sus	B♭2	B	Bm	B7	Bm7
BM7	Bm7(♭5)	Bdim7	Bsus	B7sus	B2	C	Cm (3fr.)	C7	Cm7 (3fr.)	CM7
Cm7(♭5)	Cdim7	Csus	C7sus	C2	C♯ / D♭ (4fr.)	C♯m / D♭m (4fr.)	C♯7 / D♭7	C♯m7 / D♭m7 (4fr.)	C♯M7 / D♭M7 (4fr.)	C♯m7(♭5) / D♭m7(♭5)
C♯dim7 / D♭dim7 (3fr.)	C♯sus / D♭sus (4fr.)	C♯7sus / D♭7sus	C♯2 / D♭2 (4fr.)	D	Dm	D7	Dm7	DM7	Dm7(♭5)	Ddim7
Dsus	D7sus	D2	E♭	E♭m	E♭7	E♭m7	E♭M7	E♭m7(♭5)	E♭dim7	E♭sus
E♭7sus	E	Em	E7	Em7	EM7	Em7(♭5)	Edim7	Esus	E7sus	E2
F	Fm	F7	Fm7	FM7	Fm7(♭5)	Fdim7	Fsus	F7sus	F2	F♯
F♯m	F♯7	F♯m7	F♯M7	F♯m7(♭5)	F♯dim7	F♯sus	F♯7sus	F♯2	G	Gm (3fr.)
G7	Gm7	GM7	Gm7(♭5)	Gdim7	Gsus	G7sus	G2			

Acknowledgments and copyright holders

Compiler and writer: Marilyn Comer

Reviewers: Kari Anderson, Carol Benson, Sherilyn Bergdorff, Lois Brokering, Martha Fisher, Cindy Fisher-Bronin, Nick Fisher-Bronin, Ronald A. Nelson, Scott Weidler, Wayne L. Wold

Augsburg Fortress: Norma Aamodt-Nelson, Suzanne Burke, Carol Carver, D. Foy Christopherson, Ann Delgehausen, Ryan French, Charles Humphrey, Lynn Joyce Hunter, Lynette Johnson, Aaron Koelman, Rebecca Lowe, David Meyer, Kristine Oberg, Linda Parriott, Rachel Riensche, Martin A. Seltz, Frank Stoldt, Eric Vollen, Mark Weiler

Cover art and design: Tanja Butler, Circus Design

Music engraving: Thomas Schaller, Mensura Music Preparation

Copyediting and music preparation: Becky Brantner-Christiansen, J. David Moore, Dean Niquette, Lani Willis

Material from the following sources is acknowledged: *Praying Together,* © 1988 English Language Liturgical Consultation: texts of "Glory to God in the highest" (#20), "Lamb of God" (#46), and "Our Father in heaven" (#96).

The Revised Common Lectionary, © 1992 Consultation on Common Texts.

Copyright acknowledgment: The publisher gratefully acknowledges all copyright holders who have granted permission to reproduce copyrighted materials in this book. Every effort has been made to determine the owner(s) and/or administrator(s) of each copyright and to secure needed permission. The publisher will, upon written notice, make necessary corrections in subsequent printings.

Permission information: Permission to reproduce copyrighted words or music contained in this book must be obtained from the copyright holder(s) of that material. A list of the major copyright holders represented in this book follows, with information current as of the year of publication of *LifeSongs.* Some of the songs may be covered under one or more major licensing agencies, but because this status may change from time to time, it is best to verify this information with the copyright holder or licensing agency at the time of use. For contact information of copyright holders not listed here or for further copyright information, please contact Augsburg Fortress.

AUGSBURG FORTRESS PUBLISHERS
PO Box 1209
Minneapolis, MN 55440-1209
(800) 421-0239
(612) 330-3252 FAX

AF-STIFTELSEN
Psalm Och Sang
Box 512 34300
Almhult Sweden

CHORISTERS GUILD
2834 West Kingsley Road
Garland, TX 75041-2498
(972) 271-1521
(972) 840-3113 FAX

THE COPYRIGHT COMPANY
40 Music Square East
Nashville, TN 37203
(615) 244-5588
(615) 244-5591 FAX

CRC PUBLICATIONS
2850 Kalamazoo Ave. SE
Grand Rapids, MI 49560
(616) 246-0785
(616) 246-0834 FAX

CPH PUBLISHING
3558 South Jefferson Avenue
St. Louis, MO 63118
(800) 325-0191
(314) 268-1329 FAX

DAVID HIGHAM ASSOCIATES, LTD.
5-8 Lower John Street
Golden Square
London W1R 4HA UK
011-44-171-437-7888
011-44-171-437-1072 FAX

EMI CHRISTIAN MUSIC PUBLISHING
101 Winners Circle
PO Box 5085
Brentwood, TN 37024-5085
(615) 371-4400
(615) 371-6897 FAX

FREDERICK HARRIS CO., LTD.
2250 Military Road
Tonawanda, NY 14150
(905) 501-1595
(905) 501-0929 FAX

GIA PUBLICATIONS, INC.
7404 South Mason Avenue
Chicago, IL 60638
(800) 442-1358
(708) 496-3828 FAX

HINSHAW MUSIC, INC.
Box 470
Chapel Hill, NC 27514
(919) 933-1691
(919) 967-3399 FAX

HOPE PUBLISHING COMPANY
380 South Main Place
Carol Stream, IL 60188
(800) 323-1049
(630) 665-2552

ICEL
1522 K Street Northwest, Suite 1000
Washington, DC 20005
(202) 347-0800
(202) 347-1839 FAX

INTEGRITY MUSIC, INC.
1000 Cody Road
Mobile, AL 36695
(334) 633-9000
(334) 633-5202 FAX

ISEDET
Camacuá 282
Buenos Aires 1406 Argentina
011-54-1-632-5039
011-54-1-633-2825 FAX

LEXICON MUSIC INC., USA, M.P.I. LTD
75 High Street
Needham Market
Suffolk IP6 8AN England

LIVING THE GOOD NEWS, INC.
600 Grant Street, Suite 400
Denver, CO 80203-3524
(303) 832-4427

LUTHERAN THEOLOGICAL COLLEGE AT MAKUMIRA
(Contact Augsburg Fortress for permission, or)
PO Box 55
Usa River (near Arusha)
Tanzania, East Africa
011-25-557-3858 FAX

LUTHERAN WORLD FEDERATION
Box 2100
150 route de Ferney
CH1211 Geneva 2 Switzerland
011-41-22-791-6360
011-41-22-798-8616 FAX

MANNA MUSIC, INC.
Box 218
35255 Brooten Road
Pacific City, OR 97135
(503) 965-6112
(503) 965-6880 FAX

MORNINGSTAR MUSIC PUBLISHERS
1727 Larkin Williams Road
Fenton, MO 63026-2024
(800) 647-2117
(314) 647-2777 FAX

MUSIC MATTERS, INC.
409 Blandwood Avenue
Greensboro, NC 27401-2705
(800) 216-6864

NEW DAWN MUSIC
5536 NE Hassalo PO Box 18030
Portland, OR 97218-0030
(800) 548-8749
(503) 282-3486 FAX

OCP PUBLICATIONS
5536 NE Hassalo PO Box 18030
Portland, OR 97218-0030
(800) 548-8749
(503) 282-3486 FAX

OXFORD UNIVERSITY PRESS
Walton Street
Oxford OX2 6DP England
011-44-186-555-6767
011-44-186-526-7749 FAX

PRINCE OF PEACE PUBLISHING, CHANGING CHURCH, INC.
200 East Nicollet Blvd
Burnsville, MN 55337
(612) 435-8107

SELAH PUBLISHING COMPANY
58 Pearl Street
Box 3037
Kingston, NY 12401-0902
(914) 338-2816
(914) 338-2991 FAX

WALT DISNEY COMPANY
3900 West Alameda Street
Burbank, CA 91505
818-569-3270
818-845-9705 FAX

WORLD COUNCIL OF CHURCHES
150 route de Ferney
PO Box 2100
CH1211 Geneva 2 Switzerland
011-41-22-791-6111
011-41-22-798-1346 FAX

WORLD LIBRARY PUBLICATIONS
A Division of J. S. Paluch Company, Inc.
3825 North Willow Road
Schiller Park, IL 60176-9936
(800) 621-5197
(888) 957-3291

Hymn and song suggestions for the church year

related to the Revised Common Lectionary and Life Together *resources*

Year A

Advent 1
- Pre: 4 He came down
- Lower: 2 Soon and very soon
- Upper: 1 Stay awake, be ready, *st. 1*

Advent 2
- Pre: 4 He came down
- Lower: 2 Soon and very soon
- Upper: 1 Stay awake, be ready, *st. 2*

Advent 3
- Pre: 4 He came down
- Lower: 8 The King of glory
- Upper: 1 Stay awake, be ready, *st. 3*

Advent 4
- Pre: 4 He came down
- Lower: 8 The King of glory
- Upper: 1 Stay awake, be ready, *st. 4*

Christmas
- Pre: 190 Sleep, baby Jesus
- Lower: 15 'Twas in the moon of wintertime, *refrain*
- Upper: 15 'Twas in the moon of wintertime, *st. 1 and refrain*

Christmas 1
- Pre: 17, 18 Away in a manger
- Lower: 28 Oh, sleep now, holy baby
- Upper: 29 The virgin Mary had a baby boy

Christmas 2
- Pre: 17, 18 Away in a manger
- Lower: 21 Gloria
- Upper: 21 Gloria

Epiphany
- Pre: 192 Twinkle, twinkle
- Lower: 30 We three kings of Orient are
- Upper: 38 Shine, Jesus, shine, *refrain*

Baptism of Our Lord
- Pre: 86 I was baptized, happy day!
- Lower: 85 You have put on Christ
- Upper: 85 You have put on Christ

Epiphany 2
- Pre: 77 Come into God's presence
- Lower: 32, 33 This little light of mine
- Upper: 32, 33 This little light of mine

Epiphany 3
- Pre: 193 Peter, Andrew, James, and John
- Lower: 34 I am the light of the world
- Upper: 39 Jesus brings a message

Epiphany 4
- Pre: 143 Blest are they, *refrain*
- Lower: 37 We are called
- Upper: 143 Blest are they

Epiphany 5
- Pre: 32, 33 This little light of mine
- Lower: 35 Bring forth the kingdom, *sts. 1-2 and refrain*
- Upper: 35 Bring forth the kingdom, *sts. 1-2 and refrain*

Epiphany 6
- Pre: 152 This is my commandment
- Lower: 172 The great commandments
- Upper: 172 The great commandments

Epiphany 7
- Pre: 200 Can you listen
- Lower: 142 Love God and your neighbor, *refrain*
- Upper: 142 Love God and your neighbor

Epiphany 8
- Pre: 162 In our work and in our play
- Lower: 170 I am trusting you, Lord Jesus
- Upper: 161 Fear not for tomorrow

Transfiguration
- Pre: 175 Heleluyan
- Lower: 40 Come to the mountain
- Upper: 36 I want to walk as a child of the light, *st. 1*

Lent 1
- Pre: 151 We love
- Lower: 41 I want Jesus to walk with me
- Upper: 42 Is there anybody here who loves my Jesus?

Lent 2
- Pre: 129 If anybody asks you who I am, *sts. 1-3*
- Lower: 129 If anybody asks you who I am, *sts. 1-3*
- Upper: 45 For God so loved the world

Lent 3
- Pre: 86 I was baptized, happy day!
- Lower: 46 Lamb of God
- Upper: 87 Baptized in water

Lent 4
- Pre: 34 I am the light of the world
- Lower: 34 I am the light of the world
- Upper: 42 Is there anybody here who loves my Jesus?

Lent 5
- Pre: 52 Glory be to Jesus, *st. 1*
- Lower: 144 Jesus, Jesus, let us tell you
- Upper: 144 Jesus, Jesus, let us tell you

Passion/Palm Sunday
- Pre: 48 All glory, laud, and honor, *refrain*
- Lower: 47 Hosanna! the little children sing
- Upper: 49 Filled with excitement

Easter Day
- Pre: 187, 188 Alleluia
- Lower: 54 This is the feast
- Upper: 60 This is the day

Easter 2
- Pre: 53 Do you know who died for me?
- Lower: 61 Come and see, *refrain*
- Upper: 61 Come and see, *sts. 1-3 and refrain*

Easter 3
- Pre: 77 Come into God's presence
- Lower: 103 Come, let us eat
- Upper; 103 Come, let us eat

Easter 4
- Pre: 65 The Lord is my shepherd
- Lower: 65 The Lord is my shepherd
- Upper: 171 Have no fear, little flock

Easter 5
- Pre: 195 Jesus told a story
- Lower: 105 I received the living God, *refrain*
- Upper: 105 I received the living God

Easter 6
- Pre: 61 Come and see
- Lower: 147 If you love me, *st. 1*
- Upper: 147 If you love me, *st. 1*

Ascension
- Pre: 196 This is the way we sing our praise
- Lower: 108 Go now in peace
- Upper: 62 Alleluia! Jesus is risen!, *refrain*

Easter 7
- Pre: 128 Many are the lightbeams, *st. 1*
- Lower: 128 Many are the lightbeams, *st. 1*
- Upper: 128 Many are the lightbeams

Pentecost
- Pre: 133 We are the church, *refrain*
- Lower: 133 We are the church, *st. 4 and refrain*
- Upper: 91 Every time I feel the spirit

Trinity
- Pre: 197 The creation
- Lower: 113 The Lord is great!
- Upper: 79 Listen, God is calling

Proper 3
- Pre: 162 In our work and in our play
- Lower: 170 I am trusting you, Lord Jesus
- Upper: 161 Fear not for tomorrow

Proper 4
- Pre: 118 Two little eyes
- Lower: 173 Faith that's sure, *refrain*
- Upper: 121 I'm so glad Jesus lifted me

Proper 5
- Pre: 122 Jesus, you help
- Lower: 147 If you love me, *st. 1*
- Upper: 147 If you love me, *sts. 1-2*

Proper 6
- Pre: 74 Come and sing your praise
- Lower: 186 Make a glad noise to the Lord
- Upper: 186 Make a glad noise to the Lord

Proper 7
- Pre: 115 You made every part of me
- Lower: 172 The great commandments
- Upper: 165 What does it mean to follow Jesus?

Proper 8
- Pre: 78 Won't you come and sit with me
- Lower: 73 Come! Come! Everybody worship
- Upper: 73 Come! Come! Everybody worship

Proper 9
- Pre: 92 Jesus listens when I pray
- Lower: 96 Our Father in heaven
- Upper: 169 Lord of all hopefulness, *st. 1*

Proper 10
- Pre: 150 The tiny seed
- Lower: 35 Bring forth the kingdom, *st. 3 and refrain*
- Upper: 83 Lord, let my heart be good soil

Proper 11
- Pre. 200 Can you listen
- Lower: 84 Open your ears, O faithful people, *sts.1-2 and refrain*
- Upper: 84 Open your ears, O faithful people, *sts. 1-2 and refrain*

Proper 12
- Pre: 150 The tiny seed
- Lower: 139 You are the seed, *st. 1 and refrain*
- Upper: 139 You are the seed, *sts. 1, 3, and refrain*

Proper 13
- Pre: 102 All good gifts around us
- Lower: 104 Feed us, Jesus
- Upper: 104 Feed us, Jesus

Proper 14
- Pre: 162 In our work and in our play
- Lower: 59 There's new life in Jesus
- Upper: 80 How firm a foundation

Proper 15
- Pre: 133 We are the church
- Lower: 73 Come! Come! Everybody worship
- Upper: 124 Jesus' hands were kind hands

Proper 16
- Pre: 133 We are the church
- Lower: 173 Faith that's sure, *refrain*
- Upper: 80 How firm a foundation

Proper 17
- Pre: 134 Love, love, love!, *sts. 1-2*
- Lower: 142 Love God and your neigbor
- Upper: 165 What does it mean to follow Jesus?

Proper 18
- Pre: 78 Won't you come and sit with me
- Lower: 147 If you love me, *sts. 1, 4*
- Upper: 147 If you love me, *sts. 2-4*

Proper 19
- Pre: 162 In our work and in our play
- Lower: 59 There's new life in Jesus
- Upper: 125 Forgive our sins as we forgive, *st. 1*

Proper 20
- Pre: 115 You made every part of me
- Lower: 37 We are called, *refrain*
- Upper: 37 We are called, *sts. 1-2 and refrain*

Proper 21
- Pre: 115 You made every part of me
- Lower: 97 Come, Lord Jesus
- Upper: 135 There's a Spirit in the air

Proper 22
- Pre: 160 Jesus loves me!
- Lower: 148 Let me be your servant, Jesus
- Upper: 183 Sing alleluia

Proper 23
- Pre: 65 The Lord is my shepherd
- Lower: 189 Rejoice in the Lord always
- Upper: 171 Have no fear, little flock

Proper 24
- Pre: 160 Jesus loves me!, *sts. 1, 4*
- Lower: 97 Come, Lord Jesus
- Upper: 165 What does it mean to follow Jesus?

Proper 25
Pre: 152 This is my commandment
Lower: 172 The great commandments
Upper: 142 Love God and your neighbor

Reformation
Pre: 133 We are the church
Lower: 168 God is our refuge and strength
Upper: 180 I will sing, I will sing, *sts. 1, 3, 5*

Proper 26
Pre: 118 Two little eyes
Lower: 98 God gave to me a life to live
Upper: 148 Let me be your servant, Jesus

All Saints
Pre: 164 Come, we that love the Lord, *refrain*
Lower: 164 Come, we that love the Lord, *refrain*
Upper: 164 Come, we that love the Lord, *sts. 1, 2, and refrain*

Proper 27
Pre: 162 In our work and in our play
Lower: 131 Chatter with the angels
Upper: 37 We are called

Proper 28
Pre: 74 Come and sing your praise
Lower: 79 Listen, God is calling
Upper: 183 Sing alleluia

Christ the King
Pre: 98 God gave to me a life to live
Lower: 153 When I needed a neighbor
Upper: 141 Come now, you blessed

Year B

Advent 1
Pre: 3 Light one candle: Christ is coming, *st. 1*
Lower: 3 Light one candle: Christ is coming, *st. 1*
Upper: 5 The King shall come, *sts. 1-2*

Advent 2
Pre: 3 Light one candle: Christ is coming, *st. 2*
Lower: 3 Light one candle: Christ is coming, *st. 2*
Upper: 5 The King shall come, *sts. 1-3*

Advent 3
Pre: 3 Light one candle: Christ is coming, *st. 3*
Lower: 3 Light one candle: Christ is coming, *st. 3*
Upper: 5 The King shall come, *sts. 1-4*

Advent 4
Pre: 3 Light one candle: Christ is coming, *st. 4*
Lower: 3 Light one candle: Christ is coming, *st. 4*
Upper: 5 The King shall come, *sts. 1-5*

Christmas
Pre: 15 'Twas in the moon of wintertime, *refrain*
Lower: 15 'Twas in the moon of wintertime
Upper: 15 'Twas in the moon of wintertime

Christmas 1
Pre: 15 'Twas in the moon of wintertime, *refrain*
Lower: 14 That boy-child of Mary, *refrain*
Upper: 14 That boy-child of Mary, *refrain*

Christmas 2
Pre: 15 'Twas in the moon of wintertime, *refrain*
Lower: 14 That boy-child of Mary, *sts. 1-2 and refrain*
Upper: 14 That boy-child of Mary, *sts. 1-3 and refrain*

Epiphany
Pre: 192 Twinkle, twinkle
Lower: 36 I want to walk as a child of the light, *refrain*
Upper: 30 We three kings of Orient are

Baptism of Our Lord
Pre: 86 I was baptized, happy day!
Lower: 85 You have put on Christ
Upper: 87 Baptized in water

Epiphany 2
Pre: 194 Jesus called
Lower: 31 Open our eyes, Lord
Upper: 138 Here I am, Lord, *refrain*

Epiphany 3
Pre: 193 Peter, Andrew, James, and John
Lower: 39 Jesus brings a message
Upper: 39 Jesus brings a message

Epiphany 4
Pre: 32, 33 This little light of mine
Lower: 79 Listen, God is calling, *st. 1 and refrain*
Upper: 185 Oh, for a thousand tongues to sing

Epiphany 5
Pre: 98 God gave to me a life to live
Lower: 69 Spirit Friend, *st. 1*
Upper: 69 Spirit Friend

Epiphany 6
Pre: 159 I've got peace like a river
Lower: 123 When Jesus the healer, *st. 5*
Upper: 123 When Jesus the healer, *st. 5*

Epiphany 7
Pre: 122 Jesus, you help
Lower: 123 When Jesus the healer, *sts. 1-2*
Upper: 123 When Jesus the healer, *sts. 1-2*

Epiphany 8
Pre: 106 To the banquet, come
Lower: 106 To the banquet, come
Upper: 165 What does it mean to follow Jesus?

Transfiguration
Pre: 175 Heleluyan
Lower: 40 Come to the mountain
Upper: 174 Beautiful Savior

Lent 1
Pre: 76 Hello, everybody
Lower: 41 I want Jesus to walk with me
Upper: 41 I want Jesus to walk with me

Lent 2
Pre: 43 Walk in God's ways
Lower: 41 I want Jesus to walk with me
Upper: 52 Glory be to Jesus

Lent 3
Pre: 195 Jesus told a story
Lower: 144 Jesus, Jesus let us tell you
Upper: 144 Jesus, Jesus let us tell you

Lent 4
Pre: 151 We love
Lower: 151 We love
Upper: 94 Lord, listen to your children praying

Lent 5
Pre: 181 I've got the joy, joy, joy
Lower: 55 Now the green blade rises, *st. 1*
Upper: 55 Now the green blade rises, *st. 1*

Passion/Palm Sunday
Pre: 47 Hosanna! the little children sing
Lower: 47 Hosanna! the little children sing
Upper: 49 Filled with excitement

Easter Day
Pre: 53 Do you know who died for me?
Lower: 55 Now the green blade rises, *st. 1*
Upper: 55 Now the green blade rises, *sts. 1, 4*

Easter 2
Pre: 134 Love, love, love!, *sts. 1-2*
Lower: 61 Come and see, *refrain*
Upper: 61 Come and see, *sts. 1-3 and refrain*

Easter 3
Pre: 64 Christ the Lord is risen today!
Lower: 62 Alleluia! Jesus is risen!, *refrain*
Upper: 62 Alleluia! Jesus is risen!, *st. 1 and refrain*

Easter 4
Pre: 65 The Lord is my shepherd
Lower: 65 The Lord is my shepherd
Upper: 65 The Lord is my shepherd

Easter 5
Pre: 151 We love
Lower: 128 Many are the lightbeams, *sts. 1-2*
Upper: 62 Alleluia! Jesus is risen!, *sts. 1, 3, and refrain*

Easter 6
Pre: 152 This is my commandment
Lower: 142 Love God and your neighbor, *refrain*
Upper: 152 This is my commandment

Ascension
Pre: 196 This is the way we sing our praise
Lower: 178 Oh, sing to the Lord
Upper: 62 Alleluia! Jesus is risen!

Easter 7
Pre: 116 Like a tree, *response*
Lower: 116 Like a tree
Upper: 128 Many are the lightbeams

Pentecost
Pre: 133 We are the church, *refrain*
Lower: 133 We are the church, *st. 4 and refrain*
Upper: 68 Spirit, Spirit of gentleness

Holy Trinity
Pre: 70 Holy, Holy Spirit
Lower: 129 If anybody asks you who I am, *st. 3*
Upper: 145 All around the world

Proper 3
Pre: 77 Come into God's presence
Lower: 127 Bind us together, Lord, *refrain*
Upper: 165 What does it mean to follow Jesus?

Proper 4
Pre: 73 Come! Come! Everybody worship, *st. 1 and refrain*
Lower: 73 Come! Come! Everybody worship
Upper: 79 Listen, God is calling

Proper 5
Pre: 130 We are all one in Christ
Lower: 127 Bind us together, Lord, *refrain*
Upper: 128 Many are the lightbeams, *st. 5*

Proper 6
Pre: 150 The tiny seed
Lower: 150 The tiny seed
Upper: 83 Lord, let my heart be good soil

Proper 7
Pre: 162 In our work and in our play
Lower: 41 I want Jesus to walk with me
Upper: 80 How firm a foundation, *st. 2*

Proper 8
Pre: 122 Jesus, you help
Lower: 123 When Jesus the healer, *sts. 3, 7*
Upper: 123 When Jesus the healer, *sts. 1, 3, 7*

Proper 9
Pre: 160 Jesus loves me!, *st. 1*
Lower: 123 When Jesus the healer, *sts. 6-7*
Upper: 123 When Jesus the healer, *sts. 1 and 6-7*

Proper 10
Pre: 149 Jesus wants me for a helper
Lower: 59 There's new life in Jesus
Upper: 59 There's new life in Jesus

Proper 11
Pre: 115 You made every part of me
Lower: 73 Come! Come! Everybody worship, *st. 1*
Upper: 144 Jesus, Jesus let us tell you

Proper 12
Pre: 102 All good gifts around us
Lower: 104 Feed us, Jesus, *refrain*
Upper: 104 Feed us, Jesus

Proper 13
Pre: 129 If anybody asks you who I am, *sts. 1 and 4-5*
Lower: 105 I received the living God, *refrain*
Upper: 105 I received the living God, *sts. 1, 4*

Proper 14
Pre: 170 I am trusting you, Lord Jesus
Lower: 104 Feed us, Jesus, *refrain*
Upper: 103 Come, let us eat

Proper 15
Pre: 74 Come and sing your praise
Lower: 103 Come, let us eat
Upper: 103 Come, let us eat

Proper 16
Pre: 77 Come into God's presence
Lower: 82 Alleluia. Lord, to whom shall we go?
Upper: 82 Alleluia. Lord, to whom shall we go?

Proper 17
Pre: 195 Jesus told a story
Lower: 98 God gave to me a life to live
Upper: 183 Sing alleluia

Proper 18
Pre: 200 Can you listen
Lower: 142 Love God and your neighbor
Upper: 185 Oh, for a thousand tongues to sing

Proper 19
- Pre: 77 Come into God's presence, *sts. 1-2*
- Lower: 77 Come into God's presence, *sts. 1-2*
- Upper: 165 What does it mean to follow Jesus?

Proper 20
- Pre: 160 Jesus loves me!, *sts. 1-3*
- Lower: 167 Children of the heavenly Father, *st. 1*
- Upper: 167 Children of the heavenly Father, *st. 1*

Proper 21
- Pre: 97 Come, Lord Jesus
- Lower: 135 There's a Spirit in the air
- Upper: 62 Alleluia! Jesus is risen!, *st. 2*

Proper 22
- Pre: 74 Come and sing your praise
- Lower: 97 Come, Lord Jesus
- Upper: 169 Lord of all hopefulness, *st. 3*

Proper 23
- Pre: 129 If anybody asks you who I am
- Lower: 79 Listen, God is calling
- Upper: 183 Sing alleluia

Proper 24
- Pre: 115 You made every part of me
- Lower: 148 Let me be your servant, Jesus
- Upper: 148 Let me be your servant, Jesus

Proper 25
- Pre: 118 Two little eyes
- Lower: 34 I am the light of the world
- Upper: 123 When Jesus the healer, *sts. 1, 4*

Reformation
- Pre: 200 Can you listen
- Lower: 180 I will sing, I will sing, *sts. 1, 3, 5*
- Upper: 103 Come, let us eat

All Saints
- Pre: 160 Jesus loves me!, *st. 6*
- Lower: 131 Chatter with the angels
- Upper: 80 How firm a foundation, *st. 1*

Proper 26
- Pre: 152 This is my commandment
- Lower: 147 If you love me
- Upper: 147 If you love me

Proper 27
- Pre: 149 Jesus wants me for a helper
- Lower: 37 We are called, *st. 2*
- Upper: 141 Come now, you blessed

Proper 28
- Pre: 162 In our work and in our play
- Lower: 170 I am trusting you, Lord Jesus
- Upper: 161 Fear not for tomorrow

Christ the King
- Pre: 77 Come into God's presence
- Lower: 180 I will sing, I will sing, *sts. 1 and 5-6*
- Upper: 62 Alleluia! Jesus is risen!, *sts. 1, 5, and refrain*

Year C

Advent 1
- Pre: 12 Get ready!, *st. 1*
- Lower: 7 Prepare the royal highway
- Upper: 11 People, look east, *st. 1*

Advent 2
- Pre: 12 Get ready!, *st. 2*
- Lower: 7 Prepare the royal highway
- Upper: 11 People, look east, *st. 2*

Advent 3
- Pre: 12 Get ready!, *st. 3*
- Lower: 7 Prepare the royal highway
- Upper: 11 People, look east, *st. 3*

Advent 4
- Pre: 12 Get ready!, *st. 4*
- Lower: 7 Prepare the royal highway
- Upper: 11 People, look east, *st. 4*

Christmas
- Pre: 23 Go tell it on the mountain, *refrain*
- Lower: 23 Go tell it on the mountain, *sts. 1-3 and refrain*
- Upper: 19 Sing we now of Jesus

Christmas 1
- Pre: 23 Go tell it on the mountain, *refrain*
- Lower: 14 That boy-child of Mary
- Upper: 19 Sing we now of Jesus

Christmas 2
- Pre: 77 Come into God's presence
- Lower: 21 Gloria
- Upper: 21 Gloria

Epiphany
- Pre: 119 Earth and all stars!, *refrain*
- Lower: 119 Earth and all stars!, *refrain*
- Upper: 119 Earth and all stars!, *refrain*

Baptism of Our Lord
- Pre: 159 I've got peace like a river
- Lower: 130 We are all one in Christ
- Upper: 87 Baptized in water

Epiphany 2
- Pre: 77 Come into God's presence, *sts. 1-3*
- Lower: 127 Bind us together, Lord
- Upper: 127 Bind us together, Lord

Epiphany 3
- Pre: 74 Come and sing your praise
- Lower: 135 There's a Spirit in the air
- Upper: 144 Jesus, Jesus, let us tell you

Epiphany 4
- Pre: 200 Can you listen
- Lower: 166 Walk! Walk!
- Upper: 117 Love is never ending

Epiphany 5
- Pre: 194 Jesus called
- Lower: 39 Jesus brings a message
- Upper: 39 Jesus brings a message

Epiphany 6
- Pre: 116 Like a tree
- Lower: 116 Like a tree
- Upper: 105 I recieved the living God

Epiphany 7
- Pre: 195 Jesus told a story
- Lower: 98 God gave to me a life to live
- Upper: 125 Forgive our sins as we forgive

Epiphany 8
- Pre: 149 Jesus wants me for a helper
- Lower: 109 The trees of the field
- Upper: 109 The trees of the field

Transfiguration
- Pre: 175 Heleluyan
- Lower: 40 Come to the mountain
- Upper: 38 Shine, Jesus, shine

Lent 1
- Pre: 52 Glory be to Jesus
- Lower: 41 I want Jesus to walk with me
- Upper: 41 I want Jesus to walk with me

Lent 2
- Pre: 158 Give me oil in my lamp
- Lower: 167 Children of the heavenly Father
- Upper: 105 I received the living God

Lent 3
- Pre: 43 Walk in God's ways
- Lower: 166 Walk! Walk!
- Upper: 69 Spirit Friend

Lent 4
- Pre: 195 Jesus told a story
- Lower: 105 I received the living God, *refrain*
- Upper: 105 I received the living God

Lent 5
- Pre: 97 Come, Lord Jesus
- Lower: 153 When I needed a neighbor
- Upper: 136 On the poor

Passion/Palm Sunday
- Pre: 47 Hosanna! the little children sing
- Lower: 47 Hosanna! the little children sing
- Upper: 44 Jesus, remember me

Easter Day
- Pre: 177 Halle, halle, hallelujah!
- Lower: 60 This is the day
- Upper: 19 Sing we now of Jesus

Easter 2
- Pre: 53 Do you know who died for me?
- Lower: 61 Come and see, *refrain*
- Upper: 61 Come and see, *sts. 1-3 and refrain*

Easter 3
- Pre: 118 Two little eyes
- Lower: 148 Let me be your servant, Jesus
- Upper: 194 Jesus called, *sts. 1, 4*

Easter 4
- Pre: 65 The Lord is my shepherd
- Lower: 157 Jesus, shepherd us
- Upper: 157 Jesus, shepherd us

Easter 5
- Pre: 151 We love
- Lower: 142 Love God and your neighbor
- Upper: 142 Love God and your neighbor

Easter 6
- Pre: 134 Love, love, love!, *sts. 1-2*
- Lower: 142 Love God and your neighbor
- Upper: 142 Love God and your neighbor

Ascension
- Pre: 196 This is the way we sing our praise
- Lower: 178 Oh, sing to the Lord
- Upper: 62 Alleluia! Jesus is risen!, *refrain*

Easter 7
- Pre: 129 If anybody asks you who I am
- Lower: 128 Many are the lightbeams
- Upper: 56 In the bulb there is a flower

Pentecost
- Pre: 133 We are the church, *refrain*
- Lower: 133 We are the church
- Upper: 68 Spirit, Spirit of gentleness

Holy Trinity
- Pre: 113 The Lord is great!
- Lower: 184 One, two, three
- Upper: 69 Spirit Friend

Proper 3
- Pre: 149 Jesus wants me for a helper
- Lower: 124 Jesus' hands were kind hands
- Upper: 80 How firm a foundation

Proper 4
- Pre: 122 Jesus, you help
- Lower: 123 When Jesus the healer, *sts. 1, 7*
- Upper: 123 When Jesus the healer, *sts. 1, 7*

Proper 5
- Pre: 97 Come, Lord Jesus
- Lower: 124 Jesus' hands were kind hands
- Upper: 124 Jesus' hands were kind hands

Proper 6
- Pre: 200 Can you listen
- Lower: 59 There's new life in Jesus
- Upper: 125 Forgive our sins as we forgive

Proper 7
- Pre: 122 Jesus, you help
- Lower: 79 Listen, God is calling
- Upper: 79 Listen, God is calling

Proper 8
- Pre: 43 Walk in God's ways
- Lower: 166 Walk! Walk!
- Upper: 144 Jesus, Jesus, let us tell you

Proper 9
- Pre: 118 Two little eyes
- Lower: 148 Let me be your servant, Jesus, *refrain*
- Upper: 148 Let me be your servant, Jesus

Proper 10
- Pre: 149 Jesus wants me for a helper
- Lower: 153 When I needed a neighbor
- Upper: 146 Jesu, Jesu, fill us with your love

Proper 11
- Pre: 74 Come and sing your praise
- Lower: 165 What does it mean to follow Jesus?
- Upper: 165 What does it mean to follow Jesus?

Proper 12
- Pre: 195 Jesus told a story
- Lower: 73 Come! Come! Everybody worship, *sts. 1 and 4-5*
- Upper: 90 Seek ye first

Proper 13
- Pre: 162 In our work and in our play
- Lower: 73 Come! Come! Everybody worship, *sts. 1-3*
- Upper: 161 Fear not for tomorrow

Proper 14
- Pre: 65 The Lord is my shepherd
- Lower: 157 Jesus, shepherd us
- Upper: 156 One in a hundred

Proper 15
- Pre: 34 I am the light of the world
- Lower: 59 There's new life in Jesus
- Upper: 117 Love is never ending

Proper 16		
Pre:	73	Come! Come! Everybody worship, *sts. 1-2*
Lower:	123	When Jesus the healer, *sts. 1, 5, 7*
Upper:	123	When Jesus the healer, *sts. 1, 5, 7*
Proper 17		
Pre:	106	To the banquet, come
Lower:	106	To the banquet, come
Upper:	165	What does it mean to follow Jesus?
Proper 18		
Pre:	116	Like a tree
Lower:	116	Like a tree
Upper:	147	If you love me
Proper 19		
Pre:	156	One in a hundred
Lower:	156	One in a hundred
Upper:	144	Jesus, Jesus, let us tell you
Proper 20		
Pre:	97	Come, Lord Jesus
Lower:	135	There's a Spirit in the air
Upper:	37	We are called
Proper 21		
Pre:	118	Two little eyes
Lower:	66	Gracious Spirit, heed our pleading
Upper:	148	Let me be your servant, Jesus
Proper 22		
Pre:	150	The tiny seed
Lower:	173	Faith that's sure
Upper:	173	Faith that's sure
Proper 23		
Pre:	74	Come and sing your praise
Lower:	124	Jesus' hands were kind hands
Upper:	123	When Jesus the healer, *sts. 1, 5, 7*
Proper 24		
Pre:	133	We are the church
Lower:	94	Lord, listen to your children praying
Upper:	59	There's new life in Jesus, *sts. 1-4*
Proper 25		
Pre:	195	Jesus told a story
Lower:	135	There's a Spirit in the air
Upper:	165	What does it mean to follow Jesus?
Reformation		
Pre:	129	If anybody asks you who I am, *st. 2 with added phrase*
Lower:	180	I will sing, I will sing, *sts. 1, 3, and refrain*
Upper:	105	I received the living God, *st. 3 and refrain*
All Saints		
Pre:	97	Come, Lord Jesus
Lower:	143	Blest are they, *refrain*
Upper:	80	How firm a foundation
Proper 26		
Pre:	78	Won't you come and sit with me
Lower:	41	I want Jesus to walk with me
Upper:	148	Let me be your servant, Jesus
Proper 27		
Pre:	62	Alleluia! Jesus is risen!, *refrain*
Lower:	62	Alleluia! Jesus is risen!, *refrain*
Upper:	139	You are the seed
Proper 28		
Pre:	149	Jesus wants me for a helper
Lower:	97	Come, Lord Jesus
Upper:	42	Is there anybody here who loves my Jesus?
Christ the King		
Pre:	77	Come into God's presence, *sts. 1-2*
Lower:	168	God is our refuge and strength
Upper:	44	Jesus, remember me

Scripture references

Genesis		
1:1-2	68	Spirit, Spirit of gentleness
1–2	197	The creation
Exodus		
20:1-21	10	Oh, come, oh, come, Emmanuel
20:8	73	Come! Come! Everybody worship
1 Samuel		
3:1-18	138	Here I am, Lord
Psalms		
1	116	Like a tree
5:1-3	94	Lord, listen to your children praying
8	113	The Lord is great!
8:1	120	How majestic is your name
23:1-2	65	The Lord is my shepherd
24:7-10	7	Prepare the royal highway
24:7-10	8	The King of glory
34:3	120	How majestic is your name
46	81	A mighty fortress is our God
46	168	God is our refuge and strength
46:1-3	41	I want Jesus to walk with me
47	196	This is the way we sing our praise
47:1	182	Clap your hands, all you people
62:2	173	Faith that's sure
91	163	On eagle's wings
98	24	Joy to the world
98	178	Oh, sing to the Lord
98:1	74	Come and sing your praise
98:1	119	Earth and all stars!
100:1-4	186	Make a glad noise to the Lord
100:4	77	Come into God's presence
118:24	60	This is the day
126:5	180	I will sing, I will sing
136	117	Love is never-ending
150	179	Hallelujah! Praise ye the Lord!
150:1	176	Praise God, from whom all blessings flow
Isaiah		
6:8	138	Here I am, Lord
7:14	10	Oh, come, oh, come, Emmanuel
9:2	37	We are called
9:6	120	How majestic is your name
11:1	10	Oh, come, oh, come, Emmanuel
40:3-5	7	Prepare the royal highway
40:9-10	23	Go tell it on the mountain
40:11	80	How firm a foundation
41:10	80	How firm a foundation
43:1	129	If anybody asks you who I am
43:2	80	How firm a foundation
46:4	80	How firm a foundation
48:18	159	I've got peace like a river
55:12	109	The trees of the field
60:1-3	38	Shine, Jesus, shine
60:1-3	5	The King shall come
60:1-4	10	Oh, come, oh, come, Emmanuel
66:12-13	159	I've got peace like a river
Joel		
2:28-29	68	Spirit, Spirit of gentleness
Micah		
6:8	37	We are called
Zechariah		
9:9	8	The King of glory
Matthew		
1:20-21	1	Stay awake, be ready
1:20-21	12	Get ready!
1:21	29	The virgin Mary had a baby boy
1:23	14	That boy-child of Mary
2:1-12	30	We three kings of Orient are
2:9-11	29	The virgin Mary had a baby boy
2:13-23	28	Oh, sleep now, holy baby
3:1-2	3	Light one candle: Christ is coming
3:1-6	6	On Jordan's banks the Baptist's cry
4:4	90	Seek ye first
4:18-22	39	Jesus brings a message
4:18-22	193	Peter, Andrew, James, and John
4:18-22	194	Jesus called
5:3-12	143	Blest are they
5:13-16	35	Bring forth the kingdom
5:13-16	139	You are the seed
5:14-16	32	This little light of mine
5:14-16	37	We are called
6:9-13	195	Jesus told a story
6:12	125	Forgive our sins as we forgive
6:25-34	161	Fear not for tomorrow
6:25-34	167	Children of the heavenly Father
6:33	90	Seek ye first
7:7	90	Seek ye first
7:24-27	80	How firm a foundation
11:4-6	123	When Jesus the healer
11:28-30	169	Lord of all hopefulness
12:25-29	81	A mighty fortress is our God
13:1-23	83	Lord, let my heart be good soil
13:31-32	150	The tiny seed
17:1-8	38	Shine, Jesus, shine
17:1-8	40	Come to the mountain
17:8	31	Open our eyes, Lord
18:10-14	156	One in a hundred
19:14	160	Jesus loves me!
20:26-27	137	Make me a servant
21:1-11	8	The King of glory
21:1-11	48	All glory, laud, and honor
21:1-11	50	Hosanna! This is a special day
22:34-40	142	Love God and your neighbor
22:34-40	172	The great commandments
22:39	140	Love your neighbor
24:36-44	1	Stay awake, be ready
25:1-13	158	Give me oil in my lamp
25:31-40	141	Come now, you blessed
25:31-40	153	When I needed a neighbor
25:35-36	135	There's a Spirit in the air
28:1-10	55	Now the green blade rises
28:6	57	Jesus Christ is risen today
28:16-20	79	Listen, God is calling
28:19-20	110	Go into the world
28:19-20	139	You are the seed
28:20	112	God be with you
28:20	161	Fear not for tomorrow
28:20	162	In our work and in our play
Mark		
1:1-8	6	On Jordan's banks the Baptist's cry
1:16-20	39	Jesus brings a message
1:16-20	193	Peter, Andrew, James, and John
1:16-20	194	Jesus called
3:22-27	81	A mighty fortress is our God
4:1-20	83	Lord, let my heart be good soil
4:23	84	Open your ears, O faithful people
4:30-32	150	The tiny seed
9:2-8	38	Shine, Jesus, shine
9:2-8	40	Come to the mountain
10:13-16	124	Jesus' hands were kind hands
10:14	160	Jesus loves me!
10:35-45	137	Make me a servant
10:46-52	123	When Jesus the healer
11:1-10	48	All glory, laud, and honor
11:8-10	7	Prepare the royal highway
12:28-31	172	The great commandments
12:28-34	142	Love God and your neighbor
13:32-37	1	Stay awake, be ready
13:33-37	11	People, look east
16:1-8	55	Now the green blade rises
16:6	57	Jesus Christ is risen today
Luke		
1:30-35	12	Get ready!
1:35	1	Stay awake, be ready
2:1-8	190	Sleep, baby Jesus
2:7	17	Away in a manger
2:7	18	Away in a manger
2:8-16	15	'Twas in the moon of wintertime
2:8-16	26	Silent night, holy night!

Topics and themes

Authors, composers, and sources

First lines and common titles